RETHINKING

VENEZUELAN

POLITICS

Class, Conflict, and
the Chávez Phenomenon

Steve Ellner

LYNNE
RIENNER
PUBLISHERS

BOULDER
LONDON

To Miriam Waltch (Aunt Micky),
1929–2006

Paperback edition published in the United States of America in 2010 by
Lynne Rienner Publishers, Inc.
1800 30th Street, Boulder, Colorado 80301
www.rienner.com

and in the United Kingdom by
Lynne Rienner Publishers, Inc.
3 Henrietta Street, Covent Garden, London WC2E 8LU

Hardcover edition published in 2008 by Lynne Rienner Publishers, Inc.

ISBN 978-1-58826-699-6 (paperback : alk. paper)
LC 2007042196

Printed and bound in the United States of America

⊗ The paper used in this publication meets the requirements
of the American National Standard for Permanence of
Paper for Printed Library Materials Z39.48-1992.

5 4 3 2 1

RETHINKING

VENEZUELAN

POLITICS

Contents

Foreword

AS A graduate student learning about Latin American politics in the 1980s, it was hard to avoid the study of democratic transitions. With authoritarian regimes crumbling in one country after another, scholars inevitably turned their attention to the dynamics of regime transition and the prospects for democratic consolidation. Implicitly or explicitly, the Venezuelan case weighed heavily on scholarly debates over democratization. In contrast to most of its neighbors, Venezuela had escaped the wave of military coups that swept across Latin America in the 1960s and 1970s, and the country's own democratic transition in the late 1950s was widely viewed as a model for others to follow. This transition had been carefully negotiated among rival party elites, who agreed to moderate their positions, restrain their followers, and converge on an oil-fueled model of state-led capitalist development. The outcome—so we thought—was a "pacted" democracy dominated by two stable, centrist, and multiclass parties that controlled civil society and alleviated class conflict by distributing oil rents to diverse social constituencies.

In many ways, then, Venezuela seemed like an exceptional case of political development in the Latin American region. It stood apart not only for its oil wealth but for the strength and discipline of its leading parties, the resilience of its democratic regime, and the breadth of the policy consensus secured by its political pacts. As neighboring countries struggled to restore democracy, rebuild party systems, and reduce ideological polarization, it is hardly surprising that they looked to the Venezuelan experience for guideposts to follow. Indeed, many democratic reformers sought to create a region in which Venezuela would no longer be exceptional—that is, one in which other countries had also attained democratic stability and social peace.

Venezuela did, in fact, look less and less exceptional after 1989, but not simply because other countries had advanced in their democratic development. Instead, Venezuela appeared to be converging on the patterns of institutional decay, political instability, ideological conflict, and social polarization that were widely recognized elsewhere in the region. As the oil economy entered into decline—mired in a morass of debt, inefficiency, and corruption—the policy consensus evaporated, and the ability of the regime to buy support and neutralize opposition progressively withered. The political leadership split over the desirability of free market reforms, while social mobilization intensified and the dominant parties lost their control over both civil society and voting behavior. Mass riots, several military coup attempts, and the impeachment of President Carlos Andrés Pérez in 1993 shattered the myth of Venezuela's consensual politics; by the end of the 1990s the country had elected former military coup leader Hugo Chávez to the presidency, who quickly dismantled the institutional edifice of the post-1958 democratic regime and proclaimed a "Bolivarian Revolution" in the name of the poor.

The great virtue of Steve Ellner's book is that it unearths the deep historical roots of Venezuela's Bolivarian Revolution. Rather than treating *Chavismo* as a dramatic break with the post-1958 democratic order, Ellner suggests that it is the crystallization of socioeconomic, cultural, and political tensions that had long existed in the country's social fabric—tensions that, in fact, belie conventional interpretations of Venezuelan exceptionalism, even if they were kept largely submerged for the better part of a political generation. Ellner's challenge to the exceptionalism thesis rests on a series of subtle shifts in the analytical focus of his work; he examines popular masses as well as political elites, social actors as well as formal political institutions, and conflict as well as consensus. His analysis helps readers to understand why Venezuelan society became increasingly polarized into the social and political camps that faced off in the Chávez era, while steering between the stereotypical interpretations of those camps that are often presented in public discourse.

For readers who seek to understand the historical and sociological contexts that gave rise to *Chavismo,* this book is the right place to start. Although Venezuela's transition from a pacted democracy to what Chávez describes as "socialism for the twenty-first century" is particularly dramatic, other countries in Latin America have also experienced a revival of popular movements and a repoliticization of development strategies following a period of technocratic consensus around market liberalism. By placing the Venezuelan experience within its broader regional context, Ellner not only sheds new light on what Venezuela shares with its neighbors; he also helps us to understand what lies behind the recent political turmoil elsewhere in the region. Far from being an exception, Venezuela may, in fact, be a microcosm of the sociopolitical tensions that exist throughout the region, even if they take a variety of different political forms.

This book also provides readers with an even-handed account of the dramatic changes in Venezuelan society unleashed by Chávez's Bolivarian Revolution. Ellner traces the different stages of the Chávez regime, including the political and economic reforms that have been adopted and the political conflicts they have triggered. The account explains how the reform process progressively radicalized and redefined itself over time, creating the outlines of a new economic and political model that breaks with both neoliberal orthodoxy and historical expressions of socialism and populism in Latin America. This new model has redefined property rights, social programs, and the modes of popular participation in Venezuela through reforms that include land redistribution and use rights, the promotion of service and producer cooperatives, a broad range of social "missions," the creation of local commissions to administer public works, and experiments with worker self-management in occupied or nationalized factories. Ellner analyzes both the achievements and the limitations of these diverse reforms, and in the process sheds new light on the range of developmental alternatives under debate in contemporary Latin America. As such, his book is a must-read for anyone who seeks to understand the new political and economic institutions being forged in Latin America as part of the "left turn" inaugurated by the election of Chávez in 1998.

—Kenneth Roberts

▼

Preface to the Paperback Edition

EVEN MORE so than when the hardcover edition of this book was published some two years ago, the attention of commentators across the political spectrum is centered on Venezuelan political developments. This spotlight is relatively new for the country. In the first decades of Venezuela's modern democratic period, beginning in 1958, Latin America specialists tended to underestimate the country's importance. But this treatment did not accord with Venezuela's status as a major oil producer and, during the 1960s and 1970s, the only stable democracy in South America. And it abruptly ended in 1998 with the ascent to power of Hugo Chávez, who has since become a household name not only in Latin America and the United States, but throughout the world.

Much of the media has focused attention on Venezuela for the wrong reasons. The country is often portrayed as unstable and on the verge of a catastrophic change—perhaps the establishment of a dictatorial communist regime or a military dictatorship, or the outbreak of a bloody national confrontation. Fortunately, this characterization, at least until now, has been inaccurate.

Venezuela's importance stems from the transformations currently under way and the nation's uncharted course. Success or failure will be determined by the *Chavista* movement's capacity to identify and analyze errors, which are inevitable in any experimental process, and to correct them. The deepening of democracy, which is conducive to internal discussion and open debate, is an essential requisite for the establishment of a viable model.

As the Chávez presidency enters its eleventh year, the direction of the *Chavista* movement and government is subject to considerable debate. Many Venezuelans, and political analysts in particular, maintain or imply that the nation's course depends entirely on Chávez's aspirations. Some of them argue that Chávez has always harbored plans to establish a communist-style dictatorship, while others point to his eclecticism, which makes predictions tenuous. Nevertheless, Chapters 6 and 7 of this book point to a rich internal, albeit largely informal, debate within the *Chavista* movement that has influenced actions and policies from the outset.

Since the publication of the hardcover edition, radicalization and other developments under Chávez's government have reinforced the tendencies and general directions outlined in Chapters 5–8. Chapter 5 discusses the *Chavista* strategy of taking advantage of each political victory by acting quickly to deepen the process of change. Recent electoral triumphs include the presidential elections of December 2006, the November 2008 local elections in which *Chavista* gubernatorial candidates emerged triumphant in 17 of 22 states, and a national referendum in February 2009 that approved Chávez's proposal to eliminate term limits on elected officials.

The Chávez government implemented radical changes in the wake of these triumphs. Thus, Chávez decreed for the first time the nationalization of strategic sectors of the economy in accordance with the nation's Constitution of 1999. The takeovers of the steel company SIDOR in 2008 and Cerámicas Carabobo the following year were important because they culminated prolonged labor conflicts during which union leaders had called on the government to take control of the firms and Chávez had threatened intervention if the disputes were not settled. The SIDOR nationalization in particular invigorated the highly divided pro-*Chavista* labor movement. Following the takeover of Cerámicas Carabobo, Chávez declared that the workers would now play a more central role in the process of change in Venezuela. Nevertheless, the continued factionalism in the pro-*Chavista* labor confederation limits the possibility that the workers movement will spearhead additional changes.

The internal conflict in the Chávez movement between hard-line and soft-line currents, as discussed in Chapter 6, has in large part intensified over the past two years. The hard-liners applauded the nationalizations after 2007 as a step in the direction of socialism and freeing the nation of foreign control of the economy. In contrast, some of the soft liners, grouped in the Podemos party and to a lesser degree the Patria para Todos (PPT), objected to the centralization of power and specifically the concentration of decisionmaking authority in Chávez's hands. In 2007, Podemos left the governing coalition and opposed a constitutional reform proposal that was defeated by a narrow margin in a December 2007 referendum. Podemos leaders criticized, among other provisions of the proposal, the increase of executive power that would result from the elimination of the Central Bank's autonomy and steps that would roll back decentralization.

The two currents have also clashed on the ideological front. Hardline writers heavily attacked the prominent soft-line intellectual Heinz Dieterich for suggesting that conditions are not ripe for a socialist-style revolution and for defending a more gradual course in accordance with the pragmatic policies of the recently named president of Cuba, Raúl Castro. Dieterich points out that, without a working class "vanguard," the *Chavista* movement lacks a social agent for revolutionary transformation. The Venezuelan government should therefore concentrate its efforts on uniting the rest of the continent in an economic union that would exclude the United States.

The "grassroots" versus "statist" strategies analyzed in Chapter 7 are even more useful than the "hard-line" and "soft-line" categories for gaining insight into the *Chavista* movement over the past two years. The grassroots approach favors popular participation in decisionmaking free of bureaucratic controls. It is best illustrated by the government-sponsored community councils that have recently proliferated throughout the country. Unlike the neighborhood associations that represented thousands of communities over the previous three decades, the community councils design and execute projects and pressure contractors to employ community residents. The statist approach warns against the autonomy of the councils and supports mechanisms created by the municipal and state government to ensure against the misuse of public funds that previously characterized many of the state-financed worker cooperatives. Those defending the grassroots strategy are confident that the community councils through their own oversight committees (known as social controllerships) are capable of guaranteeing trustworthy management.

Chávez's two-pronged strategy of cultivating harmonious relations with other governments while employing a radical and defiant discourse—as discussed in Chapter 8—has continued to underlie Venezuela's actions at the international level. Chávez's stance has allowed him to become an icon for many of the poor throughout the region, as well as for leftists in spite of his military background. At the same time, he avoids the isolation within the Latin American community of nations that Cuba faced in the 1960s, and he is able to take advantage of a leftward swing across the continent. The most recent example of leftist inroads is the election in March 2009 of Mauricio Funes as president of El Salvador. Even before his inauguration, Funes traveled to Venezuela to reverse his predecessor's policy of rejecting various Venezuelan-sponsored programs for the sale of oil under special terms and economic cooperation.

The tension between Chávez's radical rhetoric and his friendly gestures to nonleftist governments is best illustrated by his recent relations with neighboring Colombia and with the United States. After facilitating the release of various hostages in the hands of Colombian guerrillas with the approval of President Álvaro Uribe in 2007, the two governments engaged in harsh name-calling. The discord culminated with Chávez's decision to send 6,000 soldiers to the Colombian border and the mutual withdrawal of ambassadors. More recently, however, the two countries reestablished diplomatic relations and Chávez hosted President Uribe in Caracas, where various agreements were signed. Similarly, one month before this writing, Chávez had a well-publicized, all-smiles encounter with President Barack Obama at the Summit of the Americas in Trinidad. Amazingly, the meeting was preceded just weeks before by Obama's statements accusing the Venezuelan government of exporting terrorist activity, to which Chávez responded by calling the US president "a poor, ignorant man."

*   *   *

During the two years that I worked virtually full time on this book, many people provided help in diverse ways. Conversations with Fred Rosen, then editor of *NACLA: Report on the Americas*, and Anna Hardman of Zed Books helped me to develop ideas and to frame issues for the book. Philip Oxhorn (McGill University), Judith Ewell (William and Mary College), Miguel Tinker Salas (Pomona College), Susan Berglund (Universidad Central de Venezuela), Peter Winn (Tufts University), Charles Bergquist (University of Washington), and Ralph Van Roy read one or more chapters of the manuscript and provided useful insights and suggestions. I am also thankful to the Comisión de Investigación of the Universidad de Oriente–Anzoátegui, where I have taught since 1977, for financial assistance for the numerous trips I made to Caracas and elsewhere. I would like to make special reference to the commission's personnel for their efficiency and unrestrained good humor.

Lengthy formal and informal conversations with Venezuelan friends and acquaintances have influenced my thinking in numerous ways and enhanced the quality of my work. I will name just a few of those who have been most helpful: Eligio Damas, Margarita López Maya, Luis Lander, Irán Aguilera, Andrés Alfonzo, Rodolfo Magallanes, and Thamara Alvarez. Finally, my wife, Carmen Hercilia, deserves considerable credit for the final product of my research. As I worked on this project, Carmen was patient, supportive, encouraging, and loving— descriptive words that cannot be overstated.

1

▼

Introduction:
Rethinking
Venezuelan Politics

EVENTS during a given historical period shape the tools and frameworks used by people to understand the past and the present. The political setting during each decade or two after the United States Civil War, for instance, influenced the predominant interpretations of the causes of that conflict, which differed in fundamental ways from those of previous years (Pressly 1954). It should not be surprising therefore that the dramatic changes and radical discourse ushered in with the election of Hugo Chávez in 1998 have affected the thinking of Venezuelans of diverse political, social, and educational backgrounds. Not only is there greater interest in the nation's past but also a tendency to reexamine social attitudes and celebrate the defense of national autonomy and independence on political and economic fronts.

In some cases, this new interpretation of the past reinforces political and historical scholarly analyses that were undertaken over a period of several decades prior to Chávez's assumption of power.[1] In addition to this revisionism, Chávez himself has forcefully put forward fairly original interpretations in response to the challenges his movement has faced, as will be discussed in subsequent chapters. I believe that political imperatives have sometimes led Chávez to overstate his case.

My basic objective in this book is to take a close look at struggles over issues of substance in Venezuela, particularly political expressions of class and racial cleavages. Much historical and political writing over the years has failed to attach sufficient significance to these sources of conflict during various periods in the nation's history and instead has overemphasized personal ambition and discourse. Many writers have been influenced by the "Venezuelan exceptionalism thesis," which is a

1

central concern of this book. The exceptionalism thesis argues that modern Venezuelan history has been exempt from the internecine struggles, acute class conflicts, and racial animosities that have characterized other Latin American countries. For many years, political analysts, along with those close to the circles of power in Washington, presented the exceptionalism view by labeling Venezuela a model democracy due to its stability, marginalization of the left, and avoidance of militant independent trade unionism.

Exceptionalism writers extolled the leadership of the nation's dominant modern democratic parties. According to their view, the modernizing middle-class elite that rebelled in 1928 against longtime dictator Juan Vicente Gómez (1908–1935) established the bases for a stable democracy by founding the multiclass parties Democratic Action (AD) and Committee of Independent Political Electoral Organization (COPEI), which contained class conflict. By glorifying the "generation of 1928" and democratic leaders who emerged in subsequent years, these writers downplayed the contribution of struggles and transformations from the previous century. Exceptionalism thus reinforced traditional historiography, which presented a monochromatic view of the nineteenth century that wrote off all political movements for change as complete failures with no long-lasting impact. AD held power from 1945 until 1948 when it was overthrown by military dictator Marcos Pérez Jiménez, who ruled until 1958. Subsequently, the moderate AD for the most part alternated power with the equally moderate COPEI. During these decades, the exceptionalism focus became the generally accepted explanation of Venezuelan politics. Only in the 1990s was the stability interrupted and the political system thrown into crisis. The massive nationwide disturbances during the week of February 27, 1989, were followed by the abortive military coup headed by Hugo Chávez in 1992, the impeachment of AD's Carlos Andrés Pérez the following year, and several months later (for the first time) the election of a presidential candidate, Rafael Caldera, who did not belong to either AD or COPEI.

The exceptionalism thesis does contain elements of truth. Certainly Venezuelan politics in the twentieth century was not subject to the class-based parties that emerged in Chile, nor did the Venezuelan government apply brutal repression against working-class protests as occurred in Argentina, Bolivia, and elsewhere. There were good reasons why Venezuela appeared to be class-conflict free. Ample resources, for instance, underpinned the practice of clientelism, which discouraged collective struggles. Furthermore, multiclass parties created internal mechanisms to broker class disputes. Finally, class mobility, which was particularly pronounced within the armed forces, at times eased social tensions. Indeed, the middle- and lower-middle-class backgrounds of most Venezuelan military officers contrasted with the more privileged background of their counterparts throughout the hemisphere.

Nevertheless, the appearance of social harmony during the modern period and the claim that Venezuela was a model democracy misled scholars, who for the most part failed to foresee the political crisis of the 1990s. Most important, many political writers and the media in general failed to look at electoral fraud and state repression committed against political and labor activists who were outside of the political system. In some cases the omission was deliberate in that it was intended to preserve Venezuela's image as a model democracy. The harsh critique presented by Chávez and *Chavista* leaders of Venezuela's "exceptional" post-1958 democracy, while exaggerated in some aspects as will be discussed in Chapter 3, exposes the fallacies of exceptionalism thinking.

Political scientists writing on the post-1958 period have also minimized the importance of tension and struggle within the mainstream AD and COPEI organizations. In both parties, left-leaning factions emerged but were the victims of heavy-handed treatment and violation of internal democratic rules on the part of party machines. The leaders of these factions articulated positions on social inequality, severance of dependency on foreign capital and technology, assertion of an independent foreign policy, and internal democratization. They failed, however, to put forward an all-encompassing strategy to achieve these goals or to rally public support for them. Nevertheless, they raised issues, albeit timidly, that later were to become focal points of the *Chavista* movement. Writing that denies the programmatic and ideological implications of the factional conflicts within AD and COPEI parties coincides with the claims of the spokesmen for the dominant factions of both parties who at the time accused the dissidents of being motivated solely by personal ambition. Many writers (including leftist ones) who accept these arguments attribute the factional struggle to the eagerness of the minority factions to gain control of the abundant oil-derived resources at the disposal of those in the seats of power.

In this book, in keeping with my focus on substantive issues and especially issues of socioeconomic change, I scrutinize governments and their policies that laid the groundwork for radical transformation. Powerful establishment groups have always had a special fear of charismatic leaders with a radical discourse who implement policies that have a potential for setting off far-reaching change. These leaders, albeit inadvertently in some cases, provide the popular sectors of the population with a sense of empowerment. I analyze three cases in which governments set the stage for transformation and as a result faced the hardened opposition of establishment forces: the AD government of 1945 to 1948; the first administration of Carlos Andrés Pérez between 1974 and 1979; and the Chávez government after 1998. Concrete economic policies contrary to the immediate interests of powerful economic groups are important for understanding political conflict, but in themselves do not explain the depth of reaction (to argue otherwise would be to fall into the error of economism). The combination of policies with transformational potential and a discourse that empowers people was particularly evident in the case of the Chávez government and explains why (more than in the two other above-mentioned cases) it faced open resistance from the business sector and the US government.[2]

▶ The Paradigmatic Significance of the Chávez Phenomenon

The tendency to downplay substantive issues and to concentrate instead on personality, personal ambition, and self-serving behavior has particularly manifested itself in the writing and general discussion on the government of Hugo Chávez. In the process, many political writers have sidetracked the basic issues, particularly those related to social, economic, and national interests. In addition to specific zero-sum game policies that favor one class at the expense of another, Chávez's government has begun to promote a new model, which recognizes the rights of the private sector but also its obligations in the context of broader social and national goals. The possibility of a "demonstration effect," in which Venezuela serves as an example for the rest of Latin America and an alternative to the existing capitalist system in those nations, weighs heavily on the actions of Chávez's most influential enemies. Political analysts for the most part, rather than focus on the demonstration effect, concern themselves with Washington's claim that Chávez is using oil money to finance the Latin American left. In doing so, they pass over the real significance of what is occurring in Venezuela. In short, while political analysts and journalists have tended to emphasize the roles of personality and rhetoric in understanding the Chávez government, zero-sum game policies and the contours of the new emerging model should instead be at the center of analysis.

The degree to which the government has prioritized the development of a new viable economic model is open to debate. At the level of discourse, Chávez insists that social goals are more important than economic ones since the basic thrust of the revolution is "humanistic" and increased production does not necessarily resolve the pressing problem of poverty. Furthermore, the *Chavista* movement has refrained from engaging in a formal debate over ideology and strategy that would define the relationship between small-scale production, which the government has made an all-out effort to stimulate, and large-scale production. Finally, Chávez's appeal to voluntarism, solidarity, and good intentions on the part of small-scale producers, who receive generous amounts of credit from the state, detracts from the establishment of mechanisms that guard against misuse of public funds and ensure the viability of these new forms of production.

The discourse and actions of the Chávez presidency and movement have influenced the way Venezuelans view themselves and in the process have encouraged a reexamination of Venezuelan society, politics, history, and ethnicity. The Chávez phenomenon has also brought into the open controversial topics such as racism that were previously discouraged or ignored. This new political atmosphere is bound to frame the issues of political and intellectual debate as well as academic research for many years to come. The reconsideration of long-held assumptions may also go well beyond Chávez's supporters. Intense polarization notwithstanding, political actors and observers have reached a virtual consensus that, regardless of the duration of Chávez's stay in power, his election in 1998 signaled definitive changes and the nation will never be the same.

The Chávez government's prioritization of lower-class needs, as reflected in rhetoric and budgetary allocations, and the social polarization in Venezuela manifested in voting preferences since 1998, have influenced analysts and actors (including those of the opposition) to pay greater attention to class concerns. This new orientation contrasts with the behavior of political parties across the political spectrum over previous decades. In the 1960s, for instance, Venezuelan leftists strayed from Marxist class analysis and ignored the advice of proleftist trade union leaders who cautioned against taking up guerrilla warfare in sparsely populated rural areas far removed from the working class (Ellner 1993, 41). The largest leftist party in the 1970s and 1980s, the Movement Toward Socialism (MAS), also eschewed class politics and emphasized political reforms and elections at the expense of social demands. Similar to what has happened on the political front, scholarly research has begun to look more at class issues, in contrast to the more institutional approach that characterized it in the past. Thus various, particularly

young, scholars have taken a close look at the urban poor, unlike in previous years when, with the exception of one study (Ray 1969), writers
largely ignored the topic (Hansen, Hawkins, and Seawright 2004;
Canache 2004; Valencia Ramírez 2007; Fernandes 2007).

President Chávez's interpretations of Venezuelan history, which are
shaped by political considerations and imperatives and are designed to
stimulate national pride, also clash with traditional views. Most important, Chávez's version of the nation's history puts in relief popular causes and the role of heroic leaders, other than those of the War of
Independence, whom historians have always glorified. Along these
lines, Chávez frequently extols the Indian martyr Chief Guaicaipuro,
who confronted the Spanish at the time of the founding of Caracas in the
mid-sixteenth century; Chávez named an Indian assistance program
Mission Guaicaipuro and rebaptized the "Day of the Race" (Columbus
Day) as the "Day of Indian Resistance."[3] The Venezuelan leader who
most benefits from this historical reevaluation is Cipriano Castro, long
considered lustful and irresponsible. Chávez often compares his own
predicament at the time of the coup and general strike in 2002 and 2003
with that of Castro, who in 1902–1903 resisted the European blockade
of Venezuelan ports hailed by his financially powerful adversaries.

Chávez's views of modern democracy also diverge sharply from
generally accepted ones. Chávez's condemnation of Venezuela's party-
based democracy of 1945–1948 and after 1958 has been more severe and
all-encompassing than even the accounts of many Venezuelan leftists.
The *Chavistas* label the overthrow of dictator Marcos Pérez Jiménez on
January 23, 1958, a "popular insurrection" (rather than a simple military
coup) and accuse the political party elites of having hijacked the movement in order to gut it of its social and leftist content. This critique helps
justify the February 1992 attempted coup staged by Chávez, which laid
the groundwork for his rise to power in 1998. Chávez's criticism of the
nation's modern democracy will undoubtedly leave an indelible imprint
on political historiography and do much to bury the Venezuelan "exceptionalism thesis," which views the nation's democracy as having been
stable, unique, and superior to the rest of Latin America.

Issues of ethnicity and racism have also been thrust to the center of
national discussion as a result of attitudes assumed by President Chávez
and the opposition. On the one hand, Chávez frequently appeals to racial
pride; the *Chavista* Constitution of 1999 calls on the state not only to
accept Indian languages and culture but to promote their "appreciation
and dissemination" (article 121). On the other hand, during the height of
political tension between 2001 and 2003, individual members of the

opposition used racist slurs against the *Chavistas*, while racism also manifested itself in graffiti in wealthy zones and even occasionally in the media. At the same time, the opposition accused Chávez of playing the race card (Herrera Salas 2007, 112–113; Velasco 2002, 43–44). This open clash of positions represents a break with the past when the issue of racism was widely spurned and the myth of Venezuela as a racial democracy served to underpin discriminatory practices (Ishibashi 2001). The current polemical setting is conducive to studies that deepen the scholarly research of the last half century on the cultural contributions of blacks and Indians and to the systematic diffusion of these findings. The present period also encourages analysts to go beyond the cultural focus by examining the class and political implications of racism (Velasco 2002, 24; Herrera Salas 2007, 105–106).

▶ Longstanding Notions About Venezuelan Society and Politics

The Chávez era has not only changed the focus of political debate in the present but has also called into question the validity of deeply rooted concepts and notions. Three in particular have profound implications for political analysis and scholarly work. While containing elements of truth, these propositions require reexamination in light of recent developments:

1. *During the modern period beginning in 1936, Venezuelans have exhibited relatively low levels of class conflict and tension and have avoided ongoing internecine political confrontation.* Venezuelans in general and observers in particular often draw a profile of the Venezuelan character to support the claim that twentieth-century Venezuelan history is devoid of the acute social confrontations, deep-seated political animosity, and xenophobic attitudes that have characterized other Latin American countries. Some traditional writers, for instance, claimed that even as far back as the colonial period Venezuela was free of "grave uprisings" of slaves (Uslar Pietri 1959, 4).[4] Other writers have pointed out that throughout its history Venezuela has never fought in a foreign war and that in the modern period guerrilla warfare was not as bloody, repressive governments not as harsh, and street protests not as frequent as elsewhere in the continent (Naím and Piñango 1984, 553).[5]

Many observers attribute the "aversion to conflict" among Venezuelans to their faith that thanks to abundant oil income their material expectations will eventually be satisfied (Naím and Piñango 1984, 563). Others assert that the informality of the daily behavior of Venezuelans, the looseness of social distinctions, and racial tolerance explain the allegedly low levels of class conflict over an extended period of time.[6] The renowned Venezuelan intellectual Mariano Picón Salas, for instance, argued that the breakdown of social stratification dates back to the dislocations of the War of Independence when the "struggle for life, food, and living quarters diminished the rigidity of social frontiers" and "the classes drew close to one another," including slaveholders and slaves. Picón Salas claimed that until then, class distinctions were as sharp as in the other Spanish colonies (Picón Salas 1949, 118, 120). In a similar vein, some political scientists rely on public opinion surveys to demonstrate that during the post-1958 period class cleavages were poor predictors of preferences toward AD and COPEI and support for the democratic system (Baloyra 1977, 57).

A related explanation for alleged social harmony is class mobility, which historically distinguishes Venezuela from other Latin American nations such as Colombia and Chile. The Venezuelan armed forces, more than in other nations in the continent where the institution is a preserve of the upper class, has served as a mechanism to allow lower- and lower-middle-class men to improve their social status. These characteristics give credence to the "exceptionalism thesis," which views the nation as exempt from the acute conflicts that have occasionally racked other Latin American nations.

2. *Venezuelan political conflict has centered on power for power's sake while issues of substance, particularly socioeconomic ones, have not had long-lasting significance.* Many historians and political scientists have downplayed the importance of concrete issues and demands in political struggles taking place since the War of Independence. Traditional historiography underestimated the impact of the demands formulated by popular sectors between Simón Bolívar's death in 1830 and the modern period in 1936. Some of these historians stressed the wanton destruction and class animosity of the nineteenth century without seriously considering the aspirations of the popular classes (Vallenilla Lanz 1990, 126–127; see also Wright 1990, 38–39).

Historians writing in this vein viewed the decades-long rule of the Liberal Party after its triumph in the Federal War (1859–1863) as representing a continuation of the past and its program of direct elections, alternation in power, equality before the law, and abolition of capital punishment as nothing more than demagoguery (Uslar Pietri 1959, 4). Likewise historians belittled the slogan "New Men, New Ideas, New Methods," coined by Cipriano Castro upon taking power in 1899, and considered his government a continuation of past deceit and mismanagement. Finally, traditional historians demonized Castro's successor, Juan Vicente Gómez (1908–1935), and in doing so ignored the institution building spurred by oil money in the 1920s. Even Gómez's traditional enemies, who formulated democratic demands and faced relentless persecution, were dismissed as "caudillo" types. This low regard for political leaders of all types can partly be explained by the antimilitary bent of traditional historiography and the predominance of military actors throughout the nineteenth century—one of the few exceptions being the much-venerated but politically ineffective José María Vargas in the 1830s.

Michael Coppedge, in his influential *Strong Parties and Lame Ducks: Presidential Partyarchy and Factionalism in Venezuela*, adheres to a similar perspective by pointing to the increasing superficiality of the differences among the political actors of proestablishment parties during the modern democratic period. His analysis centers on institutional factors and the role of abundant oil money. According to Coppedge, Venezuela's presidential system and electoral rules discouraged electoral alliances and focused the attention of politicians on the prize of the presidency. This dynamic subordinated programmatic and ideological commitments to pragmatic strategies of gaining power. Coppedge adds that by the 1980s party factionalism and interparty rivalry were completely lacking in substance (Coppedge 1994, 162). Chapters 3 and 4 of this book will attempt to demonstrate that the conflicts between centrist and left-leaning currents in both AD and COPEI revolved around substantive issues and had ideological implications, even though major actors in both camps were inconsistent over a period of time. By the mid-1990s the lack of firmness and vacillation reached a new threshold as leaders of the left-leaning factions of the AD and COPEI parties and the proleftist parties, MAS and the Causa R, were won over to neoliberal positions, thus generating widespread disillusionment. These developments set the stage for the electoral triumph of the outsider Hugo Chávez in 1998.

3. *The conflict-management capability of strong institutions and the moderation of leaders during the second half of the twentieth century explain the absence of internecine confrontations.* Scholarly writing in the latter part of the twentieth century has often privileged the role of political moderates in the achievement and preservation of Latin American democracy.[7] This is particularly true in the case of Venezuela. Daniel Levine, one of the outstanding US political scientists writing on Venezuela, has argued that efficacious political institutions dominated by the moderate parties AD and COPEI channeled political conflict along

peaceful lines and provided the nation with protracted stability. Levine points to AD's and COPEI's mass base and linkages with civil society, organized labor, and university bodies as the key behind successful institutionalization. Levine also highlights "political learning" in which moderates of the post-1958 period learned from the mistakes of the short-lived democracy of 1945 to 1948 by toning down their rhetoric, pursuing interparty alliances with fellow moderates, and avoiding the hegemonic strategies that were threatening to powerful established interests. Levine not only underscores the role of moderates but views the exclusion of the left after 1958 as necessary on grounds that it was a destabilizing force. Although he does not oppose the left's proposed reforms, he argues that they had to be delayed until after the achievement of democratic consolidation and stability in the 1960s (Levine 1978, 107).

Terry Karl in her seminal essay "Petroleum and Political Pacts: The Transition to Democracy in Venezuela" also credits moderate leaders with achieving democratic stability but, unlike Levine, attributes their predominant position to the nation's status as an oil producer. She argues that moderate political leaders basically represented the middle class and avoided the extreme positions of labor and peasant leaders on the left and the landowners on the right. She attributes the political success of the nonleftists to the impact of oil on classes and specifically its tendency to favor the middle-class moderates at the expense of more radical class-based positions. Oil production in Venezuela largely displaced agriculture by attracting the rural population to oil and urban areas, thus weakening the peasantry and the oligarchy. The emerging working class was also politically weak as well as fragmented because the economically strategic oil workers were geographically isolated and limited to about 2 percent of the work force, while the urban-based manufacturing sector was late in developing. In contrast, the "unusually large middle class fostered by petrodollars" played a critical role in maintaining stability with moderation (Karl 1987, 87). Its leaders enjoyed a degree of autonomy that enabled them to reconcile conflicting interests of the politically weak classes. In doing so, the moderates were aided by abundant oil resources that served to win over or neutralize recalcitrant sectors and interest groups (see also Salgado 1987, 100).

▶ Partisan Historiography

Venezuelan historiography and political studies demonstrate the applicability of the adage "History is written by the victors" (Ellner 1995, 91).

The writings of members of the ascendant parties founded after the death of Juan Vicente Gómez in 1935 molded the thinking of the general population and were reflected in much of the scholarship on politics and history. The arguments put forward in the published works of AD's leading figure Rómulo Betancourt, and particularly his *Venezuela: Política y Petróleo* (published in 1956), were assimilated by party sympathizers, political analysts, and the population in general. Likewise, the prolific Juan Bautista Fuenmayor (1969), who headed the Communist Party of Venezuela (PCV) in the 1930s and 1940s, influenced leftists, as did other contemporary Communist intellectuals such as Rodolfo Quintero and Salvador de la Plaza. After 1958, a new generation of politician-historians—such as Gehard Cartay Ramírez, José Rodríguez Iturbe, and Rodolfo José Cárdenas (of COPEI); and Eduardo Morales Gil, Manuel Vicente Magallanes, and Rubén Carpio Castillo (of AD)—defended their respective parties' positions on major events. The polarizing atmosphere of the Cold War added to the partisanship and reductionism of much of this writing.

Simplistic, black-and-white notions of political history were evident from the outset of the modern period in 1936 as a result of the influence of the writing of political actors. Those belonging to AD and the PCV, who wrote about the immediate past, converged in characterizing Gómez as nothing more than a ruthless caudillo. This portrayal was not surprising since the founding leaders of both parties initiated their political careers in the struggle against Gómez's twenty-seven-year rule. The AD and PCV leaders viewed themselves as putting an end to the country's semifeudal and barbarian legacy, and thus denigrated the leading pre-1936 political figures in general, and not just Gómez and his supporters. During their early years, Betancourt and other future AD members even clashed with anti-*Gomecistas* who had originally been associated with the Gómez regime and that of his predecessor, Cipriano Castro. In addition to generational and ideological gaps, Betancourt and his political companions were suspicious of the military background of the old-time anti-*Gomecistas*. This antimilitarism led AD and PCV writers to condemn Venezuelan governments going back to independence, which consisted of one military ruler after another.

AD had a special reason for severely criticizing and questioning the ethical conduct of Gómez and everyone who was associated with him, including his successors Eleazar López Contreras (1936–1941) and Isaías Medina Angarita (1941–1945). The main justification of AD leaders for the coup they spearheaded on October 18, 1945, was that it represented a rupture with *Gomecismo* (which López and Medina allegedly formed part of). Similarly, writers belonging to AD, the PCV, COPEI, and the Republican Democratic Union (URD)—Venezuela's four major parties that participated in the 1958 overthrow of the military dictatorship—underscored the nefariousness of Marcos Pérez Jiménez and in doing so ignored certain progressive and nationalistic aspects of his decade-long rule.

The argument in favor of the 1945 coup was as much a political imperative for AD as was the justification of the abortive 1992 coup for the *Chavistas*.[8] The defense of the motives of both coups legitimized the subsequent positions and actions of AD and the *Chavistas*. Thus the legitimization of the 1945 coup and concomitantly of AD's rule of 1945–1948 helped refute the rationale for the November 1948 coup and in turn delegitimized the military dictatorship of 1948 to 1958. This line of reasoning also served to justify the overthrow of Pérez Jiménez in 1958 and in turn underpinned the defense of the post-1958 democracy in response to those who attacked it for falling short of the material achievements of previous years.

Similarly, the fervent justification of the 1992 coup by the *Chavistas* had implications for their future political actions. Chávez was an unknown in 1992 and his appeal in subsequent years was contingent on widespread sympathy for the coup's objectives. The *Chavistas* argued that the 1992 coup attempt paved the way for Chávez's assumption of power in 1998. Undoubtedly the coup radicalized the general population and thus contributed to Rafael Caldera's electoral triumph in 1993 on an anti-neoliberal platform, and subsequently influenced the widespread disapproval of his government when it abandoned those positions in 1995. The resultant combination of popular expectations and disillusionment with proestablishment politicians like Pérez and Caldera was an essential ingredient for Chávez's election in 1998.

The basic rationale for the *Chavista* movement's drive for power was that the post-1958 democracy had betrayed national interests, neglected the poor, and was riddled with corruption. The unswerving rejection of the post-1958 governments makes Chávez's arguments in favor of the need for a "revolutionary" break with the past more compelling. Indeed, the *Chavista* term "revolutionary process," referring to the changes after Chávez's assumption of power in 1998, recalls AD's characterization of the 1945 coup as the "Revolution of October."[9] The plausibility of the *Chavista* interpretation of events notwithstanding, it is my belief that—short of extreme circumstances involving recurring atrocities against the population—a military coup against a democratically elected government is unjustifiable.

In short, politically inspired writing on the post-1936 modern period—like the opinions on the nation's past often expressed by Chávez—largely ignored the complexity of historical developments. These writers simplified the critical junctures of 1936, 1945, 1948, and 1958 by judging resultant changes in absolute terms, depending on the position of the writers' respective parties at the time. The *Chavistas* in power after 1998 have questioned the accuracy of the political literature that was highly partial in favor of post-1958 governments. The *Chavista* experience has also encouraged a reexamination of the three above-mentioned notions of Venezuelan politics and society: that Venezuela historically was characterized by low-levels of conflict; that issues of substance largely have been lacking in political struggles; and that solid political institutions have minimized open expressions of conflict. This book proposes a systematic revision of these assumptions regarding Venezuela's past and present. In doing so, it profits from scholarship over the last several decades that has questioned traditional views on specific periods of Venezuelan history.

▶ Toward Rethinking Venezuelan Politics

The view of Venezuela's past and present put forward in this book calls for a greater examination of important political and social actors that analysts have often excluded or left on the sidelines. Most important, the book questions the long-held assumption that class mobility in Venezuela has minimized social strains and thus explains the allegedly low levels of class-based politics. The fallacy of the assumption was demonstrated by the War of Independence, when racial and class tensions came to the fore in spite of the considerable mobility produced by interracial unions during the colonial period. Similarly, in spite of the social mobility facilitated by the windfall of oil revenue in the 1970s, Venezuela since the late 1980s has witnessed a high degree of social tension and conflict.

The approach proposed in this book takes issue with three broad historiographic schools and interpretive tendencies. First, traditional historians writing in the nineteenth and much of the twentieth century emphasized the random violence of the War of Independence and its long-term aftermath, while minimizing the importance of political and especially social demands and aspirations that had important repercussions in the period after 1936. Second, politically motivated interpretations from Betancourt to Chávez have simplified and distorted history.

Third, exceptionalism literature and thinking, which portrayed the post-1958 democracy as a model for the rest of Latin America, also presented unbalanced views. The perspectives and viewpoints in all three cases have affected the thinking of writers about Venezuela, as well as Venezuelans in general, to this day.

In analyzing Venezuelan history and politics, I borrow from the theoretical formulations of various recent schools of historiography that call on historians to explicitly recognize their own values, ideological orientations, and viewpoints.[10] The following chapters, and particularly the discussion of pre-1958 history, rest on the proposition that political movements best serve the nation by combining efforts to achieve four critical goals, as opposed to the promotion of one or two of them to the exclusion of the others. The four battle fronts are: (1) the struggle for social justice; (2) the struggle for democracy; (3) the effort to promote national economic development; and (4) the adoption of economic and political nationalism.

This approach is intended to be a corrective to positivism, which guided late-nineteenth-century and early-twentieth-century rulers and has also been reflected in traditional Venezuelan historiography and even current political thinking (Ellner and Hellinger 2003, 225–226). Positivism during Venezuela's premodern period stressed the promotion of national development and envisioned gradual material progress, while failing to address the other three above-mentioned aspirations. Chapter 2 discusses the shortcomings of the positivist approach as well as traditional historiography. It is argued that the struggles for democracy, nationalist ideals, and social justice must be valued in their own right, rather than dismissing them as futile causes simply because concrete gains were not registered in the short- or medium-term future. It is my belief that these types of struggles invariably remain in a nation's collective consciousness and that their goals are sometimes achieved in unpredictable forms many years after they were apparently defeated.

The banners that have been raised during the modern period since 1936, and specifically after 1998 under Chávez, have to be understood in this larger historical context. Indeed, the evaluation of the phenomenon of *Chavismo* in this book reflects my appreciation of the importance of all four goals and the belief that no one of them should be prioritized at the expense of the others. *Chavismo* represents a reaction to the tendency of the neoliberals (like the positivists before them) to subordinate issues of social justice and national sovereignty to the goal of economic growth, which is assumed will be forthcoming once promarket reforms are implemented. The *Chavistas*, however, have overreacted to the past emphasis on economic goals and developmentalism by privileging the banners of social justice and nationalism while failing to address systematically the need to create a viable economic model with the aim of promoting efficiency and increasing national production.

Chapter 2 of this book discusses radical and popular banners dating back to the nineteenth century that represented an important antecedent to the modern period. Chapter 3, covering 1958–1988, looks at political currents both within and outside of the establishment parties whose struggles against the nation's dominant leadership and its policies pointed to the fundamental shortcomings of Venezuelan democracy during that period. The chapter also, however, highlights the system's progressive features. In Chapter 4, dealing with the years of neoliberal ascendance in the 1990s, I trace the political elite's abandonment of economic policies favoring state interventionism and argue that this general turn to neoliberalism at leadership levels paved the way for the rise of the *Chavista* movement. Chapter 5 examines the dynamic of the Chávez phenomenon of continuous radicalization and the simultaneous emergence of the outlines of a new model reflected in social and economic fields. The next two chapters demonstrate the complexity of the *Chavista* movement, as shown by both internal ideological conflicts (Chapter 6) and by cleavages separating those who support a party strategy from those who manifest antiparty attitudes and insist on a grassroots approach (Chapter 7). Ideological differences in the realm of foreign policy express themselves along similar lines, as discussed in Chapter 8. Finally, Chapter 9 relates the Venezuelan case to various theoretical formulations regarding national specificity, "people's history," and the role of the state.

▶ Notes

1. Traditional historiography prior to the modern democratic period, which was questioned by professional historians graduating from the first schools of history founded in the Universidad Central (UCV) and the Universidad de los Andes (ULA) in the 1950s, has influenced the thinking of Venezuelans to this day, as will be discussed in Chapter 2 (Ellner 1995, 93).

2. Ernesto Laclau (1977) formulated the thesis that nonrevolutionary populist governments sometimes set the stage for revolutionary transformation. Laclau, however, limited his analysis to discourse while failing to underline the importance of concrete policies that also contribute to creating a prerevolutionary situation (Raby 2006, 242–243).

3. Proposals to bury Guaicaipuro's symbolic remains in the National Pantheon long failed to materialize (Hellinger 1991, 15–16) until a presidential decree in 2001 ordered the burial.

4. The Venezuelan historian Federico Brito Figueroa attempted to refute the traditional notion that denied the occurrence of a significant number of slave revolts in Venezuela (Brito Figueroa 1985, 243–245).

5. Nevertheless, throughout the modern democratic period Venezuela has exhibited high levels of interpersonal and criminal violence (see Márquez 1999).

6. Thus, for example, the tendency to use *tu* instead of *usted* for the word "you" (known as *tuteo*) reflects the informality that characterizes the everyday behavior of Venezuelans. For a fuller description of the personal characteristics discussed in this paragraph, see Fergusson (1939, 320–331) and Leeuw (1935, 159–166).

7. Samuel Huntington (1991), for instance, in his influential book *The Third Wave: Democratization in the Late Twentieth Century*, credits moderates and moderate strategies, as opposed to leftist ones, particularly those involving violence, with achieving democracy throughout history, specifically in Latin America in the 1980s. Ruth Collier (1999) presents an alternative view that stresses the role of the labor movement and worker mobilization in the reestablishment of Latin American democracy during the same period. The assertion by political scientist Giovanni Sartori (often applied to Latin America) that a two-party system with minimum ideological differences is conducive to stable and authentic democracy also, in effect, privileges political moderates (Sartori 1976; see also Duverger 1954). A third example of a theoretical approach that celebrates the role of moderates is the four-volume *The Breakdown of Democratic Regimes*, edited by Juan Linz and Alfred Stepan, which credits cautious and prudent leadership of centrists and moderates with the avoidance of democratic breakdown (Linz and Stepan 1978).

8. The justification of the February 4, 1992, coup attempt based on the Pérez government's corruption and betrayal of national interests is an article of faith among the *Chavistas*. One coup participant who has expressed misgivings is Ronald Blanco La Cruz, an army captain who was wounded in action and in 2000 was elected governor of the state of Táchira on the *Chavista* ticket.

9. The case for the perniciousness of the post-1958 governments was enhanced by Chávez's refusal to accept the traditional left's absolute condemnation of dictator Pérez Jiménez, whom he actually invited to his presidential inauguration in 1999 (Caballero 2002, 215).

10. Writers belonging to the "postmodernist" school of history, among others, defend this approach (Jenkins 1997).

2

▼

From the
Colonial Period to 1958:
A Brief Overview

UNTIL the boom in university-promoted, social-science research in Venezuela in the latter part of the twentieth century, studies on the nation's history and politics were characterized by a focus on individual actors that put forward black-and-white explanations of the past. Thus, for instance, beginning in the nineteenth century, writing on Simón Bolívar amounted to, in the words of one prominent revisionist historian, a "cult of the hero" that vilified royalist forces, even though initially the popular classes sympathized with the Spanish monarchy and the independence movement was identified with the Creole aristocracy (Carrera Damas 1969). Writings by members of the generation of 1928 who founded the first modern political parties further simplified long-standing political processes. Similar to the messianic impulses of other generations that believed they were destined to radically change society, the generation of 1928 belittled all past struggles since independence, dismissing that protracted period as a lost century. Those generation members who wrote on contemporary politics viewed the regime changes of 1936, 1945, 1948, and 1958 as the dawning of new eras that were either overwhelmingly positive or catastrophic, depending on each writer's political sympathies and party affiliation.

These politically motivated interpretations passed over continuities and gradual trends produced by structural transformations, specifically social and economic ones. Indeed, the dramatic developments on political and socioeconomic fronts after 1936 did not occur in a historical vacuum. The Venezuela of 1936 was hardly the same society as that of 1830. Had the years 1830 to 1936 been truly static without the occurrence of significant events, as implied in traditional historiography, the far-reaching slogans, demands, and programs that were formulated and received popular support following the death of Juan Vicente Gómez would have been hard to explain.

The policies and strategies of various governments during the nineteenth and early twentieth centuries encouraged, if not promoted, the changes that set the stage for the modern period. It is true that positivist thinking—which was often openly racist, disregarded democratic ideals, and spurned the aspirations of the popular sectors—was the ideological prompt of the longest governments in Venezuelan history, namely those of Antonio Guzmán Blanco (1870–1888) and Juan Vicente Gómez (1908–1935). Nevertheless, to their credit, both positivist-inspired regimes promoted national development and state building through incipient national institutions.

In addition to national development, the three other ideals discussed in Chapter 1 (nationalist aspirations, democracy, and social justice) lay behind ongoing struggles and formed part of the national collective consciousness that would be embedded in the popular movement in 1936. Nationalism found expression in the positions assumed by various governments, specifically those of Guzmán Blanco and Cipriano Castro. In contrast, the causes of democracy and social justice championed by the Liberal Party during the bloody Federal War (1859–1863) were shunted aside once Guzmán Blanco reached power and were not taken up by subsequent governments. In spite of this abandonment, however, both banners inspired struggles in the years to come.

Commitment to democracy, for instance, characterized the opposition to Gómez, beginning with the demand for the enforcement of the no-reelection provision of the Constitution in 1914, and inspired the armed struggles undertaken by the dictator's powerful and wealthy adversaries, such as José Rafael Gabaldón in 1929. Furthermore, students who participated in movements against Gómez in 1919 and 1928 were linked to the dictator's older political adversaries as well as discontented elements within the military. Historians have generally underscored the importance of the movement of the generation of 1928, and its complete break with the nation's political past, at the expense of these former struggles. Indeed, most writing on the period labels the older anti-*Gomecista* leaders self-serving "caudillos" and characterize those opposed to Gómez prior to 1928 as disillusioned and lacking in credible leadership and political orientation (Fuenmayor 1978, 266; Morón 1971, 323).

The accumulation of experiences in the struggle for far-reaching change over an extended period of time helps explain the outpouring of popular energy beginning just days after the death of Gómez. The zeal

in favor of social justice and democracy and the expression of nationalist sentiment manifested themselves in 1936 in many forms: the spontaneous street actions that forced the foreign employees of oil companies
to seek refuge in ships anchored in the Lake of Maracaibo (nationalism);
the civic strikes in May and June of 1936 to protest legislation abridging
democratic rights (support for democracy); and the proliferation of labor
unions (the struggle for social justice). While ideological currents from
Europe molded the thinking of members of the generation of 1928 who
formed part of the leadership of these movements, the rank-and-file participants in 1936 were influenced by the rich tradition of protest in
Venezuela dating back to the nineteenth century.[1]

Of the four historical banners referred to in Chapter 1, scholars and
analysts have paid the least attention to the struggle for social justice
and the related phenomena of class and racial tensions. The exceptionalism thesis, which denied the existence of acute social conflict in
Venezuela, gained widespread acceptance during the modern democratic
period after 1958. In addition, some political scientists viewed
Venezuela as a neocorporatist society in which state structures governed
labor relations and straightjacketed the labor movement, thus thwarting
expressions of worker conflict (Salamanca 1998, 31–88). Other studies,
which viewed unions as beholden to political parties, also minimized the
importance of rank-and-file struggles and cases of worker movement
autonomy (Fagen 1977, 189–192). Finally, the portrayal of the nation as
a racial democracy denied the prevalence of racial tensions, even though
animosity between whites and people of color played a key role in the
War of Independence and nineteenth-century civil wars, and has manifested itself, albeit in more subtle forms, ever since.

Of the four above-mentioned goals, the efforts to promote national
development have received by far the most attention. This trend began
with the works of Germán Carrera Damas who questioned the notion of
the 1830–1936 period as a lost century (Carrera Damas 1984).
Nevertheless, the interpretations by Carrera Damas and other authors
who have underlined the significance of political movements and struggles of the premodern period have not been assimilated by much of the
nation. In recent years, educators in the field of history have discussed
this dilemma at meetings such as the Conference on Research and
Teaching of the Science of History (Jornadas de Investigación y
Docencia en la Ciencia de la Historia), held every two years since 1985.
Participants have expressed particular concern over the predominance of
just a few textbooks approved by the Ministry of Education for classroom use. Some educators argue that these texts reflect a "Euro-Centric
vision" (Del Valle 2005) that downplays Indian resistance to the Spanish

conquest and the rebellions of black slaves and denigrates all nineteenth-century military leaders.[2] The Democratic Action party (AD) and Committee of Independent Political Electoral Organization party (COPEI), which for many years controlled the Ministry of Education, had a vested interest in viewing Venezuelan politics prior to the modern period as a manifestation of backwardness since this portrayal bolstered their own legitimacy and that of the governments they headed after 1945.

In spite of barriers, examples of recent changes in perception of historical figures and events abound. Thus, for instance, as a result of AD's loss of prestige beginning in the 1990s, Rómulo Betancourt is no longer revered as in previous decades. Furthermore, the anniversary of the February 27, 1989, disturbances involving lower-class Venezuelans now receives greater attention than that of the AD-led coup of October 18, 1945.

President Chávez's condemnation of traditional political historiography as "bourgeois history" based on an "imported" model (Blanco Muñoz 1998, 103), his praise for such historical figures as Cipriano Castro, Isaías Medina Angarita, and Luis Beltrán Prieto Figueroa, and his refusal to vilify Pérez Jiménez have encouraged his followers and even many outside of his movement to rethink the nation's past. Diverse trends under Chávez's presidency have also stimulated reexamination through new lenses that focus on the four historical banners discussed earlier. Developments that have influenced interpretations along these lines include the emergence of new social organizations representing Indians, blacks, women, and the marginalized sectors of the population; the incorporation of a radical democratic model in the 1999 Constitution; the government's explicitly anti-imperialist foreign policy; and social polarization along political lines.

The following sections will argue for drawing the connection between the nation's rich heritage of political struggle and transformations prior to 1936, on the one hand, and the modern period on the other. In doing so, it explores the contours of revisionist thinking designed to fill gaps in the existing literature, particularly with regard to social conflict and class interests, and suggests avenues of inquiry that may contribute to a comprehensive picture of the nation's past.

▶ The Colonial Period

An underlying thesis proposed in this book is that Venezuela has historically been characterized by class fluidity, but, contrary to what is often assumed, mobility has not translated itself into social harmony. The colonial period puts these characteristics in sharp relief. Even though, as many historians have noted, racial stratification in colonial Venezuela was less rigid than in neighboring colonies due largely to miscegenation (Salcedo-Bastardo 1979, 151), racial and social tension was more intense (Lombardi 1982, 117). Resentment and confrontation along class and racial lines fed into the War of Independence and helps to explain why the movement against Spain consolidated itself in Venezuela sooner than for the rest of the continent.

Colonial Venezuela's salient characteristic that accounts for both its social and racial fluidity and the colony's lead role in the War of Independence was its backwater setting. Venezuela's marginal economic value was due to its lack of both precious metals and a hierarchical structure of the Indian population that would have been conducive to intense labor exploitation. As a result, few Spanish women immigrated to the colony and married into the Creole elite, thus encouraging miscegenation that represented a form of class mobility. In addition, owing to Venezuela's limited economic importance, the Spanish crown's presence was weak and colonial institutions were rudimentary. Venezuela was a fragile link in the Spanish empire, which was bound to break at an earlier date than it did within other Latin American nations.

Colonization got off to a bad start with the concession granted the German trading company Welser in 1528 for the conquest and settlement of Venezuela. In their unyielding but futile search for precious metals, the Germans failed to fulfill their end of the bargain of founding towns, building forts, and bringing Indians under control in order to incorporate them into the *encomienda* labor system. Not only did the Welsers enslave the Indians, but they sold goods to the Spanish at elevated prices and tried to avoid payment of taxes, provoking grievances from residents of the capital city of Coro as well as government functionaries. After two decades, the Spanish crown revoked the Welsers's concessions.

Following the exit of the Germans, settlers made several attempts to found Caracas, beginning in 1555, but the achievement was held back by the Spanish zeal in searching for gold, as well as resistance from local tribes. Under the united leadership of the legendary Carib cacique Guaicaipuro, the Indians of the region held the Spanish at bay and at one point forced them to flee to the island of Margarita (Sanoja and Vargas Arenas 2002, 57–59). Caracas was finally founded in 1567 and became the nation's capital ten years later. Indeed, throughout much of the colonial period, recalcitrant Indian resistance impeded the consolidation of Spanish rule in Venezuela. The two main Indian groups, the Caribs and

the Arawaks, lacked regional organization other than for military purposes and consequently were harder to subdue in their entirety.

Venezuela's rugged coastline also impeded the assertion of Spanish
authority since it discouraged settlements that would have served as a
check on foreign intruders. This geographical liability contributed to the
movement of independence. Thus in the eighteenth century, the extensive contraband that grew out of Spain's inability to effectively patrol
the Venezuelan coast facilitated the entrance of pamphlets espousing
free trade, democracy, and other subversive ideas from Europe.

Fragmentation further weakened Spanish rule in Venezuela. The
colony consisted of three distinct regions that were isolated from one
another and had commercial ties with different foreign markets. One
consisted of Caracas and Aragua to its west, along with the plains to the
south of both. A second region took in the eastern part of the colony
including the coastal cities of Barcelona and Cumaná and the cattle-
raising plains to their south. The third region was in the west, which was
tied commercially to the Venezuelan city of Maracaibo and to Bogotá.

The modernizing Bourbon kings of the eighteenth century reacted to
Venezuela's increased economic importance as a result of its production
of cacao by taking steps to centralize control over the colony. In 1728
the crown granted the Basque-owned Guipuzcoana Company special
privileges to monopolize foreign commerce and assert authority over the
entire colony from Caracas. Centralization advanced further in 1777
when the crown converted Venezuela to the status of captaincy general,
whose leading figure reported directly to the crown, thus relieving the
colony of its dependence on the Viceroyalty of Bogotá. The crown's
decision in 1786 to grant Venezuela its own *audiencia*, located in
Caracas and under the direction of Spaniards, had a similar centralizing
impact. With the tightening of Spanish authority in the eighteenth century, the Creole elite-run city councils (*cabildos*), which in Caracas had
occasionally taken over from the governor during his absence from the
colony, had their power reduced to routine secondary matters, as was
their intended function.

The centralization under the Spanish Bourbon kings led to rebellion
and other forms of resistance from diverse sectors of the population,
which highlighted not only conflicting class interests but also acute
social tensions. Class differences were particularly well defined in one
of the most important preindependence rebellions led by Canarian
immigrant Juan Francisco León in 1749. León marched on Caracas from
the east with 800 armed men and surrounded the governor's house,
demanding the expulsion of the Guipuzcoana Company's functionaries.

Support for León at first crossed class lines. Members of the elite sympathized with his cause, as demonstrated by the position assumed by Caracas's *cabildo* as well as by university authorities, until the movement went beyond protest to armed uprising. The elite's initial favorable reaction reflected the discontent of local planters due to the drastically reduced prices the Guipuzcoana Company paid for cacao and the inflated prices on imported goods. Less wealthy planters, who increasingly saw their aspiration to become slaveholders thwarted, also held the company responsible for their economic predicament. Like León, many of the members of this middle sector were Canary Islanders who were subject to discriminatory treatment and sometimes considered an inferior race (Ferry 1989, 138). Once the rebellion was crushed, the Spanish authorities meted out punishment according to class. Concessions were made to the elite, in sharp contrast to the exemplary measures taken against the nonprivileged. Most graphically, the nailing of a mulatto's head to the door of León's house in 1751 was intended as a warning, particularly to blacks and multiracial colonists (known as *pardos*). The veritable alliance of the oppressed *pardos* with the middle sectors that lay behind the León movement was an ominous sign for the crown that its Spanish representatives in Venezuela in no way ignored (Ferry 1989, 175).

During the colonial period, the racial fusion of members of the popular sector became more pronounced than elsewhere in the continent. To a greater extent than in other colonies, agricultural laborers who owned their own subsistence plots (known as *conucos*) enjoyed freedom from forced labor. These laborers (who were *pardos*) had greater black and Indian features than the supposedly "white" members of the elite. In addition to their *conucos*, the *pardos* worked as free laborers on haciendas alongside, and at "similar and complementary tasks" as, blacks and Indians, who were subject to servitude. Due to the impoverishment shared by the popular sector in general, the daily interaction of free laborers, blacks, and Indians led to a high incidence of interracial unions and broke down interracial barriers to procreation, thus swelling the ranks of the *pardo* population. By the time of the War of Independence, the *pardos* constituted 50 to 60 percent of the colony's population. Venezuela was also characterized by cultural fusion, as demonstrated by its most popular cult, that of María Lionza. Dating back to the fifteenth century, María Lionza was an Indian legendary figure but in succeeding centuries acquired considerable European and African traits (Wright 1990, 18–20).

Racial fluidity, however, did not translate itself into racial harmony. Even though the *pardos* imitated the upper class in dress and social

customs, and in some cases purchased from the crown certain privileges reserved for the elite, they were generally excluded from participation in the colony's institutions. Toward the end of Spanish rule, the
Bourbon kings supported measures of equality that had the effect of
emboldening the *pardos* and galvanizing tensions between them and
the Creole elite.

The resistance of the elite to the social aspirations of the *pardos* was
demonstrated by their reaction to the "gracias al sacar" royal order
issued in 1795, which allowed those of mixed blood to buy their way
into the upper class. The elite-controlled *cabildo* of Caracas, which in
the past had requested that the king rule out this type of practice and
pressured to deepen racial divisions, now decided to ignore compliance
with the order (Herrera Salas 2007, 102). Indeed, the Venezuelan elite's
opposition and resistance to the "gracias al sacar" measure were more
intense and efficacious than in neighboring colonies (Carrera Damas
1984, 41). The elite's fear of challenges from below was aggravated by
the Haiti slave uprising in 1791, followed by the three-day bloody revolt
of racially diverse nonprivileged sectors in Coro led by José Leonardo
Chirinos, a free farmer of Indian and African descent. The racial and
class frictions that intensified during the latter years of Spanish rule culminated with the War of Independence. This sequence is a clear demonstration that the high degree of class mobility characteristic of
Venezuela, both as a colony and a nation, has historically failed to
reduce class distinctions or to contain socially driven conflict.

▶ The War of Independence

The period from April 19, 1810, when colonists forced the crown-
appointed captain general to step down, until the death of Simón Bolívar
in 1830 exemplifies a pattern described throughout this book in which
leaders vacillate and reverse their stands while popular sectors defend
ongoing demands and goals. The radical changes in the positions of
political leaders were evident in the nineteenth century (to be discussed
later in this chapter) and the post-1958 democratic period (discussed in
Chapters 3 and 4). Nevertheless, the pattern was particularly striking
during the struggle for independence in that both sides in the conflict
did complete turnabouts. In the course of just a few years the royalists
abandoned their appeal to the popular sectors, while the independence
forces—at first representing the colonial elite exclusively—succeeded in
filling the resultant vacuum.

The reversals explain in large part the outcome of the independence struggle. When the Spaniards were finally defeated in the early 1820s and popular support was no longer critical, some independence leaders, such as José Antonio Páez, turned their backs on the popular sectors (from which they had come). The conservative backlash was strengthened by the return of émigrés in the 1820s and it resulted in the postponement of the abolition of slavery, even though halfway measures such as manumission of slave offspring were implemented. In contrast, Bolívar defended the absolute abolition of slavery and called for Latin American unification, a position that appeared advanced for the time. These controversial stands generated resistance from vested interests, thus contributing to the tragic end of Bolívar's life that included the assassination of his trusted general Antonio José de Sucre and his own banishment and isolation at the time of his death in 1830, so graphically described by Gabriel García Márquez (1990) in *The General in His Labyrinth.*

The major turning point in the realignment of classes during this period occurred at the outset of the so-called Third Republic that began with the landing of a Bolívar-led expedition on the island of Margarita in May 1816. Lessons from the defeats of the first two republics were not lost on Bolívar. The First Republic began with the dislodging of Spain's maximum representatives on April 19, 1810, until the surrender of Francisco de Miranda to Spanish forces in July 1812. Bolívar noted that the independence forces were plagued by a lack of centralized political leadership. He was particularly critical of, and even attempted to modify, the Constitution of 1811, which maintained regional autonomy by establishing a federal system of government. The colonists paid heavily for the error as the repression unleashed by the Spaniards was unexpectedly harsh and produced a veritable bloodbath in Caracas. The main lesson of the Second Republic that spanned from Bolívar's arrival from the west of Venezuela in May 1813 until May 1815 was equally compelling. During this period the independence leaders failed to appeal to the popular classes. The leading commander of the royalist forces, José Tomás Boves, took advantage of the association of the independence cause with the privileged sectors by appealing to the anti-elite and antiwhite feelings of his soldiers. A large number of them were seminomads from the plains region who held Boves in high esteem because of his acceptance of pillage as a facet of military warfare.

These experiences molded Bolívar's thinking and actions at the time of the Third Republic. Bolívar's famous speech at the Congress of Angostura (today Ciudad Bolívar) in 1819 attacked federalism, and this same line of thinking was reflected in the Constitution of Bolivia (then Upper Peru), which he drafted in Lima in 1826. In addition, a number of decisions taken by Bolívar helped win over the nonwhite population to his side. At the outset of the Third Republic, in the city of Carúpano, he decreed the liberty of slaves who joined his army. His Law of Distribution of National Property as Compensation to Officers and Soldiers in 1817, which turned over the land and possessions of Spanish loyalists to his troops, also favored nonprivileged sectors with the aim of shoring up the military (Irwin 2004, 96). In addition, the return of the reactionary Fernando VII to the Spanish crown in 1814, following the defeat of Napoleon, helped change the allegiance of large numbers of nonwhites. Not only did the king eliminate reforms and practices of the past that had helped break down race distinctions in the colonies, but he sent a 15,000-man army under General Pablo Morillo to replace the rag-tag forces under Boves, who had died in battle in December 1814.

Traditional historiography presents a particularly one-sided view of two important episodes during the period that had implications for class and nationalism. One is the execution of the second in command of the eastern forces, Manuel Piar, a staunch opponent of the system of slavery whose mother was a mulatto and whose soldiers were predominately nonwhite. Many traditional historians attribute Piar's defiant behavior to his jealousy of Bolívar, due to the latter's superior social status. Some of them, such as the renowned writer José Gil Fortoul, argue that the main issue at stake was simply the ambition of power (Siso Martínez 1973, 89). In general, traditional historians accept at face value the accusations formulated against Piar of promoting insubordination, separatism, and conspiracy as well as caste warfare (Morón 1971, 187). The gravest allegation against Piar was that he had preached hatred of whites and called for their murder.

Leftists and other writers deny the main charges against Piar and claim that the witnesses who testified against him were his personal enemies while the "white" army hierarchy lacked impartiality (González 1979, 202). Some of these historians argue that over the last two centuries the concerted effort to portray Bolívar as infallible has produced intentional distortions about Piar's actions (Salas 2004, 189, 193, 211).

Class and race were the real issues that mattered in the verdict against Piar. Indeed, if the other charges such as conspiracy and desertion had influenced the decision to execute Piar, then it would have been impossible to explain why harsh measures were not also taken against other commanders in the east (such as Santiago Mariño, the leading officer) who also staunchly promoted separatism and opposed Bolívar's centralized authority. Leftist historian Asdrúbal González describes the atmosphere prevailing at the time as "a revolutionary fervor with the potential of transforming the war of independence into class warfare" and goes on to point out that Piar "at that historical moment was the popular leader most capable of carrying out the struggle to its ultimate consequences" (González 1979, 185). González, however, disagrees with the view eventually embraced by Bolívar that Piar had become a symbol of race and class hatred (Lynch 2006; I. Quintero 2004, 160) and instead argues that Piar's social animosity was directed against the Spanish. In short, Piar expressed the attitudes and interests of the non-privileged, but exactly how his convictions and leadership would have played out, and whether the buoyancy of the lower-class troops in the wake of military victories would have led to infighting and chaos, was impossible to determine. In any case, the execution of Piar did serve its intended purpose of helping Bolívar consolidate his command, thus making possible subsequent military successes throughout the colony and much of the rest of Spanish America.

The second event that traditional historiography failed to explore in depth and place in a broader context was the Panama Congress convoked by Bolívar for the newly independent Spanish American republics in 1826. The congress made plans to establish a loose confederation of Spanish American nations to assume responsibility for the collective defense of the region. Nevertheless, with the exception of Colombia, none of the governments that sent representatives to Panama ratified the agreements. This failure led historians to minimize the importance of the congress and dismiss its proposals as futuristic, if not utopian.

Bolívar, however, had good reason for calling the congress. The prospect of a foreign military intervention in the continent was very real and was heightened by the Monroe Doctrine issued in 1823 and the prevalence of the conservative order imposed on Europe by Metternich. The congress also called for the liberation of Cuba and Puerto Rico from Spanish rule as well as enforcement of the abolition of the slave trade. These proposals were hardly quixotic but did clash with US and European interests (Ortega Díaz 2006, 46–47). Indeed, US and English diplomats opposed Bolívar's plans and attempted to discredit the congress (Pividal 1979, 163–179). Bolívar originally favored inviting only Spanish American countries to the congress. Nevertheless, after invitations went out to other countries, including the United States, he accepted broader participation. For this reason, many historians pass over Bolívar's fear of Washington, which he expressed at the time of the congress, and fail to point out that the Panama meeting embraced the banner of Latin American unity, as opposed to "Pan-Americanism," which would have taken in North America (see, for instance, Morón 1971, 210–211). In contrast, leftist writers, including pro-*Chavistas*, harp on Bolívar's warnings regarding US imperial intentions (Ortega Díaz 2006).

Bolívar created the Gran Colombia Republic, taking in Venezuela, Colombia, and Ecuador, in 1821 as a first step toward Spanish American unification. Páez, however, led Venezuela's withdrawal in 1830 and Ecuador followed suit the same year. Pro-Chávez historians accuse Great Britain of playing a key role in the destruction of the Gran Colombia. They also claim that the goal of reestablishing the Gran Colombia was defended in subsequent decades by various top officers who had served under Bolívar as well as Venezuelan heads of states (such as José Gregorio and José Tadeo Monagas in the 1840s and 1850s) and was incorporated in the Constitutions of 1857 and 1864 (Toro Jiménez 2006a; 2006b, 48–52). In fact, after a short-lived government in 1835 that sought to revive the Gran Colombia, the project was doomed and hardly emerged as an issue of contention or point of reference in Venezuelan politics. Indeed, the attempt to demonstrate the continuity of the spirit of Gran Colombia is politically charged. Chávez frequently appeals to its legacy to support his call for Latin American unity in the face of US imperialism.

Traditional historians emphasized the violence and destruction unleashed by the War of Independence in Venezuela, which far surpassed the devastation in other Spanish colonies. Thus, for instance, the renowned positivist intellectual Laureano Vallenilla Lanz described in detail lower-class animosities as manifested by the slogan "death to the whites." He pointed out that by the 1820s the situation had degenerated. "Spontaneous anarchy" forced Páez and other independence leaders to give orders to shoot against "those bands that ravaged the countryside, looted and burned down towns, hounded authorities, and killed white people" (Vallenilla Lanz 1990, 167–168). Other writers have explained the switch in loyalty (from Spain to the patriots) of the popular sectors, which are depicted as ignorant masses, to the death of their caudillo, Boves, and his replacement by Páez.

In dwelling on irrational, vacuous, and unruly behavior, traditional writers ignore or play down the concrete aspirations and goals of the popular sectors. In order to present a balanced picture of class motivations, historical studies need to focus on three key policies of the army's command that drew the popular classes to the ranks of the independence forces: the liberation of slaves, the distribution of land to the soldiers, and the promotion of lower-class soldiers (such as Páez) to top positions. In addition, the practice of pillage and confiscation of property, which also helped convert the War of Independence into a popular struggle, needs to be placed in proper perspective. Traditional historians underlined the horrors of pillage while various others have exaggerated its transformational nature (Fernández Avello 1974). As the historian Germán Carrera Damas demonstrates, pillage hardly represented the precursor of agrarian reform, nor was its acceptance by both Boves and Bolívar part of a larger plan of redistribution of wealth (Carrera Damas 1972, 247–251). Nevertheless, Bolívar was aware of the class appeal of his Law of Distribution of National Property and viewed it as an acceptable alternative to class warfare. The law in effect substituted the anarchical seizure of enemy possessions with the regulation of the distributive process (I. Quintero 2004, 159).

Beginning with Antonio Guzmán Blanco in the latter part of the nineteenth century, Venezuelan political leaders eulogized Simón Bolívar as part of an effort to promote a national identity and the centralization of power. More recently, Chávez has called Bolívar "Latin America's first anti-imperialist," in accordance with the Venezuelan president's appeal to nationalist sentiment and his anti-US rhetoric. In both cases, political imperatives underlined the defense of historical interpretations that center on Bolívar's attractive qualities and achievements. Traditional writers have also glorified Bolívar and have thus reinforced the "cult of Bolívar." At the same time they have repudiated the "exaggerated" attempts by historians such as Carrera Damas to demythologize Bolívar (Morón 1971, 176) and to present a more balanced picture of the man in the context of his era.

The veneration of Bolívar passes over his human qualities and errors in judgment. An example of such a folly often ignored by historians is when he impulsively arrested Francisco de Miranda for having reached an agreement with Spanish authorities that put an end to the First Republic.[3] More important, Bolívar's vacillations and identification with the elite, as well as at times his pragmatism, detracted from his credentials as a champion of egalitarian ideals and uncompromising nationalism. Bolívar, for instance, while in exile in Jamaica following the defeat of the Second Republic, appealed to England to provide arms and men for the independence cause by offering the nation a special commercial relationship. Furthermore, in spite of his compassion for the plight of nonwhites and his liberation of all of his more than 100 slaves, Bolívar dreaded the prospect of a "pardocracy" in a country where the *pardos* far outnumbered whites, a fear that was reinforced by memories of the racially motivated destruction perpetrated by Boves's army (Ugalde 2004, 48; Wright 1990, 27–28; Lynch 2006). Bolívar's support for a strong central government was intended as a guarantee against social upheaval. In short, the politically inspired historiography of the War of Independence has up to the present lent itself to views that de-emphasize or distort social demands and aspirations and other key issues of the period.

▶ The Nineteenth-Century National Period, 1830–1899

At first glance, the period from the death of Bolívar in 1830 until the end of the nineteenth century would appear to confirm the view of traditional historiography that those years were characterized by a series of betrayals of ideals, destructive civil wars, and the absence of significant transformations. Traditional historians labeled major nineteenth-century leaders—such as José Antonio Páez, Ezequiel Zamora, and Antonio Guzmán Blanco—"caudillos" and downplayed their redeeming qualities. The somber view of the nineteenth century was expressed by writers influenced by positivism who counterposed the "barbarism" of the past to the "civilization" that set in, according to some, in the late nineteenth century and, according to others, at the outset of the modern period in 1936 (Howard 1984, 96–104).

The blatant corruption of the two nineteenth-century leaders who remained in power the longest, Páez and Guzmán Blanco, and the failure to establish electoral democracy, unlike in other nineteenth-century South American countries, lent themselves to the negative viewpoint of traditional historiography. The dominant political figure in the 1830s and 1840s was the Conservative Party's Páez, an independence war hero of humble origins who died one of the richest men in the country in 1873. The Conservative Party's rival, the Liberal Party (founded in 1841), at first defended agricultural interests that faced foreclosure and successfully lobbied for the repeal of the Credit Law of April 10, 1834, which left debtors vulnerable to loss of property. The Liberal program included popular elections, alternation in power, equality before the law, religious liberty, and abolition of slavery, capital punishment, and imprisonment for debt.

The Conservative-Liberal rivalry culminated with the Federal War of 1859–1863. Traditional historians generally stressed the random violence and lack of military coordination of the five-year conflict, which resulted in an estimated 100,000 deaths and reduction in the number of cattle by over 50 percent. The Liberal triumph with the signing of the Treaty of Coche provided the Liberals with a golden opportunity to achieve the democratic and social ideals they had been preaching. The Liberals in power, however, failed to live up to their political promises. The main Liberal leader, Antonio Guzmán Blanco (1870–1888), engaged in electoral fraud and reneged on the pledge to tolerate a free press. Although the Liberals stood for limitation of central governmental power, Guzmán Blanco weakened the state governments by seizing control of custom houses and mining and salt concessions at the same time that he abolished internal tariffs. Traditional historians attributed the *caudillismo* of Guzmán Blanco to the nation's backwardness and its political culture in particular (Wise 1951, 177; Morón 1961, 371, 402, 441).

Writers identified with the Communist movement, who shared the "lost century" view of the period, and blamed Guzmán Blanco and those closest to him for betraying the progressive banners of the Liberal Party, particularly its radical wing led by Zamora. Thus while Zamora participated in one of a series of urban and peasant uprisings in the 1840s, the more conservative leaders of the Liberal Party attempted to reach an agreement with Páez and subsequently accepted a key government ministry. Similarly, Zamora's slogan, "Horror to the Oligarchy," and the banner of land distribution were abandoned by fellow Liberals following his death in 1860 (Brito Figueroa 1960, 329–331; de la Plaza and Duclos 1973, 39–40). In affirming the essentially static nature of the period, Communist ideologue Salvador de la Plaza denied that the nation's semifeudal system in the countryside was modified in any way (de la Plaza 1973, 102–111).

All historians to varying degrees recognize some of Guzmán Blanco's positive features and accomplishments. Guzmán Blanco promoted national identity and pride through the glorification of Simón Bolívar and the state's assumption of such tasks as civil registry and official marriages, activities that were previously performed by the church. To his credit, Guzmán Blanco decreed obligatory education, thus generating a near ten-fold increase in the number of schools. He also pursued an assertive foreign policy and at one point broke diplomatic relations with Great Britain in protest against that nation's encroachment on Venezuela's gold-rich Guayana region. Indeed, for the first time in Venezuelan history, Guzmán Blanco used nationalistic language in his dealings with European nations. Finally, Guzmán Blanco and other Liberals vigorously defended national sovereignty in the face of the anonymous appeal by landed interests to England to establish a protectorate in Venezuelan territory (Carrera Damas 1984, 95; Brito Figueroa 1960, 322–333).

During the modern democratic period, beginning in 1958, a revisionist school has questioned the assumptions of traditional historiography. The most renowned revisionist historian, Germán Carrera Damas, has argued against the negative line of thinking on nineteenth-century developments adhered to by both traditional and Communist historians. He responds to Communist writers who blame Guzmán Blanco for failing to make good on the promises of land distribution to the peasants by denying that agrarian reform was among the fundamental objectives of the Federal War. He also accuses Communist writers of distorting history by attempting to demonstrate Zamora's "socialist intentions" (Carrera Damas 2000, 68). Furthermore, Carrera Damas denies that the triumphant Liberals completely turned their backs on social concerns. Not only did they block the reestablishment of slavery (which had been abolished in 1854), but in 1863 issued the Decree of Guarantees that established equality before the law, thus consenting to the demands of multiracial Venezuelans (known as *pardos*). Other revisionist writers claim that Guzmán Blanco rewarded individual *pardos* for the participation of nonwhites on the side of the Liberals in the Federal War (Nava 1965, 531).

Carrera Damas's principal argument is that Guzmán Blanco represented the more advanced fraction of the dominant class by promoting a "national project" consisting of developmentalist policies and encouragement of foreign investments. The advanced sector confronted a backward fraction (known as the *godos*), which had governed Venezuela prior to the Federal War. Carrera Damas argues that the "perfection" and implementation of the national project was made possible by the pacification of the popular classes, whose members the Liberals had incited in the 1840s and 1850s but then demobilized upon reaching power following the Federal War (Carrera Damas 2000, 67). In putting forth his case, Carrera Damas implies that Liberal support for equality, liberty, and restriction of central governmental power was really designed to enhance the position of free enterprise by protecting it from arbitrariness and state-imposed restrictions and that the achievement of democracy per se was virtually irrelevant. Other historians build on Carrera Damas's concept of a "national project" to show that impressive road and railroad construction promoted commerce and united the nation. They point to a four-fold increase in exports during the period of Liberal rule from 1863 to 1888 and a favorable balance of trade in all but four of those years (Rodríguez Campos 1994, 96).

Hugo Chávez's attempt to reinforce Venezuelan nationalism by exalting past leaders such as Bolívar, Zamora, and Cipriano Castro, and his questioning of the use of the pejorative term *caudillo* for the period (Blanco Muñoz 1988, 103), is not without its detractors. The staunchly anti-*Chavista* historian Manuel Caballero accuses Chávez of systematically distorting historical facts and affirms that Zamora, far from being an antioligarch, was himself a slaveholder (Caballero 2002, 222). Elías Pino Iturrieta, another prominent Venezuelan historian who for years was instrumental in promoting revisionist history that put forward a balanced picture of Guzmán Blanco and Castro, became an ardent adversary of Chávez. Pino Iturrieta questions the motives behind Chávez's pronouncements on Venezuelan history by attributing them to his ambition for power and authoritarian mentality. Pino argues that the tendency of caudillo rulers to invoke the image of Bolívar reached "gross levels" with Guzmán Blanco, whom he calls a "self-worshiper," and has continued with Chávez. He adds that the manipulation of history by Chávez represents the "main dish" that forms part of the "menu" of justifications for his antidemocratic behavior (Pino Iturrieta 2003b; 2004).

All four ideals discussed in the last paragraphs of Chapter 1 of this book were key elements in the social and political struggles of the nineteenth century and the main political issues that emerged. Thus, for instance, the Liberal-inspired movements that led into the Federal War raised the banners of social equality and democracy. In addition, developmentalist policies and a foreign policy with nationalist overtones became prominent features of the rule of Guzmán Blanco. Much of the historical literature analyzed above focuses on just one of the ideals to the exclusion of the other three and thus presents an unbalanced view of the period. Some revisionist writing on Guzmán Blanco, for instance, centers on his successful programs of economic growth and in the process passes over the social and political shortcomings and deficiencies of his dictatorial rule. A similar error was committed by the Communist writers (with whom Carrera Damas took issue) who dwelled on the banners of social equality and land distribution while ignoring Guzmán Blanco's economic and cultural accomplishments as well as the nationalist thrust of his foreign policy.

Traditional historians who minimize the importance of political struggles during the nineteenth century on the grounds that they failed to make democratic breakthroughs, also present a distorted picture. From a long-term perspective, the social and political banners of the Liberals cannot be dismissed as futile. Indeed, historical studies need to scrutinize the ongoing struggles of the nineteenth century that led into the real democratic and social gains made during the modern period after 1936. The utilization of a bottom-up approach to the nineteenth century, and specifically with regard to political struggles and class and racial tensions, would go a long way toward documenting this continuity.

▶ The Governments of Cipriano Castro and Juan Vicente Gómez, 1899–1935

The year 1899 promised to usher in an era of transformation in Venezuela, as did the Liberal triumph in the Federal War several decades before. An army of sixty men led by Cipriano Castro and Juan Vicente Gómez invaded Venezuela from Colombia under the slogan "New Men, New Ideals, New Methods." Castro governed until 1908, when he was betrayed and overthrown by Gómez, who in turn ruled until his death in 1935.

The Castro and Gómez governments failed to fulfill expectations in favor of electoral democracy, but to their credit they promoted far-reaching changes, the most important of which was the creation of national institutions essential to stability and centralization. As a result, the Castro and Gómez regimes put an end to the nineteenth-century tradition of civil wars led by regional caudillos. The last such revolt, called the Revolución Libertadora, broke out in 1902 and was financed by the banker Manuel Antonio Matos, who was tied to foreign investors. Beginning in the 1920s when petroleum displaced coffee and cacao exports, oil production and oil revenue injected into urban areas by the government gave rise to new middle sectors and an industrial working class. The democratic sympathies of these emerging groups were reflected in the student protests against Gómez in 1928 that debuted leaders of the "generation of 1928," who were to be major political actors for the subsequent half a century.

Traditional historiography emphasizes Castro's lustfulness and Gómez's accumulation of wealth through heavy-handedness while characterizing the entire period as backward, repressive, and detrimental to national interests. Specifically in the case of Castro, the affirmation that he had "almost no moral scruples" (Rippy 1958, 432) led one Venezuelan historian to use the term "black legend" with reference to his reputation throughout the years (Pino Iturrieta 1991, 10–14). A more recent book by British historian Brian McBeth, while recognizing that the European blockade of Venezuelan ports in 1902–1903 was unjustified, blamed Castro for provoking it, stating that he acted in a "contradictory and megalomaniac manner" and showed a "complete disregard of the rights of foreign subjects" (McBeth 2001, 265–266).

The negative characterizations of Castro by traditional historians, while probably not exaggerated, obscure his redeeming qualities (Pino Iturrieta 1991, 13). Most important, Castro defended nationalistic positions, leading him to clash with foreign interests throughout his entire life. Even before coming to power, Castro lashed out at Great Britain for encroaching on Venezuelan territory in the Guayana region. As president, Castro's treatment of foreign capital was uncompromising, as demonstrated by his revocation of the concession granted the New York and Bermudez Company in 1885 for the exploitation of asphalt in the Venezuelan state of Sucre, and his requirement that the company pay indemnification. According to one account, Venezuela received greater benefits from investments than did Mexico under Porfirio Díaz's presidency, partly as a result of his mining code of 1904, which centralized mining concessions (Tinker Salas forthcoming, chapter 2). Castro's casual attitude toward the payment of foreign debts led to the blockade by Great Britain, Germany, and Italy in 1902–1903. The three countries were irked not so much by Castro's fiscal irresponsibility as by his defiant attitude, and thus they at first ruled out Venezuela's proposal (backed by Washington) to settle the matter by arbitration (Collin 1990, 96, 104). Castro reacted to the aggression by attempting to rally the country and by encouraging Venezuelans to enlist in the fight against the foreign invaders, although he quickly turned to diplomatic mechanisms.

Several years later, the administration of President Theodore Roosevelt, after considering military action against Venezuela, which it claimed was "exhausting the patience of the United States," sent war ships to the coastal area off of La Guaira in support of Juan Vicente Gómez's takeover (Polanco Alcántara 1990, 113; Ewell 1996, 104). For the remaining sixteen years of his life, Castro continued to pay a heavy price for his defiance of foreign powers. Castro became at the time, in the words of *Harper's Weekly*, "a man without a country" (Polanco Alcántara 1991, 54); he was denied entrance into various Caribbean nations by English and French authorities and was carefully tracked by the US Navy (as requested by the Gómez government), which thwarted his plans to return surreptitiously to Venezuela (Caballero 1993, 126).

Castro's unyielding nationalism, the multiple efforts of foreign interests to oust him from power, and his tragic final years in exile make him an appealing figure. But in spite of Castro's clashes with foreign powers and economic interests, writers across the political spectrum have generally refrained from praising him (Fuenmayor 1978, 108; Betancourt 1979, 28–30; Consalvi 1979, 10). (For a positive view by Venezuelan leftists see Ruptura 1977, 31–32.) Over time, this unsympathetic or lukewarm treatment of Castro was a lost opportunity for the nationalistic left (Ellner 1999c, 130–131). Chávez, on the other hand, has exploited Castro's legacy and has compared banker Manuel Antonio Matos with his own political adversaries, whom he claims are also tied to foreign powers. Chávez arranged to have Castro's remains brought to the National Pantheon on February 14, 2003 (as he had done in 1999 with Antonio Guzmán Blanco).

During the week of the ceremony at the National Pantheon, two editorials in the opposition newspaper *El Nacional* compared the demagoguery of Castro and Chávez, called them self-proclaimed revolutionaries, and pointed out that their offensive language created enemies at home and abroad. *El Nacional* added that Castro governed "through violence, scandals, and disorders . . . [and] practically the whole country rose up against" him. The editorials also pointed to the limited reach of Castro's nationalism, adding that by flaunting the European powers, Castro cemented Venezuelan ties with the United States, which ended up arbitrarily settling the claims dispute (*El Nacional*, February 11, 2003, A-8; February 17, 2003, A-8). By inveighing against Castro, the editorials in effect absolved the United States, the European invaders, Juan Vicente Gómez, and banker Manuel Antonio Matos of responsibility for having spurned national sovereignty. The two articles seemed to have been suggesting that Chávez ran the risk of suffering the same fate as his predecessor.

Another *Chavista* critic, historian Elías Pino Iturrieta, who had previously praised Castro as a "transitional" figure, accused Chávez of being an apologist for the former Venezuelan leader and being motivated by the desire to elevate his own "stature" (Pino Iturrieta 2003a). Pino and other anti-*Chavista* historians claim that Chávez's glorification of the strongman Castro is designed to prepare public opinion for his own dictatorial designs. They add that Chávez's self-serving interpretation of the past (in the words of *El Nacional*) "demonstrates he knows our history in a deficient and fragmentary way" (*El Nacional,* February 17, 2003, A-8; Caballero 2002, 215). Thus one century after Castro's overthrow, the evaluation of his rule is politically charged and has a direct bearing on current political struggle.

Castro and Gómez were different from nineteenth-century caudillos in other fundamental ways. Most important, the national standing army and other institutions created by both governments contributed to the establishment of a modern state. Castro decreed the founding of the Military Academy in 1903 and Gómez took advantage of increased revenue, mainly from oil, to centralize the military command; professionalize the officer corps; standardize uniforms, equipment, and instruction; and create the air force in 1920. Gómez's government also created a centralized and efficient Treasury Ministry by eliminating the practice of farming out tax concessions. Revisionist historian Carrera Damas calls for a nuanced evaluation of Gómez and rejects the longstanding notion that he was a mere agent of foreign powers (Carrera Damas 1995, 135). Another historian attempts to demonstrate that Gómez's absolute control of the cattle industry facilitated the extension of state power throughout the country and mechanisms of submission that had no equivalent in the rudimentary structures created by caudillo rulers of the previous century. One implication of this thesis is to deny that Gómez was a mere puppet of the foreign oil companies (Yarrington 2003, 10–12).

During the Castro and Gómez rules, the struggle for democracy, dating back to the second half of the nineteenth century, continued even though no democratic inroads were made. Indeed, Gómez's assumption of power created expectations due to the beginning of a democratic opening and promises of a presidential election in 1914. Gómez's refusal to comply with this pledge produced the first open confrontation of his rule and the defection of many of his original supporters. The anti-*Gomecistas* who opposed Gómez's permanence in power in 1914 and insisted on elections had diverse trajectories. Among those who went on to fight against the dictator during his lengthy rule were Emilio Arévalo Cedeño (who led his first of various anti-Gómez armed revolts in 1914), José Rafael Gabaldón (who, after urging Gómez to step down and call elections in 1928, led an uprising in the state of Portuguesa), Pedro Pérez Delgado ("Maisanta," Chávez's great-grandfather, himself the son of Pedro Pérez Pérez who had fought with Zamora), and Gustavo Machado and Salvador de la Plaza (who became leading, lifelong Communists). Machado and de la Plaza participated in student protests that led to the dissolution of the General Association of Students and the closing of the University of Caracas in 1912 and raised the banner of free elections and freedom of the press. They then joined a conspiracy within the military in 1919 that was accompanied by additional popular mobilization. Their activism originally reflected the Caracas elite's disgust with Gómez's monopolization schemes and was encouraged by President Woodrow Wilson's democratization zeal (D. A. Rangel 2001, 62; de la Plaza 1993, 93–94; de la Plaza and Duclos 1973,

25–26). Gabaldón (in addition to Machado and de la Plaza) embraced leftist causes for decades to come. Other anti-*Gomecistas* who predated the 1928 student movement, such as Régulo Olivares and Nestor Luis Pérez, were to form part of the succeeding government of Eleazar López Contreras and were identified with democratic and progressive positions. Another anti-*Gomecista* from the early years was the poet Andrés Eloy Blanco, who went on to become a leading member of AD.

Writers belonging to the generation of 1928 and political parties formed after 1936 play down these past struggles and continuities at the same time that they credit new political actors with initiating democratic and nationalistic banners following Gómez's death (R. Quintero 1970, 37; D. A. Rangel 1998, 98–99; see also Levine 1978, 86). Many historians have built on this perception by pointing to the "intellectual void" of the older anti-*Gomecistas* and the "impotence of their opposition . . . and way of engaging in politics" (Caballero 1998, 49). It is true that the older anti-*Gomecistas* were in many respects heterogeneous and, in trying to achieve unity in the struggle against Gómez, sacrificed specific well-defined positions (Sosa and Lengrand 1981, 47–48). Furthermore, many of these anti-*Gomecistas* were opposed to Gómez's despotism and monopoly control originally because of the dictator's violation of property rights for the sake of personal enrichment that came at their expense (as was the case with Arévalo Cedeño). Nevertheless, in characterizing the movements as elite-led, anachronistic, and "caudillo"-based (the same term used against them by the younger anti-*Gomecistas* after 1928), the generation of 1928 writers generally pass over the democratic commitments and goals of Gómez's older adversaries.

The discussion presented above of the 1899–1936 period is part of a larger critique of traditional historiography. That body of literature, which was influenced by the writings of members of the generation of 1928, underestimated the role of popular struggles during an extended period of time prior to 1936 as well as the transformations that took place during those years. A similar shortcoming characterizes much writing on the post-1958 period and even more so on the Chávez years, which tends to downplay conflict over concrete demands, particularly of a socioeconomic nature. Struggles in defense of class and national interests are overshadowed by discussion of (in the case of the pre-1936 period) power conflicts among the elite that are devoid of substantive issues and (in the case of the Chávez presidency) discourse and style.

The static view that belittles the importance of popular struggles and political change prior to 1936 is particularly questionable for the Castro and Gómez years. In the first place, the struggle for democracy during both governments, although not resulting in gains during the period, would form part of the nation's collective memory and would influence events after 1936. In the second place, both rulers distinguished themselves from nineteenth-century caudillos in that they were instrumental in transforming Venezuela into a modern state in large part as a result of the creation of a standing army and the organization of a modern national treasury. Finally, nationalist sentiment, which has expressed itself on diverse fronts in the modern period, manifested itself prior to 1936. Never, since the beginning of the independence period, had Venezuela clashed head-on with foreign interests as it did during Castro's rule. Subsequently, under Gómez, the foreign penetration of the nation's main export industry galvanized nationalist sentiment. Thus, for example, during these years the petroleum company practice of creating parallel towns for their work force alongside existing ones generated conflict and unleashed nationalist passions on the part of local residents in the oil state of Zulia.[4]

▶ The Governments of López Contreras and Medina Angarita, 1936–1945

In many ways, the ten years following the death of Juan Vicente Gómez in 1935 represented a rupture with the past, even though the two presidents who ruled during this period came from the ranks of the *Gomecista* armed forces. The years 1936–1945 were characterized by the gradual extension of democratic liberties and the creation of institutions and formulation of policies designed to promote economic development and the general welfare. The National Congress, whose members had been appointed by Gómez, elected Eleazar López Contreras president in 1936. Five years later, Congress elected López's minister of war, Isaías Medina Angarita, for the succeeding presidential term over the symbolic candidacy of renowned novelist Rómulo Gallegos, who was endorsed by AD's precursor party and the Communist Party of Venezuela (PCV). Medina immediately legalized AD and, toward the end of his government, the PCV, which had entered into an electoral alliance with the president's Venezuelan Democratic Party (PDV). Although Medina enacted progressive legislation, his failure to go beyond the system of indirect presidential elections led AD to support junior officers in the military coup of October 18, 1945.

The degree to which the López and Medina presidencies embarked on a new course in favor of democracy and national development is a source of historical debate with important implications for the post-1958 period and the present. The justification of the 1945 coup against Medina is predicated on the argument that both he and López were *Gomecistas* who brought about few changes during their administrations and that only a clean break with the past could have led the country out of its morass of backwardness and undemocratic rule. The legitimacy of the post-1958 governments in turn depends on the perception that the AD governments of the 1945–1948 period deserved credit for the authentic democracy that in no way resembled the political systems of Medina, López, and Gómez. Thus given the continuity between the 1945–1948 years and the post-1958 period, the analysis of the López and Medina governments heavily influences opinions regarding contemporary Venezuelan democracy.

Both AD and COPEI historians avidly defend the October 1945 coup (which the future *Copeyano* leaders supported at the time) and in doing so affirm the legitimacy of the governments of both parties after 1958 (Suárez Figueroa 1982). Chávez, on the other hand, and writers associated with his government, laud Medina and condemn the 1945 coup (Battaglini 1997). Looming behind these contrasting assessments are distinct attitudes toward the Venezuelan military. AD always identified itself with the civilian movement dating back to 1928 that confronted military rule. Chávez, on the other hand, whose cornerstone strategy is a "civilian-military alliance," has had positive words for various military rulers including General Pérez Jiménez, who for many years was anathema to civilian politicians including those on the left.

The approach adhered to in this book, which recognizes historical continuities and positive developments over an extended period of time, coincides with the favorable evaluation toward Medina put forward by pro-PCV and *Medinista* writers (Bustamante 1985) and thus rejects the justification of the 1945 coup. In doing so it questions the millennialism of the generation of 1928 with its blanket condemnation of all governments prior to the modern period. Nevertheless, unlike *Medinista* and Communist writers (see Fuenmayor 1969, 319–320), this book does not view the AD governments of 1945–1948 as opportunistic or as a simple instrument of US imperialism. On the contrary, it recognizes the radical potential of AD rule of those years, which was threatening to powerful economic interests (to be discussed in the next section).

The popular effervescence in 1936 following twenty-seven years of repressive rule demonstrated that popular energy, class consciousness, and nationalist sentiment dating back to the nineteenth century were never eradicated. Historians have traditionally credited the political parties that were precursors of AD and the PCV with having organized and given direction to the popular movement in 1936 (Levine 1978, 86). More recently, some writers on the period have emphasized the role of popular movements (Battaglini 1993, 121–150), but the lack of studies on their autonomous actions in 1936 (and succeeding years as well) represents an important lacuna in Venezuelan political historiography.[5] Although many of the leaders of social organizations, particularly labor unions in 1936, went on to play important political roles in future years, the parties that emerged in 1936 lacked the organizational strength to have assumed a hegemonic role at the time.

López's progressive measures in 1936, including the Labor Law (in effect until 1990) and the "February Program," which committed the government to the promotion of the general welfare, were a response to popular mobilization more than they were handouts by a paternalistic "conservative modernizer."[6] López's most important contribution to democratic liberalization was his application of the principle of no-reelection of presidents, a long-standing slogan of Venezuela's democratic movement, and his reduction of the presidential term from seven to five years.

The ebbing of the popular movement in early 1937 coincided with López's repressive policies, which included the suppression of a forty-three-day oil workers' strike in January and then the exile of forty-seven leftist leaders. While twenty-three of them left the country on the ship the *Flandre* en route to Mexico, Rómulo Betancourt and Juan Bautista Fuenmayor evaded capture and assumed the leadership of what became the PCV (founded in 1937) and AD.

Medina far surpassed López in extending democratic liberties. Most important, he permitted unionization, which led to the signing of the first collective bargaining agreement in the oil industry in 1945. His government also assumed a nationalist position toward the foreign-owned oil companies, particularly with the promulgation of the Hydrocarbons Law of 1943, which obliged them to build refineries in Venezuela, and the income tax law passed in the same year. In response to the exigencies of World War II, Medina implemented emergency measures favoring national production, which he did not completely lift once the war ended (*Pensamiento Politico* 1987, 427).

The PCV characterized Medina as a representative of the "progressive bourgeoisie," which favored democracy and clashed with foreign capital. The PCV's support for Medina generated a split within its ranks with nearly half of its members (known as the "Black Communists") leaving to form the rival United Venezuelan Communist Party (PCVU).

The Black Communists were more critical of Medina and rejected the party's World War II no-strike policy. Ironically, they resisted the overthrow of Medina with arms in their hands, while the PCV also condemned the coup. One of the Black Communists who initiated the exodus from the PCV as far back as 1943 was labor leader Luis Miquilena, who half a century later would emerge as President Hugo Chávez's right-hand man during his first years in office.

▶ The Trienio, 1945–1948

A seven-man Revolutionary Government Junta headed by Rómulo Betancourt assumed power on October 18 and governed the nation until presidential elections were held in December 1947. The junta consisted of four AD members, an independent, and two military officers, even though the plotters against Medina in the armed forces were originally assured equal weight in the provisional leadership. This misunderstanding contributed to military unrest throughout the three-year AD rule, known as the *trienio* (1945–1948). AD won all three elections held during the period with over 70 percent of the vote, and the party's Rómulo Gallegos assumed the presidency in February 1948. Nine months later he was overthrown by a coup spearheaded by Marcos Pérez Jiménez and Minister of Defense Carlos Delgado Chalbaud, both leading members in the conspiracy against Medina, as well as Luis Felipe Llovera Páez.

Coinciding with the onset of the Cold War, the *trienio* was characterized by intense political conflict involving the nation's four political parties (AD, the PCV, COPEI, and URD), mushrooming labor union and peasant movements, and elite groups represented by the recently founded business organization FEDECAMARAS (Venezuelan Federation of Chambers and Associations of Commerce and Production), the church, and the armed forces. Many, if not most, political analysts (including Betancourt in a self-criticism of his own party) attribute the political clashes leading to the 1948 coup to the sectarianism of AD, which failed to respect the political spaces of the opposition as well as traditional sectors (Betancourt 1959, 163–164). These writers consider the prevailing perception of AD's hegemonic ambitions that threatened to exclude other actors as a major factor contributing to the coup (Levine 1978, 89–92). The explanation presupposes a liberal definition of democracy (in contrast to a Rousseauan one) in which minority rights (including the rights of property) are a basic requisite that all democratic governments must safeguard, even those (like the *trienio*) that are elected by an overwhelming majority of votes.

A few writers explain the 1948 coup as a reaction against AD's reformist policies and a reflection of class interests. This view is adhered to by some former AD leaders who participated in the party's left-wing splits in the 1960s and who underline the progressive orientation of the party during its early years. The former leader of the Movement of the Revolutionary Left (MIR), Moisés Moleiro, for instance, rejects the argument of Venezuelan Communists that AD conspired with the oil companies to topple Medina in 1945. Moleiro attributes the 1948 coup to the mild reforms enacted by the *trienio* government that propelled the right-wing COPEI and the church hierarchy to prod the military to intervene. The coup succeeded, according to Moleiro, because of AD's overconfidence and its failure to mobilize its mass base to resist the military (Moleiro 1979, 135–136; 1998, 93–94, 108). Another founding leader of the MIR and a leading intellectual, Domingo Alberto Rangel, has claimed that the *trienio* government faced "obstruction from reactionaries" who masterminded the 1948 coup, while he criticizes the AD government for not being sufficiently revolutionary (D. A. Rangel 1988, 61).

This thesis is not shared by other writers on the left, including *Chavistas*, who condemn AD of those years for having betrayed popular and nationalist banners and for embracing anticommunism (Sanoja and Vargas Arenas 2004, 32–33). Not surprisingly, the anti-AD writers reject the characterization of the 1948 coup as a rightist reaction to leftist policies. Kléber Ramírez, for instance, an early leading civilian member of Chávez's movement, wrote that the *trienio* regime was "paternalistic," "repressive," "sectarian," "presidentialist," "anti-democratic," and "tied to transnational interests," thus explaining why the worker, peasant, and youth movements refrained from "mobilizing themselves to defend the government" in opposition to the November 1948 coup (Ramírez 1991, 60–62). Another historian associated with *Chavismo*, Oscar Battaglini, viewed the *trienio* as a retrogression for Venezuela in that the government distributed oil revenue to an "unproductive (parasitic) oligarchy" that took in FEDECAMARAS and was nurtured by party clientelism. Battaglini calls Betancourt's anti-imperialism "pure rhetoric" (Battaglini 2001, 119).

The emphasis on continuity presented in this book has a direct bearing on the debate regarding the nature and profundity of the changes brought about during the *trienio*. Pro-AD historians claim that the *trienio* government created a modern state, thus breaking with the nation's semifeudal and military past. In doing so, the pro-AD writers, like AD politicians who led the coup, embrace a "barbarism versus civilization" duality that views the nation's previous 100 years as lacking in significant changes. An alternative revisionist view attempts to counter this simplification of the past and instead underlines the contributions of actors and struggles to the process of democratization and national development over an extended period of time. With regard to the immediate past, far from viewing Medina as an autocrat and *Gomecista*, revisionism emphasizes the policies he implemented and that AD ended up building upon during the *trienio* government (Bustamante 1985).

AD has assumed credit for political and economic breakthroughs made during the *trienio*, while ignoring evidence that the advances were the end result of measures taken under the López Contreras and Medina governments. One of AD's most celebrated achievements in oil policy, for instance, was the "fifty-fifty" decree of Gallegos in 1948, which established government oil-derived revenue at no less than 50 percent of company pre-tax profits. Nevertheless, the Hydrocarbons Law of 1943 introduced the "fifty-fifty" percentages as a guideline for devising taxes and royalty, although in practice government revenue failed to reach that level under Medina (Rabe 1982, 87). Similarly, AD has always assumed complete credit for initiating direct universal suffrage during the *trienio*. In fact, political liberalization during the previous ten years laid the groundwork for full-fledged electoral democracy after 1945. Medina granted women the right to vote in the municipal elections of 1944, selected a civilian (Minister of Agriculture Angel Biaggini) as the pro-government presidential candidate, and promised direct elections for the electoral contests that were scheduled to take place at the end of the 1946–1951 term.

In one respect, however, the *trienio* differed qualitatively from the pre-1945 period. The political climate in the nation under AD rule was conducive to far-reaching socioeconomic transformation. AD's overwhelming electoral triumphs, its mobilization capacity as demonstrated by union organizing drives and rank-and-file participation in party activity, the socialist conviction of many AD members who assumed socialism to be an unstated party goal, and the sharp increase in government oil revenue all contributed to a sense of empowerment and optimism regarding the possibilities for radical change. Betancourt and others in the AD leadership were wary of these attitudes and deplored the unrestrained militancy of local party labor leaders who tried to "outdo the Communists in action and rhetoric" (Betancourt 1979, 363). The fear of a radicalization process, more than AD's reform program per se, explains the staunch opposition of traditional sectors who along with members of the US Defense Department backed the coup against Gallegos (Ellner 1992, 166–169).

The above interpretation is compatible with this book's approach emphasizing the participation and potential of non-elite sectors of the population. In doing so, it borrows from the theoretical writing of Ernesto Laclau and others who view populist governments as emerging in unstable situations in which the "hegemonic bloc" divides, and one of the resulting fractions attempts to bolster its position by appealing to the popular sectors through employment of a radical discourse. At such a critical juncture, popular mobilization often gets out of hand, in which case anything is possible, including revolutionary change. Populist parties that reach power in these situations, although they sometimes hold back the struggle for meaningful structural change, inadvertently unleash forces that threaten the existing system (Laclau 1977, 175; Raby 2006, 230–250). This scenario of radicalization propelled by high levels of mobilization, under a government that may go beyond its original policies and stated aims, describes the *trienio* period and its possible future directions at the time of the 1948 coup.

Certain policies and measures during this period, which were not radical in themselves, had far-reaching implications. Thus, for instance, the Gallegos government obliged foreign oil companies to pay one-fourth of their royalty in kind in order to sell it abroad for the purpose of determining the true price of crude for tax purposes. AD leaders close to Gallegos always denied that the government intended to compete with oil companies on the world market (L. Lander 1981). Nevertheless, the oil companies viewed this commercial activity as an incursion into the industry's most profitable terrain. They realized that, regardless of the government's original motive for selling the oil, it now had options that it could exploit at a future date.

Another development that frightened conservative sectors was the emergence of a militant leftist current within AD, particularly among trade unionists. At the local level these AD members defied the government policy of social harmony by participating in strikes and clashing with members of the conservative COPEI party.[7] In the last days of the *trienio*, the national leadership of the Workers' Confederation of Venezuela (CTV) favored calling a general strike to stave off the impending coup, but the proposal was vetoed by party leaders who pursued a strategy of negotiations with the military conspirators (Ellner 1982, 146).

The military officers who overthrew Gallegos were especially aware of the danger posed by AD's leftist current, which they mistakenly assumed was headed by Betancourt. Indeed, the coup leaders justified their actions by declaring that "the extremist faction that controlled AD initiated a series of maneuvers designed to dominate . . . the armed forces, trying to sow discord and disunion within it" (Ellner 1992, 164). The origins of the left-wing factions that emerged in the 1960s and 1970s (to be discussed in Chapter 3) date back to the 1940s.[8]

AD was slightly to the left of other parties of the noncommunist left that reached power in Latin America during these years. In the first place, in spite of Betancourt's rabid anticommunist rhetoric, the government resisted pressure to outlaw the PCV at the outset of the Cold War when the governing Radical Party of Chile proscribed Communist activity. Furthermore, AD labor leaders refrained from joining the Interamerican Confederation of Workers (CIT), which was promoted by the American Federation of Labor (AFL) as a counterweight to the pro-Communist Workers' Confederation of Latin America (CTAL) and whose founding conference was hosted by labor leaders of the Popular American Revolutionary Alliance (APRA) in Peru in 1948. Unlike the Perón government in Argentina, which shied away from transformation in the countryside, AD promoted structural changes in the rural areas at the same time that it drafted an agrarian reform. Finally, the AD-led CTV took in both trade unions and peasant organizations, unlike its counterpart in Mexico, which was organically divorced from the agrarian movement. For all these reasons, political scientists Ruth and David Collier, in their seminal comparative study *Shaping the Political Arena*, consider the *trienio* experience more radical and far-reaching than the other postwar reformist democratic governments in Latin America (Collier and Collier 1991, 196–201; see also Ellner 1992, 169).

▶ The Military Regime of Marcos Pérez Jiménez, 1948–1958

The dictatorship that ruled Venezuela for over nine years following the overthrow of Gallegos in 1948 was in many ways typical of military regimes in Latin America considered reliable allies by Washington in the context of the Cold War. General Marcos Pérez Jiménez quickly emerged as the strong man and was elected president in fraudulent elections held in 1952. Upon seizing power, the military government outlawed AD, and did the same to the PCV following the outbreak of an unsuccessful oil workers' strike with insurrectional intentions in 1950. Both parties condemned Pérez Jiménez for selling out to foreign interests and were particularly critical of the Reciprocal Trade Treaty of 1952 with the United States and of the oil concessions granted in 1955–1956. The treaty sacrificed Venezuelan industrial interests by reducing the nation's tariffs on a wide variety of products, in return for US maintenance of existing levels of imports of Venezuelan crude in spite of new sources of production in the Mideast. Several years later, the Pérez Jiménez government discarded the policy of "no more concessions," which dated back to the *trienio* period, by opening up oil fields to a multiplicity of companies.

Several of Pérez Jiménez's policies and actions had nationalist overtones that went unrecognized by AD, the PCV, and other adversaries. Thus Pérez Jiménez scrapped a plan to turn over steel production to a Venezuelan capitalist group, headed by Eugenio Mendoza and tied to US Steel Corporation and other foreign interests, and instead created the state-owned company SIDOR (Siderúrgica del Orinoco). At the same time, he created state enterprises in the petrochemical industry (with the construction of a plant in Morón), the hydroelectric industry (with the construction of the Macagua Dam), and the telecommunications sector (with the purchase of the English-owned CANTV). In addition, at the Inter-American conference in Panama in 1956, Pérez Jiménez called for a Marshal Plan for Latin America to be financed by a 4 percent tax on the budgets of all nations in the hemisphere, a proposal accepted by some governments but adamantly rejected by the Eisenhower administration (Rincón N. 1982, 156–157). Finally, the Pérez Jiménez regime encouraged artistic expressions of national culture, particularly the Indian past (Mayhall 2005, 135). In recent decades, revisionist scholars, many of leftist persuasions, have credited Pérez Jiménez with assuming bold positions along these lines (Rincón N. 1982; Castillo 1990; Maza Zavala 1986, 100).

In spite of differences among writers regarding the government's economic and cultural policies, few deny the ruthlessness of the political repression of those years. At the time of the coup in 1948, the intensity of the military intervention as well as its intended duration were not clear. Some political leaders minimized the importance of the decree outlawing AD and put their faith in the ruling junta president, Carlos Delgado Chalbaud, whom they hoped would take immediate steps to restore democratic rule. In one manifestation of anti-AD sectarianism, former PCV secretary-general Juan Bautista Fuenmayor opposed the 1950 oil workers' strike on grounds that the Communists, by carrying out actions with underground AD labor leaders, ran the risk of losing their legal status (Fuenmayor 1981, 322–451).

While the soft-liners in the military headed by Delgado Chalbaud intervened in politics in 1948 as a corrective to what they perceived as temporary political instability, Pérez Jiménez and other hard-liners viewed AD leftists with their mass popular support as having set the stage for a full-fledged revolution. The Pérez Jiménez faction thus favored the military's consolidation of power in order to deliver the leftists a heavy, long-lasting blow.[9] The hard-line strategy, which implied intense repression, became apparent with the assassinations of Delgado Chalbaud in 1950 under obscure circumstances and that of AD secretary-general Leonardo Ruíz Pineda in 1952, as well as the imprisonment and death of his successor Alberto Carnevali (due to lack of adequate medical attention) the following year.

The specter of a long, repressive military rule helped unify the four parties of the opposition. The Communists first promoted broad-based unity against the government by replacing slogans of national liberation with more moderate democratic ones, a policy that facilitated the formation of the Patriotic Junta (Junta Patriótica) in 1957 (Ellner 1988, 38). The junta took in not only AD, which along with the PCV bore the brunt of the government's repressive measures, but URD and COPEI as well. When in December 1957 Pérez Jiménez held a plebiscite to ratify his rule, which promised to be as fraudulent as the 1952 elections, the junta called for abstention. The junta's resistance galvanized opposition from diverse sources, including church leaders, various professional organizations, leading businessmen (such as Eugenio Mendoza), and even the US State Department.

Some commentators claim that the overthrow of Pérez Jiménez was mainly a military affair and emphasize the importance of the January 1 revolt headed by Colonel Hugo Trejo (later to become an idol of the *Chavista* movement because of his call for a civilian-military alliance along the lines that Chávez advocates). Indeed, top military officials alone assumed power on January 23 and named Admiral Wolfgang Larrazábal provisional president on the basis of his seniority in the institution, thus spurning the idea of a joint civilian-military government as was called for by the Junta Patriótica. Nevertheless, the popular resistance that culminated in a general strike on January 21 was essential in prodding the military to act and Pérez Jiménez to flee the country. The version of events underlining the role of clandestine political and popular movements in the overthrow of Pérez Jiménez accords with this book's approach, which questions the validity of historical interpretations that downplay struggles outside of closed elite circles.

The case for the legitimacy of the post-1958 democracy was contingent on the thorough condemnation of the Pérez Jiménez government and its policies on all fronts. The democratic governments after 1958 committed many of the same abuses for which Pérez Jiménez was held responsible, such as violation of human rights and corruption. Thus the legitimization of post-1958 democracy depended in large part on the argument that the Pérez Jiménez government, unlike successive democratic ones, favored foreign interests at the expense of national ones. Pro-AD and COPEI writers defended this line of thinking by contrasting the post-1958 economic policies of high tariffs and subsidies that promoted national development with the allegedly laissez-faire approach of the 1948–1958 period.

Certain features of the Pérez Jiménez regime contradicted the widely accepted characterization of Latin American military rule as inherently "right wing" and as the antithesis of such progressive economic strategies as state intervention in the economy. The Pérez Jiménez period, however, was more complex than this. Thus, for instance, the government put a halt to import substitution policies and subsidies to promote economic growth, as put in evidence by the 1952 commercial treaty. At the same time, however, the government strengthened the public sector by creating state companies in the steel, petrochemical, hydroelectric, and telecommunications sectors and by devising elaborate development plans at all levels. This complexity is typical of other periods in Venezuelan history (such as the Federal War, the rule of Cipriano Castro, and the 1945 coup) that have been simplified for political reasons by leaders across the political spectrum, such as Betancourt, Fuenmayor, and Chávez, who have heavily influenced historiography and political analysis.

▶ Notes

1. Scholarly debate on the origins of the *Peronista* movement in Argentina illustrates this same dichotomy between imported ideologies (promoted by immigrant workers) and homegrown slogans (embraced by workers recently arrived from the countryside), which grew out of political movements dating back to the nineteenth century (Baily 1967; Murmis and Portantiero 1971).

2. In one example of a grade-school text that dismisses the importance of the changes ushered in by nineteenth-century Liberal rule, Aureo Yépez Castillo and Emilia de Veracoechea quote historian Benjamán Frankel: "Guzmán Blanco's reign was the same traditional ballet in which the land, wealth, and power changed from one group of military landowner chiefs called Conservatives, *Godos*, and Oligarchs to another group of caudillo landowners

called Liberals, Revolutionaries, Anti-oligarchs and Federalists." The same text goes on to indicate that "the national prosperity [of those years] was a shadow of the wealth accumulated by Guzmán Blanco" (Yépez Castillo and Veracoechea 1997, 68). Other texts, however, provide a more nuanced view of the nineteenth century that credits a modernizing urban middle sector with promoting centralization (Arias Amaro [1985?], 19).

3. Bolívar did not realize at the time that Miranda had accepted the accord in hopes of buying time to regroup and continue the struggle at a future date (Mijares 1993, 223–227). After his arrest, Miranda was turned over to Spanish authorities and was sent to Spain where he died in a dungeon in 1816.

4. Some towns demanded establishing a limit on the size of the adjacent oil camps (Tinker Salas forthcoming, chapter 3).

5. An example of this autonomy vis-à-vis political parties in 1936 was the popular mobilizations in opposition to the Gómez-appointed National Congress and in favor of the holding of a constituent assembly. In contrast, the leftist parties accepted the Congress's selection of López Contreras as president of the nation in spite of the nomination's dubious legitimacy (Fuenmayor 1969, 150–151).

6. The term *conservative modernizer* refers to presidents in the first decades of the twentieth century (such as Arturo Alessandri in Chile) who implemented some pro-worker measures but refrained from promoting popular mobilization, a strategy that Ruth and David Collier call "project from above" (Collier and Collier 1991, 172–178). The concept is less applicable to Medina Angarita, who spoke to large crowds throughout Venezuela to rally support for his 1943 oil legislation and allied himself with Communists who controlled the labor movement. Nevertheless, Medina's Partido Democrático Venezolano was mainly a party of public employees with little popular participation.

7. Indeed those AD members who subsequently split off to form leftist parties in 1962 and 1967 opposed Betancourt's conciliatory attitude toward COPEI (Ellner 1980, 14). In doing so, they were motivated by both clientelism (refusal to share the spoils with members of other parties) and ideological imperatives (hostility to the conservative COPEI).

8. The approach proposed in this book underscores the endurance of demands, slogans, and goals in time, as was the case, for example, with the impact of nineteenth-century struggles on twentieth-century politics.

9. The leaders of the April 11, 2002, coup against Hugo Chávez split along similar lines. The provisional president, Pedro Carmona, who turned his back on democratic procedures, represented a hard line that favored a thorough break with the *Chavista* past (see Chapter 5).

3

Venezuela's "Model" Democracy, 1958–1989

THOSE who ruled Venezuela following the overthrow of dictator Marcos Pérez Jiménez in January 1958 encountered an increasingly receptive climate in Washington. At the time, the administration of President Dwight D. Eisenhower was beginning to revise its Latin American policy, which had previously viewed military governments as the most effective bulwark against Communism. In the mid-1950s, for instance, Secretary of State John Foster Dulles had praised Venezuelan dictator Pérez Jiménez and his openness toward foreign capital, predicting that if followed by the rest of the continent "the danger of communism in South America . . . will gradually disappear" (Rabe 1988, 94). In August 1958, Eisenhower drew considerable attention in Latin America when he enthusiastically received the new Venezuelan ambassador and for the first time explicitly called for the establishment of representative governments in the continent. Subsequently, Dulles's replacement, Christian Herter, committed Washington to "all of the public support we can give" to the recently elected president Rómulo Betancourt, whom he had admittedly once considered to be a "leftist" (Rabe 1988, 145). Relations between the two nations became even closer under President John F. Kennedy, who developed a personal friendship with Betancourt and visited Venezuela in December 1961. Kennedy adviser Arthur Schlesinger Jr. wrote that many in the administration considered Venezuela "a model for Latin American progressive democracy" (Alexander 1982, 554).

Washington's announced preference for democratic government in Venezuela coincided with most academic writing, which at the time, and for several decades to come, lauded the nation for representing a "showcase" democracy. Over the same period, political analysts praised Venezuelan moderate leaders for putting aside differences and designing alliances and coalitions that governed the nation during three presidential terms: AD's Rómulo Betancourt (1959–1964), AD's Raúl Leoni (1964–1969), and COPEI's Rafael Caldera (1969–1974). Special praise was extended to AD leaders in 1969 for resisting internal party pressure and handing power over to COPEI. In the subsequent two decades, political scientists praised Venezuela for developing a near two-party system similar to that of the US, which had long been considered the most conducive to democratic stability (Duverger 1954). These governments included AD's Carlos Andrés Pérez (1974–1979), COPEI's Luis Herrera Campins (1979–1984), and AD's Jaime Lusinchi (1984–1989).

The staunch defenders of Venezuelan democracy and of Rómulo Betancourt in particular in the years immediately after 1958 were ideologically motivated. Betancourt had no greater supporter in academia than Robert Jackson Alexander, who was a prolific writer, closely linked to the Alliance for Progress, and a "central player in US–Latin American labor, political, and scholarly affairs," and who received generous travel support from the notoriously anticommunist International Department of the AFL-CIO and the CIA (French 2004, 315, 320; Berger 1995, 262). Alexander approved of Betancourt's role in isolating Cuba from the Latin American community of nations including his proposal for Organization of American States–imposed economic sanctions. Alexander also justified Betancourt's hard line against the Communist Party of Venezuela (PCV), which influenced it to take up arms against the government in 1962. Indeed, Alexander attributed the PCV's support for the guerrilla movement, which went against the general line of pro-Moscow Latin American Communist Parties, to its desperation over AD's popular backing. The PCV's increasing isolation, according to Alexander, demonstrated "the degree to which a government of the democratic left . . . can undercut the bases of a Communist Party" (Alexander 1969, xix).

Given his social-democratic commitment, it is not surprising that Alexander praised AD's moderate economic reforms, including government intervention in the economy, high tariffs, and land distribution with compensation. Another well-known scholar stated that the AD government had become the "major experimental center" for social-democratic policies in Latin America, replacing its counterpart party in Costa Rica (Silvert 1961, 256–257). Influential scholars who wrote favorably on AD shared Alexander's positive evaluation of the party's economic program and claimed that the democratic government after

1958 achieved more with the resources derived from declining oil revenue than did the previous military regime (Taylor 1968, 67; Lieuwen 1965, 177–184). Betancourt's social-democratic orientation also coincided with the Kennedy administration's support for Latin American land and tax reform, social change, economic integration, and control of the violent fluctuation of international prices of third-world export commodities.[1]

The shadow of leftist populism—along with conflicting attitudes and interpretations of that phenomenon—was cast over the analysis of Alexander and others who compared AD favorably to other noncommunist leftist parties. Most important, Betancourt's AD was less personalistic and more organizationally developed than caudillo-type populist parties. Thus Betancourt, as provisional president during the *trienio*, refrained from running in the 1947 presidential elections and then maintained a low profile in order to avoid undermining the credibility of the government of Rómulo Gallegos. Furthermore, after Betancourt finished his term in 1964, he left Venezuela to avoid accusations that he manipulated the successor government of fellow party member Raúl Leoni and abstained from running for president in 1973, even though he had a constitutional right to do so.

Academic writers differentiated AD from its populist counterparts elsewhere in Latin America, including APRA (which was often considered a "cousin party"), on grounds that leaders such as Víctor Raúl Haya de la Torre were heavy-handed in party matters and failed to develop a well-integrated internal structure (Alexander 1973, 20; Martz 1966, 367; Whitaker and Jordan 1966, 197–198). Alexander especially condemned the Perón government, which he called a "totalitarian regime sui generis," even though he recognized that it implemented long overdue economic reforms (Alexander 1962, 265–266). Perón nationalized foreign-owned industries and pursued an independent foreign policy, unlike Betancourt who avoided, in the words of Alexander, "xenophobic nationalism," contained labor conflicts, and shied away from participation in the movement of nonaligned nations (Alexander 1964, 138, 315).[2]

With the string of military coups beginning in Brazil in 1964, Venezuela and Colombia became the only long-standing democracies in South America. Political scientists called both nations "pacted democracies" because interparty agreements had laid the basis for the reestablishment of democratic rule in the late 1950s. The two countries were particularly praised for pioneering interparty pacts, which were to pave the way for reemerging democracies in much of the rest of Latin

America in the 1980s. Political scientists, however, wrote more favorably of Venezuelan democracy than that of Colombia. Not only did Venezuela, unlike its neighbor, overcome the guerrilla violence of the 1960s but its party system was open to small parties, in contrast to the Colombian Liberals and Conservatives, which refused to incorporate other political forces at any level (Herman 1988, 4–5; Hartlyn 1998, 111–116).

Political scientist Daniel Levine stressed these auspicious characteristics and in doing so argued for the uniqueness of the nation's institutions within the Latin American context and even established comparisons with Western Europe. By going beyond individual personalities, Levine provided the most scholarly version of the "Venezuelan exceptionalism thesis," which posited the superiority of the nation's democracy. Levine maintained that Venezuela's democratic institutions effectively channeled conflict rather than checked it. The basic ingredient of Venezuela's success was moderate and responsible leaders, who fashioned interparty alliances in order to avoid the AD hegemony of the *trienio* period and to marginalize the left. Venezuela's pacted democracy provided moderates "mutual guarantees" and "incentives to moderation and compromise" while its basic principle of "accept and live with diversity" evidently excluded rightists and leftists, at least for the time being (Levine 1978, 102). Levine underscored the importance of moderation by ending his book *Conflict and Political Change in Venezuela* with the statement, "In Venezuela, the future lies with cautious men" (Levine 1973, 259).

A second theory regarding Venezuela's democratic success centered on the nation's status as an oil-exporting nation and reflected the way many Venezuelans understood the longevity of their nation's democracy. The "staple theory" attributed Venezuelan stability to the relative strength of the international oil market over the previous half-century (Bergquist 1986, 205–214). Terry Karl (1987) argued that the oil economy and the resultant extensive state bureaucracy created opportunities for the middle class, whose representatives played leading roles in favor of political moderation and class conciliation. During the critical year of 1958, this moderate leadership along with oil revenue helped avert internecine conflict resulting from the demands and expectations built up during the military dictatorship. Thus, for example, the government allocated funds to an ambitious employment program for the poor (known as the Emergency Plan) while the labor movement (including the Communists) reciprocated by agreeing to refrain from pressing for new contracts (Ellner 1993, 6). In addition, the government used oil money to aid the business sector by recognizing the private debt (of dubious legality), at the same time that it promised the church increased subsides and satisfied the material expectations of military officers. Karl's theory reflected the thinking of many political analysts who accepted the assumption that Venezuela's oil wealth translated itself into social harmony and political stability. Nevertheless, Karl, writing in the mid-1980s recognized (more than most political scientists at the time) the downside and potential dangers of the Venezuelan democratic model.

The upbeat academic analyses of Venezuelan democracy throughout the 1980s ignored specific trouble signs that manifested themselves. On the economic front, the run on the bolivar and sudden capital flight in 1983, which forced the Herrera Campins government to implement exchange controls, together with the sharp and unexpected decline in international oil prices in 1986, demonstrated the vulnerability of the nation's economy. The exceptionally poor leadership qualities of Jaime Lusinchi and his dubious ethical behavior undermined credibility in spite of his uncanny ability to maintain high levels of popularity. Lusinchi certainly did not live up to the image of the mature, judicious leader that Levine and others credited with assuring democratic stability. Lusinchi's replacement, Carlos Andrés Pérez, in 1989, was given an impossible mandate, namely restoring the prosperity that had character-ized his first administration in the 1970s. Finally, the surprising success of a rank-and-file movement in elections held in the all-important steel workers' union in 1987, following years of repression against the rebel trade unionists, underscored the widespread disillusionment with the tra-ditional leadership of popular organizations. All these developments pointed to difficult times ahead, which the exceptionalism thesis, with its exaggerated notions of the virtues of the Venezuelan political system and political culture, was unable to foresee.

At a moment when Venezuelan democracy appeared most stable, a political analyst with considerable experience in Latin America, Norman Gall, criticized academic writers for failing to look beneath the surface and examine real problems confronting the nation. In an article pub-lished in the *New York Review of Books* in 1973, Gall argued that the most distinguished Venezuelan specialists in the United States had pre-sented an "uncritical" view of Betancourt and AD and ignored the squandering of oil revenue "on a monumental scale" as well as the "widespread disenchantment . . . with the recent performance of the democratic parties." Gall made special reference to a published book on the Venezuelan peasant movement (Powell 1971), which glorified the land reform of 1960 while failing to point out that it benefited not so much the peasants as the landowners, who received the lion's share of the two billion dollars spent on the program (Gall 1973).[3]

This chapter attempts to address Gall's plea for a more balanced approach to post-1958 Venezuelan democracy. On the one hand, the analysis presented in this book recognizes democracy's achievements, specifically the political and economic gains that were made. Venezuelan leaders displayed a sense of "generosity" by providing those outside of the ruling circles with opportunities, though with little real decisionmaking power. Representatives of parties other than AD and COPEI occupied positions on the executive boards of major labor and student organizations, in university governments, and in the area of culture. This participation across the political spectrum contributed to stability. Economic policies that favored development included import substitution, incremental demands on foreign capital, and the creation of state companies in sectors in which private investment was unlikely to meet national needs.

On the other hand, with the exception of clientelism and corruption, which became increasingly pronounced in the 1970s, political writers downplayed the deficiencies and limitations of democracy during these years. In spite of AD's "generosity," the party leadership maintained a tight grip on social organizations as well as on its own internal organization, frequently resorting to undemocratic practices. The downside of Venezuelan democracy also included flagrant violation of human rights and electoral fraud (particularly in the 1990s). On the economic front, import substitution policies did not include an unwavering commitment to overcome dependency on foreign technology and capital. In addition, clientelism and corruption had a devastating effect on the state sector of the economy.

Special mention needs to be made of denunciations of human rights violations because of their potential to graphically impact public consciousness. Flagrant cases spanned the entire post-1958 democratic period: during the guerrilla years of the 1960s; the decade of the 1970s, when far-leftist groups phased out their remaining armed units; and the 1980s, when left-wing insurgency practically ceased to exist. At the time, these crimes were underreported in the nation's establishment media (which sometimes actually refused to run paid ads by the victims' families) and were not pursued by the system of justice, possibly because they threatened to debunk the myth of Venezuela's "exceptional" democracy.

Only after 1998 have the *Chavistas* in power revisited these cases and in the process have helped transform the image of post-1958 democratic rule. The Chávez government has named plazas, avenues, and medical clinics after martyrs of the period, while public television and radio frequently make reference to the incidents. Thus, for instance, in October 2005 in Puerto La Cruz, Anzoátegui, Governor Tarek William Saab, himself a former human rights activist, dedicated a plaza to Alberto Lovera (a Communist leader who was tortured and killed by political police in 1965 and whose cadaver was discovered on the nearby shores of Lechería) in a ceremony with his widow María del Mar de Lovera and Vice President José Vicente Rangel, who at the time had exposed the case in the National Congress.[4] In 2007 Rangel was replaced as vice president by Jorge Rodríguez, the son of a former secretary-general of the leftist Socialist League party who in 1976 was detained and assassinated by the Office of the Police Intelligence Services (DISIP), the police force of the Ministry of Interior Relations. The Chávez government has promoted investigations into the most well-known atrocities committed during those years, including the heavy bombing and machine-gun fire in Cantaura (also in the state of Anzoátegui) that killed twenty-three, unarmed sympathizers of the leftist Bandera Roja in 1982; the massacre and horrendous cover-up of sixteen fishermen who were mistaken as Colombian guerrillas in Amparo in the state of Apure in 1988; and the killings of hundreds, if not thousands, of mostly barrio residents during the week of disturbances of February 27, 1989. Some of the victims of Cantaura and Amparo were allegedly killed in cold blood (Rosas 2005). The probes have been undertaken in order to bring to justice those responsible for the atrocities.

The balanced account of 1958–1989 advocated in this chapter is meant as a corrective to the *Chavistas'* condemnation of the entire post-1958 period (pejoratively referred to as the "Fourth Republic") that fails to place in relief the disruptive changes ushered in by neoliberalism in the 1990s. At the same time, the chapter critically examines the "Venezuelan exceptionalism thesis," which takes the nation out if its Latin American context and thus ignores the structural nature of such third-world problems as dependency and chronic political instability.

▶ The Governments of Wolfgang Larrazábal and Rómulo Betancourt, 1958–1964

The overthrow of the nine-year dictatorship on January 23, 1958, and events in its immediate aftermath infused the rank and file of political and social organizations with a sense of empowerment and brought to the fore opportunities for the achievement of ambitious popular measures and nationalist goals. The legalization of trade unions opened the possibility of struggle around pent-up worker demands that had originally been formulated in the years prior to the dictatorship. Another auspicious sign was the spirit of popular unity, which initially found expression in the interparty alliance against Pérez Jiménez, known as the Junta Patriótica, and subsequently manifested itself in the labor movement's Unity Congress of November 1959. In addition, the Cuban example, in which a rebel army outside of the existing party structure toppled a repressive regime, was not lost on those who hoped that the overthrow of Pérez Jiménez would lead to a revolutionary situation. Finally, the outstanding role of the clandestine leadership of the four existing parties in the struggle for democracy and their reputation for heroism were significant. These younger party members embodied the spirit of unity, which had facilitated their clandestine work, and they tended to be more radical than the top exiled leaders such as Betancourt (AD), Rafael Caldera (COPEI), and Jóvito Villalba (URD). The nonveteran activists were also largely free of the anticommunist attitudes of their older party companions.

In the following years, the model of state intervention in a capitalist economy, and not socialism, achieved hegemony in Venezuela. The socialist left failed to take advantage of the window of opportunity that presented itself in 1958 and became increasingly isolated in subsequent years, as AD and COPEI emerged as the nation's two major parties. Political polarization pitting leftist parties against those to their right was not only detrimental to the left but also to organized labor and other social movements that suffered divisions. Despite Betancourt's efforts to demobilize the general population, his hostility to the left, and his opposition to radical change, his administration (1959–1964) favored democratic institutionalization and national development, albeit with definite constraints and effective resistance from powerful economic groups.

Shortly after January 23, 1958, Admiral Wolfgang Larrazábal was chosen provisional president, due to his hierarchical status in the armed forces, even though he had failed to oppose the dictatorship until shortly before it fell. Surprisingly, Larrazábal took popular stands and implemented popular measures. Most important was his Emergency Plan, which provided work for the unemployed, many of whom were recently arrived migrants from the countryside. Labor leaders hailed the plan and called for its "acceleration" to combat unemployment and also approved of Larrazábal's suspension of rent payment in public housing (*Tribuna Popular*, May 3, 1958, 19). In addition, Larrazábal refrained from using repression against those who, incensed by the US government's friendly relations with the Pérez Jiménez government, mobbed Vice President Nixon's motorcade during his famous visit in May. Indeed, Nixon, who called the incident "a close brush with death," blamed the Venezuelan police for not getting off their motorcycles to attempt to save his life (Nixon 1990, 180–181). In contrast to the attitudes assumed by Betancourt, Caldera, and Villalba, who scolded the protesters, Larrazábal allegedly remarked, "If I were a student I would have done the same" (Moleiro 1979, 187).

Unity among those who defended the democratic system was a natural response to the threats posed by military officers identified with Pérez Jiménez, who staged abortive coups in July and September of 1958 and then in April 1960. Leftists and members of social movements responded by calling for all-encompassing unity along with a progressive agenda. Thus, for instance, the various parties collaborated in organizing brigades to supervise the street protests in opposition to Nixon's visit as well as the military revolts led by pro–Pérez Jiménez officers. The Communists supported broad unity encompassing the formerly right-wing COPEI on the grounds that the Social Christian Party favored various progressive policies such as the creation of a state petroleum company and the maximization of oil revenue (*Tribuna Popular*, May 17, 1958, 14; November 16, 1958, 15).

A second position embraced unity from above within a corporatist framework that excluded the Communist Party but took in the top leaders of the church, the business organization FEDECAMARAS, and the armed forces, which were to be consulted on decisions affecting their respective institutions. This approach found expression in the Punto Fijo Pact and other accords among the main leaders of AD, COPEI, and URD. The agreements committed the three parties to a coalition government, regardless of which candidate won the 1958 presidential election, and called for specific policies designed to neutralize or win over powerful groups. The Minimum Program, which was the sequel to the Punto Fijo Pact, recognized the right of the church to set policies for its own schools, the property rights of landowners in the countryside, and the "primordial function" of the private sector in the economy.

For many years, historians considered Venezuela's "pacted democracy" a masterstroke, which avoided the interparty discord and clashes with the church and the military that characterized the 1945–1948 period. More recently, however, scholars have pointed to the antidemocratic aspects of the agreements: the secrecy of the original meeting of the pact's signatories; the limitations set on the terms of electoral debate, and specifically the avoidance of contentious issues such as church education and AD-COPEI relations; and the privileged treatment accorded certain elites that ossified the decisionmaking process for years to come (Karl 1987, 88–89; McCoy 2004, 265; Myers 2004, 25; Coppedge 1994, 155).

The proposals of leftists and social groups like the reconstructed labor movement's National Unified Union Committee (CSUN) to nominate Larrazábal or another independent as presidential candidate representing all four parties failed to materialize. Three candidates emerged: Larrazábal (endorsed by URD and the PCV), Betancourt (AD), and Caldera (COPEI). Larrazábal and Betancourt assumed diametrically opposed positions on relations with the PCV. Betancourt spurned the spirit of unity by harshly attacking the Communists throughout the campaign. Both Betancourt and Caldera denied that the key role of Communists in the struggle against the dictatorship entitled them to participate in interparty agreements (Barrios 1963, 65). In contrast, Larrazábal, on accepting the PCV's endorsement, stated, "I am a full-fledged patriot and aspire to be president of all Venezuelans, and thus cannot reject the backing . . . of any group" (Plaza 1978, 116).

In spite of Betancourt's comfortable victory over the left-of-center Larrazábal, the ideological sympathies of Venezuelan voters remained unclear owing to AD's left-wing origin and political heterogeneity, as was made evident by the party's three subsequent schisms. Betancourt received 49 percent of the vote, followed by Larrazábal with 36 percent, and Caldera with 16 percent. Betancourt owed his triumph to his overwhelming support in rural areas. In contrast, URD and the PCV came in first and second place in Caracas, where AD came in last. Larrazábal also triumphed in the central states of Carabobo, Aragua, and Miranda, where the manufacturing working class was concentrated, although AD won in Zulia and other oil states. The disproportionate support of leftist parties in urban areas, and particularly the nation's capital, was another indication of the left's promising prospects during these years. On the night of the elections a peacekeeping force of PCV*istas* attempted to contain violence carried out by barrio dwellers who were convinced that fraud had been committed against Larrazábal.

As president, Betancourt faced insurgencies spearheaded first by pro–Pérez Jiménez officers in 1960 and 1961 and then the PCV and MIR on the left. Leftist-inspired military uprisings in Carúpano and Puerto Cabello in early 1962 signaled the beginning of a guerrilla movement that spanned most of the decade. Betancourt's repressive policies were reflected in the phrase "Shoot first and ask questions later," attributed to his interior minister Carlos Andrés Pérez.

At the same time, Betancourt pursued certain policies and actions designed to favor national production and promote democracy at home and abroad that were favorably received by the general population. In contrast to the Pérez Jiménez regime, Betancourt established high tariffs to protect national industry and implemented fiscal policies to maximize oil revenue. These measures, however, created tension with FEDECA-MARAS, particularly among the multinational oil companies, which joined the business organization in 1959 (Ewell 1984, 134–135). Relations with the United States on economic issues were also strained by Washington's insistence on the system of import quotas on oil and refusal to provide Venezuelan petroleum a preferential or "hemispheric" treatment, as was proposed by Betancourt's minister of mines Juan Pablo Pérez Alfonzo. Washington's intransigence on this matter formed the backdrop of Pérez Alfonzo's initiatives to create the Organization of Petroleum Exporting Countries (OPEC) in 1960. In another move that met general approval, including on the left, the National Congress draft-ed a new constitution, which was ratified in January 1961. PCV con-gressmen, while formulating various objections, voted in favor of the document on grounds that it "replaces the *Perezjimenista* constitution that served the tyranny, and this fact alone signifies an important step forward" (*Tribuna Popular*, November 27, 1960, 8).

Betancourt faced the dilemma of how to proceed with economic and social reforms and viable forms of representation of the nonprivileged, without contributing to a sense of popular empowerment that would have unleashed radicalization and scared off powerful groups. The strat-egy Betancourt embraced after 1958 was designed to avoid such a chain of events in several ways. In the first place, the economic policies of import substitution and state control of various key sectors of the econo-my were not inspired by uncompromising economic nationalism, nor were they intended to sever dependence on foreign capital and technolo-gy. This cautiousness became especially evident in the oil industry. Thus Betancourt ruled out the possibility that the state-owned Venezuelan Petroleum Corporation (CVP), which he founded in 1960, would com-pete with private capital, adding that "the very modesty of working capi-tal assigned to it indicates how limited its objectives are." In order to calm the fears of the World Bank regarding government intentions to develop an independent productive capacity, the CVP signed service contracts with foreign oil companies for the exploitation of its oil fields, while its principal objectives centered on fiscal activity. This approach clashed with the more nationalist current within AD as represented by CVP president Rubén Sáder Pérez, who viewed his company as a com-

petitor in all phases of the industry and objected to the limited and dis-
persed areas assigned to it (Ellner 1987, 14–18).

In the second place, President Betancourt's staunch anticommunism
set the limits of change, confirmed the government's commitment to private property, and circumscribed the scope of social struggle by encouraging splits in social movements. Betancourt's anticommunism played a
key role at the party, national, and international levels. Thus, harsh anticommunism helped trigger the split-off of the *Fidelista* faction of AD
and its transformation into the Movement of the Revolutionary Left
(MIR) in 1960. It also hastened the withdrawal of leftist trade unionists
from the Workers' Confederation of Venezuela (CTV) in 1961, as well
as the left's decision to take up arms shortly thereafter.

Betancourt's anticommunism also thrust Venezuela into the forefront
of the campaign to isolate Cuba at the continental level. Betancourt threw
his support behind the proposition to expel Cuba from the Organization
of American States (OAS) at the foreign ministers' conference at Punta
del Este in Uruguay in January 1962. This position contrasted with that
of Latin America's principal democratic governments (Argentina, Brazil,
Mexico, and Chile), which, influenced by public opinion, resisted pressure from the Kennedy administration by voting against the proposal.
Kennedy insisted on support from democratic Latin American nations
before acting on Cuba, thus making Venezuela a key actor (Schlesinger
1965, 177–178, 225). In the final months of his administration,
Betancourt responded to the discovery of an arms cache on the desert
coast of the state of Falcón to call for Latin American sanctions against
Cuba. Betancourt claimed that he had "incontestable evidence" that the
supplies had been sent "from Havana to its Venezuelan fifth column,"
namely the Venezuelan guerrilla movement (Alexander 1982, 545).
Subsequently, however, former CIA operative Philip Agee wrote that he
was convinced that the incident was a setup, masterminded by the
agency's Caracas office (Agee 1982, 38–39). Betancourt's hard line
toward Cuba moved his party close to the centrist COPEI and triggered
the exit of the left-leaning URD from the coalition government.

In the third place, Betancourt played an active role in putting the
brakes on popular mobilization. Shortly after the overthrow of Pérez
Jiménez, he strongly encouraged labor to sign the Worker-Management
Conciliation Pact, which committed unions to refrain from renegotiating
highly questioned contracts signed under the dictatorship and implied a
no-strike policy. At the same time, he proposed that "the parties avoid
the deployment of its members on the streets for a given period of time
since a massive presence of party activists could cause alarm among

influential sectors" (Betancourt 1959, 183). Betancourt also reacted harshly to a number of strikes, including those of telephone and transportation employees in November 1960 and January 1962, respectively, and pressured party oil-worker leaders to drop a controversial absolute job security clause from the 1960 contract in order to avoid an impending labor conflict (Ellner 1993, 17–20; Coppedge 1994, 155).

Several factors explain the triumph of the centrists headed by Betancourt in spite of the favorable conditions for the left in 1958 and AD's own leftist heritage. Most important, the left committed several major blunders. Following the overthrow of Pérez Jiménez, leftists went from one political extreme to the other. In 1958, the PCV subordinated socioeconomic demands to the slogans "Immediate Elections" (*Elecciones ya!*) and "national unity." In subsequent years, PCV leaders generally recognized that they had failed to harness popular energy and enthusiasm generated by the overthrow of Pérez Jiménez. The left's defensive approach became apparent when leftist trade-union leaders signed the Worker-Management Conciliation Pact. In addition, the PCV failed to insist on the immediate enactment of an agrarian reform, which would have allowed Larrazábal's presidential candidacy to effectively challenge Betancourt in rural areas.

A related error, which holds much relevance for the current period, was the PCV's failure to mobilize support for Hugo Trejo, a nationalist officer who had led a military uprising against Pérez Jiménez on January 1, 1958. During the early months of the Larrazábal government, Trejo actively proposed the democratization of the armed forces, its participation in political debate, and the termination of its isolation from the rest of the nation in order to mend its image as an "army of occupation," following nine years of repressive military rule (Trejo 1977, 179). Rightist officers who subsequently revolted against the government successfully pressured Larrazábal to send Trejo abroad. The PCV failed to attempt to block the decision, even though it criticized Larrazábal for moving too slowly in purging the armed forces and the public administration of followers of the ex-dictator (*Tribuna Popular*, March 1, 1958, 5). Years later, at the time of the 1992 attempted coup, Chávez established contact with Trejo, whom he has called his "tutor" (Blanco Muñoz 1998, 275). Indeed, Chávez and his followers consider Trejo a precursor of their concept of the "civilian-military alliance" in which the armed forces incorporate themselves into the political and economic life of the nation, a key element of the *Chavista* political strategy.

Following Betancourt's presidential inauguration, which coincided with the triumph of the Cuban revolution in January 1959, the

Venezuelan left went to an opposite extreme. Venezuelan leftists reacted impulsively to government repression by continuously escalating their rhetoric and tactics, including increasingly militant street protests. In the words of Communist youth leader Teodoro Petkoff, "we finally realized there was no alternative" to the armed struggle (Ellner 1980, 8). In turning to insurgency, the left ignored the fundamental difference between Venezuelan democracy (with all its shortcomings) and the military regime in Cuba under Batista, as well as other Latin American nations where leftists pursued a guerrilla strategy. The leftists also mistakenly presumed that Betancourt lacked a long-term vision or a model that could successfully compete with the socialism they advocated. Longtime PCV president Pedro Ortega Díaz looked back on the 1960s and observed: "We took for granted that our model was the only attractive one around and failed to realize that Betancourt also had one based on state intervention in the economy, which at least addressed itself to the issues of poverty and national interests" (Ortega Díaz 1989).

As a result of this chain of events, Betancourt not only succeeded in isolating the far left, but he consolidated control of his own party and reined in critics of his rule. Whether or not Betancourt intentionally provoked the left into opting for the armed struggle, he deserves part of the blame for the ensuing guerrilla war. Certainly the left was ultimately responsible for its actions, but a more measured response to its excesses by the government might have avoided the high cost of the decade-long violence that racked the nation. In short, the PCV's sudden turnabout from moderation and conciliation in favor of national unity in 1958 to extremism and armed warfare can be understood at least in part as an overreaction to the repressive measures of the Betancourt government.

▶ ## The Governments of Raúl Leoni and Rafael Caldera, 1964–1974

Greater continuity characterized the change of government in 1964 and 1969 than many political leaders and pundits anticipated. Their predictions that Raúl Leoni (1964–1969) would move Venezuela to the left, and that the government of Rafael Caldera (1969–1974) would have the opposite effect, proved unfounded (Moleiro 1979, 236–237; Ewell 1984, 174). Indeed, during these years, the formerly rightist COPEI met the formerly left-leaning AD halfway, thus convincing many analysts that Venezuelan politics had become bereft of substantive differences, particularly in the area of economic policy (Coppedge 1994, 40–41).

Leoni's reformist credentials, which invigorated those left-leaning AD leaders who subsequently split off from the party in 1967 and embraced socialism, stemmed from his long-standing association with the labor movement. Leoni's key role as labor minister in the 1945–1948 period in promoting massive unionization was rewarded at AD's 1963 national convention when labor leaders formally nominated him their party's presidential candidate. Indeed, Betancourt, who was intent on strengthening AD's ties with the centrist COPEI, feared that Leoni's candidacy would be unacceptable to that party and thus attempted to block his nomination. Leoni won with a mere 33 percent of the vote, followed by Caldera with 20 percent, Jóvito Villalba (URD) with 18 percent, and the renowned writer and intellectual Arturo Uslar Pietri, who defended conservative economic policies, with 16 percent.

In a few ways, the Leoni administration assumed positions that were on the left of the political spectrum. In its foreign policy, for instance, the government refused to recognize the military regime that came to power in Brazil in 1964, condemned the US invasion of the Dominican Republic in 1965, as well as the Vietnam War, and began to support third-world causes at international forums such as the United Nations.

Nevertheless, on the two essential goals of a peaceful resolution to the guerrilla struggle and the strengthening of the state sector of the economy, Leoni proved to be a disappointment for the left-leaning current headed by the party's secretary-general Jesús Angel Paz Galarraga. Within the party, the Paz group criticized Leoni's hard-line approach to the nation's leftist insurgency and the resultant failure to find a peaceful solution to the conflict. Political leaders across the political spectrum, including COPEI, accused the government of human rights violations. National Deputy José Vicente Rangel, a human rights champion, blamed Minister of Interior Gonzalo Barrios for the weakening of civilian power and failing to oversee the "obscure and marginal activity" carried out by security forces, including his ministry's notorious General Office of Police (DIGEPOL) (Sanin 1983, 266). Moisés Moleiro, a leading guerrilla of the 1960s and author of a critical study of AD, claimed that tortured political prisoners numbered in the hundreds and that an even greater number of leftist sympathizers disappeared during this period (Moleiro 1979, 239). Leoni failed to follow up on the meetings carried out by Paz Galarraga and other left-leaning AD leaders with the guerrilla heads with the aim of reaching a negotiated settlement. Indeed, by 1965, the PCV had indicated its willingness to abandon the guerrilla struggle by raising the slogan "Democratic Peace."

At the outset of his presidency, Leoni faced resistance from business interests over his economic policies. The oil companies in particular at first refused to pay retroactive taxes in compensation for their deceitful long-standing practice of exporting crude to their own affiliates at a discount. Under an agreement reached in 1966, the companies accepted payment of back taxes while the government pledged itself to refrain from setting prices (known as "reference prices") for the purpose of determining true profits. AD's left wing, headed by Paz Galarraga along with OPEC founder Pérez Alfonzo, criticized the compromise arrangement for holding back the effort to establish effective ongoing mechanisms for calculating taxes.

Paz Galarraga and his followers defended other positions compatible with their commitment to socialism, which they proclaimed upon separating from AD in 1967. Thus they proposed assigning the entire internal market for gasoline to the state-run CVP, and not just the 33 percent decided upon by the Leoni administration. Paz's supporters in AD also favored nationalization of Caracas's electricity utility (which Chávez was to take over in 2007), as well as the expropriation of companies in banking, transportation, and basic industry. Paz defended the airline Aeropostal and other public enterprises against charges of inefficiency leading to heavy losses, claiming that those accusations were a smokescreen designed to justify privatization. He attributed Aeropostal's financial difficulties to its mismanagement during the military dictatorship and added that the company's main objective should be to serve national interests, not maximize profits (Ellner 1987, 5–10). Paz's group also lobbied to accelerate land distribution to the peasantry in accordance with the Agrarian Reform passed in 1960. Finally, Paz and his followers objected to Betancourt and Leoni's appointment of representatives of powerful economic groups, specifically the Eugenio Mendoza and Vollmer families, to key government positions in charge of economic decisionmaking.

Scholars and AD leaders alike have played down or (as in the case of Betancourt) completely denied the ideological and programmatic content of the People's Electoral Movement (MEP) split, as well as AD internal conflicts in general after 1960 (Lieuwen 1965, 188; Martz 1970, 55; 1966, 183, 279–280; Alexander 1964, 133–134; 1982, 599–600). Instead they attributed the divisions to presidential aspirations, which indeed precipitated the schisms both in the case of the "ARS" party (formed in 1962) and the MEP. Even prior to the MEP split, Betancourt claimed that Paz's supporters "constitute a non-ideological current motivated by the hunger for power whatever the price may be," although at the same time he accused Paz of raising "extremist banners" and professing adherence to a "nearly pure Marxism" (Rivas Rivas 1987, 77; Ellner 1980, 16).

This view of Paz's behavior as based on personal ambition takes the various schisms out of the broader historical context. As early as 1935, Betancourt had proposed to Leoni and other future AD leaders a dual approach of publicly embracing one set of programs and strategies while adhering to more radical ones that were not to be revealed in order to avoid alarming powerful groups (Ellner 1982, 136). At the time of AD's founding in 1941, this dual strategy became an article of faith among party leaders. Other populist movements in Latin America in the 1930s and 1940s were characterized by the same duality, but not to the extent of AD. Unlike Perón, Getúlio Vargas, Lázaro Cárdenas, and their followers, AD leaders early on in their political careers considered themselves Marxists and (as in the case of Betancourt) Communists. The switch from radical to more moderate positions over a period of time, and the issue of to what extent original ideas and programs were still applicable, created confusion and ambiguities that generated internal conflict. Thus, for example, at the time of each schism, MIR, ARS, and MEP leaders claimed to represent AD's initial radical doctrine, which they accused Betancourt of having betrayed. Indeed, as late as the early 1990s, one faction of AD called itself "orthodox" to identify itself with the party's original positions.

Internal differences in AD centered on timing, namely at what point would the party's unofficial goals be presented to the nation. The MIR leaders believed that with the overthrow of Pérez Jiménez in 1958, and the triumph of the Cuban revolution a year later, conditions were ripe for radical change. In contrast, future MEP leaders argued that the precariousness of the nation's fledgling democracy in 1958 required caution, but by the mid-1960s they were convinced that democratic consolidation and an improved economic situation made possible a bolder approach, which was put forward by the candidacy of Luis Beltrán Prieto Figueroa for the 1968 elections.

The MEP split, and to a certain degree that of the ARS group in 1962, was triggered by the violation of internal democratic procedures by the *Betancourista* faction of the party. In 1967, AD held internal elections for the selection of its presidential candidate in which the party's president, Prieto Figueroa, ran against Gonzalo Barrios. *El Universal* and other national newspapers reported that Prieto had triumphed in sixteen districts, with Barrios winning in six, and three others yet to report final results. Prieto's victory was not surprising given his charisma and popularity in contrast to Barrios's distance from the party's rank and file. Even before the electoral contest, Betancourt had feared Prieto's triumph and decided to return to Venezuela from his self-imposed exile in Europe in order to campaign actively on behalf of Barrios. The *Betancourista* wing of the party refused to accept the results and claimed that electoral manipulation had taken place. The claim was unconvincing given *Betancourista* control of the party's national machinery and specifically the National Executive Committee (CEN) and the National Directive Committee (CDN), both of which acted to expel Prieto's supporters from their party positions. The youth members of the Paz faction responded by protesting in Caracas's Plaza Bolívar and chanting "Oligarchy No, Socialism Yes!" This incident and others like it place in doubt the accuracy of Venezuela's reputation as a model democracy promoted by writers who defended the exceptionalism thesis.

AD's division in 1967 made possible Caldera's triumph in the presidential elections of the following year with a mere 28 percent of the vote. That percentage was far less than the combined vote of the two candidates that drew support from AD's traditional base: the party's official candidate, Gonzalo Barrios, who received 27 percent, and Prieto Figueroa with 19 percent. Miguel Angel Burelli Rivas, whose "Victory Front" candidacy was endorsed by URD and the followers of Uslar Pietri, took in 22 percent.

During his first presidency of 1969–1974, Caldera distanced himself from his image as an ultraconservative, stemming from his ties with the Spanish Falange in the 1930s, as part of a leftward drift that spanned his entire political career until his second administration in the 1990s. Nevertheless, the limits of this movement in a leftward direction were revealed by his clash with leftist currents within the international Christian movement. Thus, for instance, President Caldera (with the support of the church hierarchy) ordered the expulsion of the radical Belgian priest Francisco Wuytack from Venezuela due to his participation in social protests, including a hunger strike to press for legislation on behalf of the unemployed. Caldera's moderation was also reflected in COPEI's interparty relations. With only 19 percent of the seats in the Chamber of Deputies, COPEI was forced to forge alliances and at first reached an arrangement with the socialist MEP in addition to smaller parties. But in 1970, COPEI broke with the MEP and agreed upon the Institutional Pact with AD on a legislative program and the designation of parties to control the presidency of key congressional committees. The Pact was to survive Caldera's term in office, as did a concurrent agreement between party labor leaders whereby AD occupied the presidency of the CTV and a *Copeyano* became secretary-general.

Several of Caldera's policies and actions were applauded by the left and sharply criticized by nonleftists and the private sector. Thus he granted amnesty to leftist guerrillas and legalized the PCV in 1969 and the MIR in 1973. He also replaced DIGEPOL, which was widely held responsible for flagrant human rights violations, with the Office of the Police Intelligence Services with the aim of promoting professional police standards. AD's secretary-general Carlos Andrés Pérez criticized Caldera's leniency toward the insurgents as a sign of weakness that would encourage violence in the future. Caldera's oil policy, which paved the way for nationalization, also invited criticism from the oil companies. Most important, COPEI congressmen voted in favor of the MEP-sponsored Reversion Law, which gave the state control of all petroleum company assets in anticipation of the expiration of oil concessions in 1983. Caldera also nationalized the gas industry and established reference prices in which the government set official export prices for oil and iron. In addition, under Caldera Venezuela became a member of the Andean Pact in 1973 over FEDECAMARAS's objections. The private sector feared that the move would discourage foreign investments, undermine trade agreements with the United States, and place the nation at a disadvantage because of its higher salaries and overvalued currency. Finally, Caldera, who earlier in the decade had adamantly opposed diplomatic recognition of the nations of the socialist bloc, established relations with Hungary in 1969 and the Soviet Union the following year.

Many Venezuelans undoubtedly thought that the guerrilla defeat in the 1960s closed the doors for proposals and movements for far-reaching change. Nevertheless, events demonstrated that influential sectors of the population continued to put forward bold and innovative ideas in favor of radical transformation and were optimistic about the future. This radical potential manifested itself with the emergence of the MEP, its embrace of socialism, and its electoral alliances with Communists for the 1968 and 1973 elections. Evidence of critical radical thinking also came from an unlikely source, namely COPEI, whose youth group split into three factions in the late 1960s. The conservative "Araguatos," who were tied to Caldera, clashed with the left-leaning "Avanzados" and the "Astronauts," who were even further to the left. The latter two were inspired by the movement of liberation theology within the church and viewed COPEI's youth branch as representing the vanguard of the party. The Astronauts in particular were well versed in theoretical political writing and argued that the only way for COPEI to avoid supporting capitalism with all its pernicious effects was by explicitly embracing socialism (Carnevali 1992, 268–337; Ellner 1989, 28–34).

Two other occurrences demonstrated the zeal and persistence of Venezuelans, particularly youthful ones, who favored far-reaching change. During the first two years of the Caldera administration, Venezuelan universities were shook by a movement known as the Academic Renovation, which was inspired by the student upheavals in Paris and elsewhere in the spring of 1968. Student mobilizations put forward demands and innovative proposals for political and university transformation. One of the main slogans, "To Question" (*Cuestionar*), called for inquiry and analysis without any constraints and the rejection of all taboos. In October 1970, President Caldera blamed the authorities of the Central University of Venezuela (UCV) for student disorders and sent troops on campus, after which the rector, Jesús María Bianco, and others under him resigned in protest.

As the Renovation movement was losing momentum, members of the Communist Youth group and those Communists who had been generally most committed to the guerrilla struggle left the PCV to form the Movement Toward Socialism (MAS) in January 1971. The early MAS*istas* hardly displayed the pessimism that may have been expected from those who had just suffered a shattering military defeat. Not only did the early MAS*istas* refuse to acknowledge that the decision to take up arms had been an error (Ellner 1988, 48), but they coined the slogan "Socialism in Our Lifetime" as a corrective to the tendency of the old-time Communists to relegate the struggle for state power to the far-distant future. Along these lines, the early MAS*istas* rejected the PCV's dogmatism and, inspired by the influential Euro-Communist movement, formulated original proposals in order to break out of what its main ideologue, Teodoro Petkoff, called a "ghetto" separating the left from the rest of the nation.

These events help counter the notion that Venezuela has historically been largely free of sharp ongoing struggles around far-reaching demands and goals. Indeed, much scholarly writing downplays meaningful collective action and views politics as centered on personality struggles motivated by clientelistic considerations. Political scientists Moisés Naím and Ramón Piñango, for instance, in their often-cited *El caso Venezuela: una ilusión de armonía,* defended the notion of the political passivity of Venezuelans in general. According to them, at the height of the guerrilla period, "the majority sector of Venezuelan society that was not directly involved in those events exhibited a social and political peace that could have been the envy of any non-industrialized nation—even the ones that did not have to deal with armed insurrection" (Naím and Piñango 1984, 553). The authors attribute this social and political tranquility to the government's avoidance of zero-sum game policies, due to its refusal to define priorities, and the resultant faith among Venezuelans of all backgrounds that sooner or later they would enjoy a fair share of the pie in the form of improved material benefits. Naím and Piñango along with other writers minimize the existence of conflicts by inadvertently applying trends that occurred during the prosperous oil-boom years of the 1970s to the entire 1958–1989 period, while ignoring the diverse expressions of class tension that were often difficult to interpret because they were accompanied by political party sectarianism and personal ambition.

▶ The First Government of Carlos Andrés Pérez, 1974–1979

One of the slogans of AD's presidential candidate Carlos Andrés Pérez in the 1973 elections was "This Man Really Moves!" (*Este Hombre Sí Camina!*). Even though Pérez's energetic and youthful image contrasted with that of COPEI's lackluster candidate, Lorenzo Fernandez, important differences between the two did not manifest themselves during the campaign. Indeed, Pérez had always been identified with the centrist Betancourt, whom he had served as a personal secretary in the 1940s and interior minister in the early 1960s, when he was accused of flagrant violations of human rights. The two leftist candidates, José Vicente Rangel (endorsed by MAS) and the MEP's Jesús Paz Galarraga (backed by the PCV), stressed the similarities of the two establishment party candidates, whom they claimed represented "two sides of the same coin" (Martz and Baloyra 1976, 122, 126). Pérez did better than expected with 49 percent of the vote, in contrast to the 37 percent received by Fernández, Paz's 5 percent, and Rangel's 4 percent.

Pérez's assumption of the presidency coincided with the sharp rise in oil prices triggered by the Arab oil boycott. Pérez attempted to take immediate advantage of this unexpected opportunity by addressing the National Congress on April 29, 1974, and requesting emergency powers in order to enact legislation for the "transformation of the economic structure of the nation." The breadth of the Pérez government's state interventionism in the economy in the form of social programs, promotion of economic development, and measures inspired by economic

nationalism had no equivalent in the post-1958 period. Of prime importance, Pérez announced the nationalization of the oil industry, whose
concessions were due to expire in 1983. In his April 29 speech, he also
made known his policy of "full employment" that included the obligation to hire elevator operators and cleaning personnel in restaurant bath-
rooms as well as mandatory apprenticeship programs for the private sector. Shortly thereafter, Pérez introduced legislation providing all
workers with severance payment benefits and establishing tripartite
commissions to determine the causes of layoffs in an attempt to enhance
job security and seniority. Finally, the Fifth Plan of the Nation (the previous four had had limited impact on national development) encom-
passed massive public investments in the steel, aluminum, and electricity sectors in the Guayana region under the direction of the state-run
Venezuelan Corporation of Guayana (CVG).

Pérez's activist pro–third world foreign policy, like his interventionism in the economy, placed him to the left of the *Betancourista* wing of
the party with which he had previously been identified. Pérez's stands in
the international arena antagonized conservative sectors both in
Washington and Venezuela. Thus, for instance, at the outset of his
administration, Pérez reestablished diplomatic relations with Cuba and
then submitted a resolution to the OAS in favor of lifting its sanctions
against the Caribbean nation that fell short of the required two-thirds
vote. Pérez also supported the Sandinistas in their struggle against the
Somoza dictatorship and was one of Panamanian president Omar
Torrijos's most trusted advisers in his effort to gain control of the
Panama Canal. Venezuela and Mexico created the Latin American
Economic System (SELA) in 1975 in order to promote Latin American
economic integration and serve as a counterweight to the OAS, which
was largely perceived as dominated by the United States (Martz 1980,
26). The following year, Pérez became one of the few Latin American
presidents to visit Moscow, where he signed a treaty in which the USSR
agreed to supply oil to Venezuela's Spanish market while Venezuela was
to do the same for the Soviet market in Cuba.

Pérez viewed the strong interventionist role of the state in the economy and Venezuela's pro–third world foreign policy as part of an incremental strategy of achieving socialism and an autonomous economy vis-
à-vis the developed world. The nationalization of the oil and iron
industries represented just one step in the direction of socialism, while
the Ayacucho Plan of scholarships and the research arm of PDVSA
(Petroleum of Venezuela, Joint Stock Company), the Venezuelan
Technological Institute of Petroleum (INTEVEP), created by Pérez,

were designed to further technological independence (Peña 1979, 93). Pérez's promotion of democratic socialism at the international level bore fruit in 1977 with a meeting of the Socialist International (SI) in Caracas attended by its president, Willy Brandt, and other leading European members of the organization. Pérez identified himself with the SI's left-leaning current headed by Brandt, which he credited with contributing to the "freshness of social democratic theory in opposition to imperial-ism" at the same time that he delivered a speech criticizing the conser-vative wing headed by Helmut Schmidt for defending international capi-talism (Peña 1979, 163, 251). Pérez also praised Brandt's presidency for making efforts to reach out to third-world nations (Pérez 1982).

The leftist thrust of Pérez's policies and his charisma recalled aspects of the radical populism of the 1930s and 1940s typified by Juan Domingo Perón. Indeed, Pérez's nationalization of the iron and oil industries in 1975 and 1976 resembled the radical variant of populism whose salient feature in the case of Perón and Mexico's Lázaro Cárdenas was the takeover of foreign-owned industries. Nevertheless, Pérez's populism lacked the combative and polemical dimension of these earlier movements and contained definite limitations with regard to the realization of national goals. Unlike the radical populism of those years that lashed out at the oligarchy, Pérez refrained from employing an anti-elite discourse or openly clashing with the conservative *Betancourista* wing of AD. Furthermore, Pérez failed to play an activist role within the party, and his pronouncement that his government's nationalization of the iron and steel industries should represent a "deci-sive step toward the renovation" of AD (Peña 1979, 139–140) was not backed up by action. Pérez's weak organizing capacity was also exem-plified by his failure to follow through on his pledge to set up civic com-mittees to monitor price increases and the lukewarm support he extend-ed to his allies in the labor movement (Velásquez 1979, 424; Ellner 1993, 76–80).

Pérez's reluctance to mobilize the population, single out enemies, and engage in struggles to advance political goals was not surprising given his trajectory as a member of AD's dominant faction committed to a strategy of compromise with powerful groups. A major example of this political style was Pérez's modification of his proposed Law of Job Security, introduced in the National Congress at the outset of his admin-istration, which would have ruled out layoffs when the employer could not demonstrate a breach of labor discipline. In July 1974, FEDECA-MARAS held its annual convention in San Cristóbal where it sharply criticized the proposed legislation for threatening to undermine labor discipline, at the same time that the organization opposed Pérez's regulation of retail prices. The Pérez administration's immediate response was to modify the bill by gutting it of its absolute job security provision, instead obliging companies to pay double severance payments in cases of layoffs in which the worker was not at fault. AD's labor congressmen, including future CTV president José Vargas, justified the administration's modification and helped vote it into law. Nevertheless, even in its modified form, the law was advanced for Latin America. Not surprisingly, FEDECAMARAS assailed it for being onerous for employers until finally the legislation was reformed under the influence of neoliberalism in 1997.

A second example of Pérez's timid response to conservative criticism was the legislation nationalizing the iron and petroleum industries, which stopped short of severing foreign ties. In the former case, the government granted the US companies that had run the industry until then a supply of iron at favorable prices for seven years. In the latter case, the foreign oil companies received a generous billion dollars in compensation, even though their concessions were due to expire in 1983. Furthermore, Pérez accepted the incorporation of article 5 in the oil nationalization law, which opened the possibility of mixed companies consisting of private and state capital as long as PDVSA had the controlling share. Support for article 5 came from conservative sectors, including Betancourt, who argued that "we are in an interrelated world and no one can strive for exclusively national decisions" (Velásquez 1979, 431). Finally, undisclosed commercialization and technological assistance contracts were signed with the previously dominant multinationals, which maintained an ongoing relationship with PDVSA's affiliates. Under these terms legal disputes were handled in courts outside of the nation and individual affiliates were prohibited from sharing information with each other.

In spite of Betancourt's endorsement of the nationalization of oil, prominent members of his conservative current in AD opposed President Pérez on a number of fronts. In some cases Betancourt and his AD allies went outside the party to encourage aggressive attacks against Pérez (Ewell 1984, 209–210). The *Betancouristas* particularly objected to the Pérez government's moves away from the US orbit and flirtations with the socialist bloc. They were also critical of Pérez's identification with the left-leaning current of social democratic thinking, particularly as it related to economic policy. They favored modest projects instead of Pérez's megaprojects as embodied in the Fifth Plan of the Nation. Their favorite term, *austerity*, was a buzzword for opposition to the government's marked presence in the economy and corruption. Betancourt was also wary of Pérez's failure to rely on long-standing AD leaders for top positions and his close relations with ex-members of the MIR, ARS, and MEP who had recently returned to the party fold (Alexander 1982, 629–633).

Pérez's programs received critical support from some sectors on the left, specifically MAS and the PCV. MAS backed Pérez's request for emergency powers and favored popular mobilization to ensure his programs' success and to press for further reforms. The party claimed that the Pérez government promoted the "modernization of capitalist structure," which, although not a fundamental solution, was a step in the right direction (*Punto*, May 10, 1974, 7). MAS criticized the AD-led CTV for failing to ensure that the government did not retreat from the positions Pérez had announced on April 29, at the same time that it hailed *Carlosandresista* youth secretary Héctor Alonso López for calling FEDECAMARAS "the major spokesman for reaction in Venezuela" (*Punto*, September 4, 1974, 1). After Pérez left office, several leftist congressmen, including PCV*istas* and José Vicente Rangel, refrained from voting against him on a key charge of corruption that could have resulted in his imprisonment, arguing that the accusations were rightist-inspired reprisals for his progressive policies.

Not all political analysts viewed the rift between the Pérez and the *Betancourista* wings of the party as an expression of differences between the left and the center. One theory put forward by leftist intellectuals connected with the magazine *Proceso Político* linked Pérez with an emerging bourgeoisie that was intent on penetrating foreign markets and that confronted the traditional bourgeoisie dependent upon high tariffs (*Proceso Político* 1978, 31–62). Ex-Communist Pedro Duno derisively called Pérez's top business supporters the "Twelve Apostles." In a book by that name, Duno exposed the state–private sector nexus and resultant cases of corruption involving leading representatives of the emerging bourgeoisie (Duno 1975; Martín 1975). Other leftist analysts asserted that Pérez's activist foreign policy was designed to convert Venezuela into a "sub-imperialist" power that would check Brazil's expansionist ambitions and favor Venezuela's internationally oriented emerging bourgeoisie (Lanza 1980). Still other writers harshly criticized Pérez's costly megaprojects as wasteful and unviable. Thus, OPEC founder Pérez Alfonzo, who broke with AD, called Pérez's national development plan the "Plan of Disaster." Pérez Alfonzo favored limiting petroleum production on grounds that the nation lacked the infrastructure to absorb an enormous influx of oil money. Pérez Alfonzo's cautiousness was the antithesis of President Pérez's ambitious developmentalism.[5] Although these analyses did not readily correspond to positions on the left-right political spectrum, Luis Piñerúa Ordaz of AD's conservative *Betancourista* wing, and the conservative COPEI leader Eduardo Fernández, used concepts derived from them and terms such as the "twelve apostles" to attack Pérez.

In order to evaluate its progressive potential, Pérez's first government must be placed in a broader context. During the 1960s and 1970s, a wave of military coups overthrew Latin American governments that were accused of granting inordinate concessions to the popular classes and following a populist course. Pérez's conservative adversaries used these same criticisms against his government. In addition, the highly critical attitudes of Washington-tied circles toward Pérez reinforced the view that his government was left leaning. Nevertheless, Pérez's populism diverged from the radical populism of Peronism in that he refrained from encouraging mobilizations and taking his causes directly to the people. As a loyal member of AD, he was averse to factional struggle and thus relied on technocrats and probusiness allies to fill many top government positions, rather than appointing labor and social movement followers within the party.

In spite of Pérez's mixed credentials as a leftist, his charisma and the expectations generated by his populist policies caused alarm among conservatives and powerful economic interests. Much evidence exists that historically these sectors have feared nonrevolutionary reformers with strong leadership qualities who, although committed to the established system, provide the nonprivileged with a sense of empowerment and sometimes set in motion a radicalization process that gets out of hand (Raby 2006, 230–250). Fear of this sequence of events may explain the strong reaction of conservative sectors against Pérez and may also make clear his alleged concern about the possibility of terrorist actions designed to undermine his government.[6]

The characterization of the Pérez government and *Carlosandresista* currents within AD as left leaning has important implications for the entire 1958–1989 period. *Carlosandresistas* provided continuity to AD's left-leaning internal currents whose leaders left the party to form the MIR in 1960, ARS in 1962, and the MEP in 1967. Similarly, various COPEI youth factions in the 1960s were identified with left-leaning Luis Herrera Campins, who nearly split off from his party in 1973 when shady dealings denied him the presidential candidacy and instead favored Caldera's minister of interior Lorenzo Fernández. Thus the moderate leftist currents in AD and COPEI were victims of the undemocratic internal maneuverings of the party machines headed by Betancourt and Caldera. These dissident factions channeled the discontent and far-reaching expectations of the rank and file of the two parties and labor unions along institutional lines. The critical outlook among numerous AD and COPEI members and their disillusionment as a result of measures taken by their party's leadership found expression in the radicalization, mobilizations, and acute social confrontations after 1989. Political analysts who downplay the struggle over political ideas and reduce Venezuelan politics to personalities, as was discussed in Chapter 1, pass over this dynamic, which is essential to understanding the emergence of *Chavismo* in the 1990s.

▶ The Governments of Luis Herrera Campins and Jaime Lusinchi, 1979–1989

Even though neoliberal formulas after 1989 provoked the political crisis of the 1990s, the stage for it was set by the shortcomings of the Venezuelan political system and certain ill-conceived policies during the entire post-1958 period. Poor leadership in the face of pressing challenges was especially evident during the decade of declining oil prices of the 1980s. The governments of Luis Herrera Campins (1979–1984) and Jaime Lusinchi (1984–1989), more than previous ones, created high expectations and then disillusionment due in large part to their failure to devise a coherent and viable set of policies to face the economic deterioration of those years. This disappointing performance contrasted with the model of an energetic state that had proved attractive in the 1970s and was credited with generating the prosperity of those years.

Both Herrera and Lusinchi failed to live up to their popular and anti-elite images that had contributed to their electoral triumphs. At the time of their election, Herrera was associated with radical currents within the Christian Democratic movement inspired by liberation theology, while the humble origin and unpretentious style of Lusinchi (as well as Herrera to a certain extent) convinced many that he understood the plight of common people.

Herrera's leftist credentials stemmed from his links with COPEI's left-wing Avanzado youth faction in the 1960s. Both Herrera, who came of political age at the time of the founding of COPEI in 1946, and the Avanzados of the 1960s represented generational challenges to Caldera, whose political career dated back to 1936, and were thus seen as injecting fresh ideas into the party. Herrera, for example, embraced the concept of "communitarian property," which posited the social component and responsibilities of capitalist enterprises (Herrera Campins 1979). In his eagerness to become president, however, Herrera turned to pragmatism. Most important, he rejected the option of leaving COPEI to protest the undemocratic maneuver that deprived him the candidacy for the 1973 presidential elections, and he subsequently made his peace with the more conservative Caldera (Herman 1980, 134–135).

Herrera's campaign strategy for the 1978 presidential elections attempted to build on widespread doubts about the feasibility of Pérez's foreign and economic policies. Herrera played down foreign policy in order to reinforce his criticism of Pérez's third-world outlook for overstepping Venezuela's status as a small Latin American nation far removed from the centers of world conflict. Similarly, Herrera criticized Pérez's ambitious developmental plans as being unrealistic. He also characterized the Pérez administration as hyper-presidentialist, as demonstrated by his emergency socioeconomic legislation that was railroaded through Congress in 1974. Although AD leaders called Herrera's communitarian property concept communist inspired, his positions during the campaign capitalized on a rightist backlash against Pérez's progressive policies. The strategy paid off at the polls. Herrera's 47 percent of the vote exceeded the 43 percent of AD's Piñerúa Ordaz, while the combined vote of the four leftist candidates (José Vicente Rangel representing MAS, Américo Martín of the MIR, Prieto Figueroa of the MEP, and Héctor Mujica of the PCV) was a mere 8 percent.

President Herrera's foreign policy bore no resemblance to the left-leaning positions he had assumed earlier in his political career and also contrasted with President Pérez's bold stands in the international arena. In war-torn El Salvador, President Herrera firmly backed fellow Christian Democrat Napoleón Duarte, who refrained from challenging the right-wing movement linked to the nation's notorious death squads. Herrera's condemnation of the extremes of the Salvadorian right, on the one hand, and Cuban interventionism, on the other, served to justify support for the allegedly moderate Duarte. Herrera's staunch anticommunism strained relations with Cuba (which had improved significantly under Caldera and Pérez), as did an incident involving Cuban refugees in the Venezuelan embassy in Havana resulting in the mutual withdrawal of ambassadors.

Herrera's "pluralism" in foreign policy, which was translated into acceptance of authoritarian regimes in the hemisphere, converged with President Reagan's realism, which also downplayed concern for human rights. Venezuela's friendly relations with the United States were reinforced by Caracas's failure to condemn the US invasion of Grenada in 1983, a position that broke with traditional Venezuelan policy of opposition to military intervention, such as the invasion of the Dominican Republic in 1965. Washington rewarded Herrera for his stands with the controversial sale of twenty-four costly and sophisticated F-16 bombers, which required approval from the US Congress. Only with the US backing of Great Britain in the Falkland (Malvinas) Islands War did Caracas momentarily distance itself from Washington.

On the economic front, Herrera also reversed the policies of the Pérez presidency. Even before the price of oil began to decline in 1981, Herrera limited government intervention in the economy in an attempt to slow down growth and reduce inflation. The government cut back on plans to increase the productive capacity of the state sector, eliminated certain protective measures as well as most subsidies for industrial production, and increased interest rates and the prices of regulated products. A run on the bolivar as a result of loss of confidence in the economy at a time of declining oil prices forced Herrera to intervene in the form of implementation of exchange controls in February 1983. The controls broke with the government's macroeconomic approach by establishing a three-tier system in which dollar requests for priority imports received preferential treatment, while dollars for nonpriority ones were sold at a higher rate, and dollars for foreign travel were purchased on the open market. Had the system not been marred by corruption, which became pronounced in succeeding years, it would have served as an effective instrument to promote economic objectives.

The Herrera administration's failure to deal with the nation's dependence on the developed world was demonstrated by its handling of the foreign debt. Upon taking office, Herrera declared that he was inheriting "a mortgaged country," in reference to Pérez's illogical policy of accumulating a mammoth debt in spite of the influx of dollars as a result of high oil prices. Nevertheless, notwithstanding a second price hike in 1979 following the fall of the Shah of Iran, Herrera doubled the foreign debt.

Over the next two decades, the scourge of dependency on foreign financial institutions absorbed between one-fifth and one-third of Venezuela's annual foreign exchange earnings and increasingly limited the nation's political options. In effect, the government during this period paid interest on the debt while the principal remained about the same. Even though nearly half of the debt was short-term, Herrera resisted reaching an agreement to reschedule payment with creditors, who pressed for the implementation of a sales or value added tax, the establishment of a single currency exchange rate, and special considerations for payment of the private sector debt (*Número*, June 12, 1983, 18). The delay, however, hurt Venezuela when bankers stiffened their demands in response to the Mexican debt crisis in 1982. AD harped on this blunder and during the 1983 presidential campaign insisted on reaching an agreement with creditors without discarding the possibility of negotiating with the International Monetary Fund (IMF). In doing so, AD skirted a more important issue, namely the nearly 50 percent of the public debt that, according to President Herrera (and confirmed by AD economist Iván Pulido Mora), had been agreed upon in violation of Venezuelan law and thus implied dubious legal obligations. Another issue that was ignored by the largest party of the opposition was the government's responsibility for repayment of the private debt, particularly loans that were unrelated to the nation's economic growth (Hellinger 1991, 127). In spite of opposition from the president of the Central Bank, Leopoldo Díaz Bruzual, Herrera agreed to create an inventory of the private foreign debt in order to provide debtors with the opportunity to purchase preferential dollars.

Following five years of unbridled expansion under Pérez, the Herrera government's abandonment of development plans left highly indebted state companies with a bloated bureaucracy and an underutilized work force. As a corrective, FEDECAMARAS president Adan Celis advocated privatization. Leftist parties such as MAS staunchly rejected the proposal and insisted that employees be brought into the decisionmaking process of state firms that required reorganization (*Punto*, January 1984, 30–31). In spite of the government's macroeconomic approach, it refrained from selling off financially strapped public companies, a process which would await the neoliberal governments of the 1990s.

The nation's economic contraction coupled with inflation set off by higher exchange rates thrust the issue of economic policy onto center stage in the 1983 presidential campaign. COPEI's candidate, Rafael Caldera, following the recommendations of US campaign adviser David Garth, denied that he was the "government's candidate" and boldly acknowledged that Venezuela's economic problems were of crisis proportions. In doing so, the veteran Caldera hoped to be seen as the man of the hour with the necessary experience to lead the nation forward. The gambit failed partly because it exacerbated internal tensions within COPEI as the Herrera faction resented Caldera's refusal to defend government policy. In the face of pressing economic difficulties, AD candidate Jaime Lusinchi's popular image compared favorably with Caldera's patrician style. Large numbers of voters found Lusinchi's slogan "Jaime Is Like You" (*Jaime es como tu*) reassuring, along with his ill-defined campaign slogan "Social Pact" (which in concrete terms referred only to the modernization of the Labor Ministry and employment agencies tied to trade unions). Lusinchi won with 57 percent of the vote, the highest percentage in any presidential election since 1958. Caldera pulled in 35 percent while the leftist vote split between MAS's Teodoro Petkoff, with 4 percent, and the independent José Vicente Rangel, who was endorsed by the PCV and the MEP, with 3 percent.

The economic and political deterioration of the Lusinchi presidency further paved the way for the neoliberal governments of the 1990s. The decline of foreign reserves, which reached a mere 1.8 billion by 1985, rampant corruption and clientelism, and the debt incurred by state companies lent credibility to the neoliberal argument of the inevitability of privatization. Various leftist and nonleftist political actors who originally opposed neoliberal policies in the early 1990s blamed the private sector in collaboration with public sector managers for the ailing condition of state firms. Some of them even suggested that public companies (along with the nation's exchange control system) were intentionally run into the ground in order to pave the way for the macroeconomic formulas implemented by the second Pérez administration.[7] In opposing privatization at the time, MAS's Teodoro Petkoff, for instance, asked: "Explain to me why all the Finance Ministers and Economy Ministers who have contributed to ruining the nation's economy have come from the private sector?" (Petkoff 1989). These accusations were supported by statistics showing that sudden changes in the policies of state companies in the years immediately prior to privatization helped make them inoperative (Ellner 1999d, 114–115).

Lusinchi's generosity toward foreign creditors and Venezuelan debtors saddled the government with financial commitments that swayed left-leaning politicians such as Carlos Andrés Pérez toward austerity measures and other neoliberal formulas. Upon taking office, Lusinchi bowed to pressure, which included rumors of impending company bankruptcies, by immediately granting preferential dollars at the lowest rate for repayment of the foreign private debt. In doing so, the president ignored arguments for a more discriminatory approach. Leftist economist Domingo Maza Zavala, for instance, claimed that only four to five billion dollars of the fourteen-billion-dollar foreign private debt was legal. In addition, during his presidential campaign in 1983, Teodoro Petkoff proposed that only small- and medium-sized businessmen be eligible for preferential dollars for paying back loans on grounds that the big capitalist groups had already received a windfall for their speculative activity. Indeed, Lusinchi's outspoken planning minister Luis Raúl Matos Azócar claimed that the private sector's purchase of $200,000 a day in the weeks prior to the implementation of exchange controls in 1983 and the subsequent reconversion of the money into bolivares represented the greatest state transfer to speculators in world history. Conservatives harshly attacked Matos Azócar for his statement and within one year he was forced out of the administration, leaving economic policy largely in the hands of probusiness finance minister Héctor Hurtado (*Punto Socialista* 1984a; 1984b).

Lusinchi expressed satisfaction that early in his administration his government reached an agreement with foreign creditors without the participation of the IMF and without the customary obligation of adopting austerity policies. Leftist parties, however, considered the arrangement ill-timed. They criticized Lusinchi for turning his back on other Latin American governments such as Peru (under Alan García), which were beginning to demand a fair treatment for their foreign debt, as well as those who called for collective negotiations with creditors. Along these lines, leftist spokesmen objected to Lusinchi's statement that his government's association with economically less privileged Latin American nations in a "debtors club" would lower Venezuela's credit rating. The leftists also called the rescheduling arrangement "unpatriotic" since it committed Venezuela to resolving differences with creditors in international courts, thus spurning the nation's judicial authority. Finally, the left protested that the government failed to submit the agreement to Congress for ratification (Partido Comunista de Venezuela 1986, 141, 151).

The problems of corruption and mismanagement, which intensified under the Lusinchi administration, not only undermined the efficiency of the public administration but also the productive capacity of state companies. Lusinchi's policy of selecting AD regional secretary-generals as governors in their respective states fostered corruption by blurring the line of distinction between the party and the public sphere. These appointments were particularly detrimental because Lusinchi, unlike Pérez before him, belonged to AD's dominant faction thus making the relationship between the state and the party all the more intimate.

The widespread corruption involving the Differential Exchange Regime agency (RECADI) underscored the effect of unethical conduct on economic performance. The system of differential currency exchange went contrary to macroeconomic theory, which favored a single exchange rate or no official rate at all. The multitiered system, along with the Commission on Costs, Prices, and Salaries (CONACOPRESA), which regulated prices and salaries, demonstrated that Lusinchi's policies diverged from neoliberalism. RECADI was designed to serve as a mechanism to provide special treatment for imports essential to industrial development and the general welfare. RECADI was thus in line with the interventionist model dating back to 1958. However, from its very beginning in 1983 under Herrera, RECADI was plagued by corrupt dealings and during its six years of existence became possibly the largest source of corruption in the nation's history. These practices thwarted the achievement of the system's social and economic objectives. The disastrous experience of RECADI provided Venezuelan neoliberals with a powerful argument in favor of deregulation of exchange rates along with other areas of the nation's economy.

AD and COPEI's loss of prestige during these years encouraged the emergence of new actors and groups that rejected centralized political control. Among the most important movements to emerge in the 1980s were neighborhood associations, which in middle-class areas firmly resisted party interference in their internal affairs (Ellner 1999a, 94). In addition, the Presidential Commission for State Reform (COPRE), which was created by Lusinchi in 1984 and placed under the direction of distinguished personalities, formulated proposals designed to deepen democracy, particularly through decentralization and electoral reform. Two years after its founding, the COPRE asserted its autonomy vis-à-vis the Lusinchi government when it attributed the nation's political woes to party-based democracy (Coppedge 1994, 7–8). Lusinchi adamantly opposed the COPRE's call for replacing presidentially appointed governors with elected ones on grounds that the new state heads would represent a throwback to nineteenth-century style regional caudillos.[8]

These actors and other social and political activists who favored a reconfiguration of the democratic system moved in two opposite directions. One current was led by those who opposed privatization and in some cases represented the nonprivileged sectors of the population. MAS, for instance, rejected the sale of major state companies and was a pioneer in the support for gubernatorial elections, decentralization, and the implementation of internal party reform. The leftist Causa R party also supported radical democracy as practiced in internal decisionmaking based on the consensus of all members present. Unlike the predominately middle-class MAS, the Causa R's social base consisted of workers and other nonprivileged classes. A second current generally linked to business circles drew a connection between the deepening of democracy and the reduction of centralized political power, including party control, on the one hand, and "economic liberty" and privatization, on the other. The editorial slant of the nation's premier newspaper, *El Nacional*, and the television station Radio Caracas, which were often extremely critical of political parties, reflected the second current (Coppedge 1994, 160). In 1987 Radio Caracas president Marcel Granier led the effort to articulate the second line of thinking by coordinating the drafting of the lengthy document *Mas y mejor democracia* (Granier 1987).

The lines between the pro- and anti-neoliberal reformers were not always clearly drawn. Thus, for instance, the COPRE, which counted among its main participants leading leftists, also proposed neoliberal formulas for deepening the nation's democracy. Furthermore, neoliberals (such as those represented by the periodical *VenEconomy*, tied to Marcel Granier) converged with the Causa R in its demands to democratize the labor movement to rid it of political party interference and on the whole in embracing an antiparty discourse (Ellner 1999b, 117).

The political reform impulse of the 1980s and 1990s, with its critique of the existing system, set the stage for the changes promoted by the *Chavistas*. Indeed, some of the prominent reformers (such as the renowned constitutional experts Hernán Escarrá and Ricardo Combellas, as well as Luis Miquilena and the MAS*istas*) participated in the *Chavista* alliance during its early years. Nevertheless, the failure of these reformers to embrace an economic strategy and their ambiguity toward neoliberalism explain in large part their failure to play a more important leadership role in the 1990s and their eventual separation from the *Chavista* movement.

▶ Venezuelan Dependency During the Oil Boom and Its Aftermath

Any overall evaluation of the presidencies of Herrera and Lusinchi must place their administrations in a broader economic context. The "school of dependency," which gained widespread acceptance in the 1970s and still has much relevance for Latin America, presented a pessimistic picture of underdeveloped nations in situations in which world market conditions suddenly favor their main export commodity. These writers argued that such periods only exacerbate dependency, and that when the boom ends the country has little or nothing to show for its increased revenue as its economy soon reverts to its former backward state. Dependency school economist Andre Gunder Frank called this phenomenon "the development of underdevelopment" (Frank 1967, 201–218).

In many ways, the scenario describes conditions in Venezuela during the oil boom decade of the 1970s and its aftermath during the governments of Herrera and Lusinchi. The economic acceleration of the 1970s was followed by a sharp economic decline either because the government had failed to control the expansion or because oil prices fell, or both. As a result, the government shut down the ambitious coal project in Naricual, Anzoátegui, scrapped plans for a steel complex in Zulia and other industrial projects in the Guayana region, and cut back on scholarship money, forcing many Venezuelan students abroad to return before completing their studies. Furthermore, with declining revenue the government was forced to renegotiate its foreign debt. In doing so, it was increasingly susceptible to pressure from abroad to adopt macroeconomic policies, a salient characteristic of financial dependency. Finally, the mass disturbances of February 27, 1989, signaled a return to the social and political instability of the pre–oil boom years.

Nevertheless, the case for the "development of underdevelopment" in Venezuela should not be overstated. The real rollbacks with regard to the programs and policies of the 1970s occurred not in the 1980s, when oil prices plummeted, but in the 1990s with the application of neoliberal policies, including widespread privatization. The thesis of the concept of "development of underdevelopment," which belittles the importance of the massive state investments in infrastructure and the implementation of social programs and legislation in the 1970s, lets the neoliberals off the hook for the devastating effects of their policies in the 1990s, including the foreign takeover of entire sectors of the economy.

Furthermore, actions and programs such as the nationalization of gas, iron, and oil and the strengthening of state control of the aluminum industry in the 1970s were not completely reversed in the 1980s but rather had a long-term impact. Indeed, the anti-neoliberalism of the Chávez government after 1998 was at first defined as the defense of many of the measures taken under Pérez's first government and targeted for elimination by the neoliberals in the 1990s. Chávez's policies along these lines included the maintenance of state control of the oil and aluminum sectors as well as the restoration of social security benefits, particularly the system of severance payments enacted under Pérez in 1974. Then, beginning in 2002, the government's anti-neoliberal thrust led it to go beyond the original objectives of the 1976 nationalization of oil by consolidating the Ministry of Mines' control over PDVSA and formulating new goals for the industry. Indeed, Alvaro Silva Calderón, Chávez's minister of energy and mines, who was one of the architects of the industry's nationalization in the 1970s, called the Law of Nationalization of

1975 "a crucial landmark in the process of nationalization" but one that awaited additional measures to deepen the transformation (Silva Calderón 2006, 123). Another example of the long-term impact of the first Pérez administration was the Ayacucho Plan and other scholarship programs, whose recipients were to contribute to the research boom on campuses beginning in 1990.[9] In short, several decades of import substitution gains, culminating with Pérez's interventionist policies of the 1970s, was not undone by declining oil prices and poor leadership in the 1980s but was put in jeopardy by the neoliberal model applied after 1989.

▶ **Notes**

1. Kennedy embraced these positions in his speech on March 13, 1961, announcing the Alliance for Progress.

2. These differences were later explored by Ruth and David Collier in their study of the political evolution of eight Latin American nations in the twentieth century. According to the Colliers, AD after 1958 stood out as institutionally developed and "characterized by a party-political system that was integrative, not polarizing," that avoided "fractionalized, unstable coalitions, and that embodied important conflict-limiting mechanisms." These characteristics reduced the intensity of the "zero-sum conflict that led to policy vacillation and immobilism." In contrast, the *Peronista* and APRA parties "were overwhelmingly dominated by a single personality" (Collier and Collier 1991, 314, 483, 571).

3. In his article, Gall singles out the works of Levine (1973), Lieuwen (1965), Powell (1971), and Martz (1966).

4. The Chávez government republished *Expediente negro*, a collection of Rangel's speeches and writings dealing with the Lovera case (Rangel 1969).

5. Pérez Alfonzo's harsh critique of Pérez's first government was the point of departure for scholarly analyses of that period by Terry Karl and others who emphasized the centralism and hyperpresidentialism that suffocated private initiative (Karl 1997; McCoy 1989).

6. According to inside sources, Pérez was highly suspicious of the loyalty of Luis Posada Carriles and other anti-*Fidelista* Cubans with top positions in the Venezuelan security forces, whom he feared might be plotting to assassinate him and whom he ended up replacing (Julio Godio 1982; confidential author interview, April 13, Caracas). Charismatic liberals (such as in the case of the three Kennedy brothers in the United States) have often been subject to campaigns of complete defamation as well as assassination. One possible explanation of this treatment is the right's fear that reformist or populist governments under charismatic leaders could set in motion changes that go far beyond original intentions, a dynamic that is applicable to Venezuela's 1945–1948 period (as discussed in Chapter 2) and Carlos Andrés Pérez's first administration. For a theoretical analysis of the revolutionary potential of critical junctures under populist governments, see Laclau (1977; 2005) and Raby (2006).

7. A similar argument has been made by critics of the George W. Bush administration who claim that irresponsible fiscal policies are designed to present successive governments with a fait accompli that will force them to cut back public services and other government programs.

8. The COPRE's president, the renowned historian Ramón J. Velásquez, resigned from his post in reaction to Lusinchi's rejection of the proposal.

9. The Program of Researcher Promotion (PPI) initiated in 1990 stimulated considerable academic research by rewarding university professors with bonuses pegged to productivity.

4

▼

Neoliberal Reforms and Political Crisis, 1989–1999

VENEZUELA'S experience with free market reforms in the 1990s was as much a demonstration as anywhere in Latin America of the acute social conflict and political crisis engendered by neoliberalism and its failure to attract popular support. Venezuelans were particularly averse to accepting the neoliberal argument on the need to make sacrifices for the sake of a better future because oil wealth over a period of decades had imbued in them a sense of material entitlement. Furthermore, unlike Peru during the same period, the same political leadership (AD and COPEI) that had run the country for three decades was now calling on the general populace to relinquish benefits in order to correct erroneous policies, thus making the neoliberal message particularly objectionable. Finally, unlike in Argentina, Chile, Brazil, and Mexico, due to the weakness of the private sector, multinationals bought out privatized companies with minimum input from national capital, thus undermining the neoliberal appeal even further.

In contrast to countries such as Peru and Argentina where an anti-neoliberal-turned-neoliberal was reelected president (Alberto Fujimori and Carlos Menem, respectively), Venezuelan voters rejected neoliberal presidential candidates three times: 1989 with the triumph of Carlos Andrés Pérez (1989–1993) who, unlike his main opponent, Eduardo Fernández of COPEI, was identified with the state interventionist policies of his first government; Rafael Caldera (1994–1999) who ran on an explicitly anti-neoliberal platform, which contrasted with his three rivals in the election; and Hugo Chávez who was also the only anti-neoliberal among several presidential candidates. Once in office, Pérez and Caldera embraced neoliberalism. These reversals are typical of how neoliberal policies were implemented in Latin America in spite of their poor electoral record and striking unpopularity (Ellner 2002, 83–85). In the case of Venezuela, both the shock treatment (which Pérez opted for) and the more gradual neoliberal approach (followed by Caldera) proved to be political failures.

Ironically, the two presidents who did the most to dismantle economic interventionist and centralist structures were among the politicians most identified with that model over an extended period of time: Pérez's first administration in the 1970s had been the most interventionist presidency in the century; and Caldera had coauthored the Labor Law of 1936 establishing the severance payment system that as president he revamped in 1997.

▶ The Second Administration of Carlos Andrés Pérez, 1989–1993

Several weeks after assuming the presidency in 1989, Carlos Andrés Pérez unveiled his neoliberal economic program, which he called the "great turnabout." Indeed, the policies that he announced and that were deepened over the next ten years would put an end to the economic model of state intervention in the economy established over the previous half-century. Thus in the 1990s the telephone company (CANTV), taken over by the state in the 1950s, the state steel industry (SIDOR), dating back to the 1950s and 1960s, and the social security system, initiated in 1944, were privatized. In addition, the severance payment system established by the Labor Law of 1936 was radically modified in order to achieve "flexibilization" of the work force in accordance with the imperatives of the global economy. These and other policies designed to facilitate Venezuela's economic insertion at the international level encouraged the thorough penetration of the national economy by multinational capital. The import substitution strategy embraced by Venezuelan governments over the previous decades had formulated diametrically opposed objectives, namely the growth of internal markets and the strengthening of the national bourgeoisie. In another far-reaching change, the Law of Decentralization promulgated in 1989 eliminated the centralist model that had its origins in the Guzmán Blanco, Castro, and Gómez regimes of the late nineteenth and early twentieth centuries, as well as post-1936 governments that saw it as an antidote to regional inequality.

The repudiation of neoliberal policies in the form of widespread disturbances came on the heels of the announcement of their application by recently elected president Carlos Andrés Pérez. The *Caracazo*, during the week of February 27, 1989, began with two days of mass looting followed by several days of repression by military troops sent to slum areas, resulting in hundreds, perhaps thousands, of deaths. Actually, the term *Caracazo* was a misnomer since, unlike the overthrow of Pérez Jiménez and other important events triggered by mobilizations in Caracas, it was a nationwide phenomenon in that it broke out in the nation's capital but spread instantaneously to other urban areas throughout Venezuela. The *Caracazo* initiated a wave of protests during the Pérez administration consisting of a large number of confrontational and violent actions that were not easily contained by clientelistic arrangements or economic concessions and often called into question government legitimacy (López Maya and Lander 2005, 97–98). The *Caracazo* was followed by a one-day general strike on May 18 that was called to pressure the government into reconsidering its neoliberal policies. The social turbulence of these years fed into the abortive military coups of February 1992 led by Chávez and another staged ten months later.

Electoral trends under Pérez's presidency also demonstrated the general repudiation of neoliberal formulas and disenchantment with proestablishment politicians and those of AD in particular. In 1989 the first gubernatorial and mayoral elections in the nation's history were held. AD gained control of eleven states, while COPEI triumphed in six, MAS in two, and the Causa R in the state of Bolívar with its candidate Andrés Velásquez, a former steel workers' president. The 1992 gubernatorial contests reduced AD's control to seven states while COPEI won in eleven and MAS in three. Velásquez was reelected in Bolívar and his party's Aristóbulo Istúriz was elected mayor of Caracas.

The critical stance of the candidates nominated to run in the 1993 presidential election was also indicative of the widespread discontent among Venezuelans. Caldera, who embraced an anti-neoliberal discourse and attributed Chávez's 1992 revolt to pressing socioeconomic conditions, left COPEI to form the Convergence Party and was supported by the leftist and left-leaning MAS, MEP, and the PCV. The leftist Causa R chose Andrés Velásquez. In internal primaries, AD and COPEI nominated charismatic candidates critical of the party machine. Zulia's governor, Oswaldo Alvarez Paz, soundly defeated COPEI's secretary-general Eduardo Fernández, while former Caracas mayor Claudio Fermín also triumphed over the AD machine's favorite by a wide margin. Thus all four candidates, in different ways, could be considered "antiestablishment."

The radical changes of policy and strategy in 1989 had a major impact not only on the economy and politics but also on the social front. Structural economic changes promoted by neoliberal economic policy contributed to the expansion of the informal economy and the weakening of organized labor. Privatization reduced the effectiveness of Venezuelan trade unionists, particularly because most of them belonged to AD and COPEI, which enjoyed extensive influence in the public sector.

Pérez's Privatization Law, passed in 1992, laid the basis for the widespread privatization of key industries as well as scores of nonstrategic companies that had faced bankruptcy and were taken over by the state, which invariably paid their owners a generous compensation. Even before the law's passage, Congress ratified the privatization of the telephone company (CANTV) over objections from the Causa R, MAS, some AD leaders, and military officers who expressed concern over the industry's strategic importance. Although privatization advocates insisted that the modernization of CANTV by the company's new owners would open up job opportunities, the work force was reduced and a large number of employees were reclassified as "confidential" and were thus unprotected by the collective bargaining agreement. The second most important sector privatized under Pérez was the port system. The National Port Institute was dissolved as was the Federation of Port Workers dating back half a century. The major ports of Maracaibo, Puerto Cabello, and Guanta were transferred to state authorities. Predictably the states, which lacked resources and experience to run the ports, turned over key operations to the private sector. Thus, as was also the case with the salt industry located in the eastern state of Sucre, decentralization of the ports turned out to be a first step toward privatization. Contrary to the promises that were made, few of the former port employees were rehired by the private sector and instead they were replaced by nonunionized temporary workers (Ellner 1999d, 123–127).

Deregulation was central to Pérez's radical brand of neoliberalism. The government lifted price controls on all but a handful of basic commodities. In addition, uniform interest rates were eliminated as were fixed currency exchange rates for certain transactions. The Pérez government also removed restrictions on foreign investments in Venezuela, resulting in multinational penetration of diverse sectors such as financial institutions, gasoline retail, and fast-food restaurants. The government's sharp reduction of tariffs formed part of its "shock treatment" approach, which contrasted with the gradual decrease proposed by politician-economist Teodoro Petkoff among others. Unlike in Argentina and Peru where deregulation helped combat rampant inflation, in Venezuela the same types of measures resulted in an increase in the cost of living.

Pérez's Organic Law of Decentralization (LOD) reflected the radical approach to state reform in keeping with the "shock treatment" neoliberal strategy of drastically reducing the authority of the central government and other national institutions. The law classified education, health, sports, public housing, indigenous communities, civil defense, and consumer protection as the shared responsibilities of the federal and state governments, while the administration of ports, commercial airports, and highways became the "exclusive" responsibility of the gubernatorial government.

The LOD (in its article 35) also rescinded the Organic Law of Coordination of the Situado passed in 1975 under Pérez's first administration. "Coordination" had consisted of committees of gubernatorial and federal government representatives that designed projects financed by the investment *situado*, which was the fixed percentage of the national budget allocated to state governments for investment purposes. As a step toward decentralization, the Presidential Commission for State Reform (COPRE) had called for the abrogation of the 1975 law on coordination and its replacement by legislation that differentiated in precise terms central and state government responsibilities. The 1989 law reflected Pérez's radical neoliberalism, which was opposed to coordination on the grounds that the national executive's superior resources and access to information would allow it to dominate any joint effort and thwart local and state government participation.

In another change supported by radical neoliberals, as well as some non-neoliberals, the Pérez administration promoted the creation of new municipalities, which were sometimes justified with the argument "the smaller the better." In Caracas three breakaway municipalities were created in affluent areas (Chacao, Baruta, and El Hatillo) under the Pérez presidency, thus depriving the barrios of badly needed resources. This pattern was repeated throughout the nation during the ten-year period after 1989 when over thirty new municipalities were created at the expense of inner city and marginalized areas.

The second Pérez administration promoted a radical brand of state reform in other areas. Thus electoral reform under Pérez, which was initiated with the direct elections of governors (previously appointed by the president) in 1989, was designed to strengthen the ties between individual candidates and their local communities at the expense of the national leaderships of political parties. In all nonpresidential elections prior to 1989, voters selected political party slates, while the names of the individual candidates did not even appear on the ballot. In the 1989 state and municipal elections, Venezuelans for the first time were able to split their vote by selecting candidates from different slates. In the 1992 and 1995 electoral contests, candidates for city council and state legislature ran in single-member electoral districts; voters selected individual candidates rather than party slates to represent their respective district.

This system weakened the political parties since elected officials owed their triumph more to their own qualities than to the appeal of their party's slate. Those who championed the radical version of state reform favored additional legislation to eliminate the comparative advantages of party politicians in the hope that independents who emerged during this period would win control of local governments (Ellner 1999a, 84–85). Years later the weakening of political parties as a result of state reform (along with other developments such as the editorial slant of various influential daily newspapers against political party leaderships) was held responsible for the political crisis that led to Chávez's rise to power (Lander 2005, 28; Molina 2004, 162–169; Colomina 2000, 1–4).

Perhaps the most radical aspect of state reform implemented during this period was the provision of a *reglamento* (enabling act) of the LOD (issued under the caretaker government of Ramón J. Velásquez) that empowered governors to nominate the state-wide directors of individual ministries. This arrangement, in which the ministry's director at the state level was beholden to the governor rather than the respective minister, had no equivalent throughout the world. It also went contrary to the constitution, which defined the governor as an "agent of the federal government" and not an autonomous actor.

A backlash against the radical thrust of decentralization found expression under the Caldera and Chávez administrations. Caldera revoked the provision of the LOD's enabling act regarding the nomination of state directors and criticized the proliferation of municipalities, claiming that they duplicated bureaucracy. He also refused to grant states the right to collect retail taxes, which the LOD (in its article 12) had authorized and which the governors during this period adamantly called for. Chávez, for his part, promoted the drafting of a new constitution in 1999 that reestablished the system of coordination of state and federal governments.

Popular protest in reaction to the implementation of Pérez's economic program was immediate. On the morning of February 27, 1989, neighborhood members mobilized against hikes in public transportation fares, which had accompanied neoliberal-inspired gasoline price increases. Within hours massive looting had spread throughout the country. The failure to maintain order was a reflection not only of the magnitude of the *Caracazo*, but of state incompetence and institutional weakness. On many routes, for instance, passengers were charged far in excess of the 30 percent increase that government authorities and the transportation union known as the Federation of Transportation Workers (Fedetransporte) had agreed upon. In addition, the Metropolitan Police in Caracas tolerated and in some cases encouraged the looting, partly as a result of dissatisfaction due to internal grievances. Intelligence was also faulty, thus explaining why the national executive addressed the nation only as late as noontime on February 28 (López Maya 2003, 123–126, 129).

The official count of those killed and wounded by firearms during the *Caracazo* was 277 and 1,009, respectively, but other estimates placed the death count at above 2,000. In subsequent years, the Committee of the Families of the Victims of February–March 1989 (COFAVIC) and other human rights organizations attempted to clarify the circumstances surrounding the deaths. COFAVIC insisted that the cases be resolved in civilian as opposed to military courts and in October 1990 convinced the attorney general to order the exhumation of the skeletons in common burial pits. Three explanations for the large number of fatalities were put forward. Progovernment sources alleged that those killed were professional agitators or members of organized gangs who had resisted the efforts of security forces to recover looted merchandise. In fact, 83 percent of the registered victims had no previous criminal record, and only one of those whose cases were brought to court had been a political activist (Ellner 1990, 740). A second explanation was that a large percentage of those who were gunned down had failed to respect the government-imposed curfew. The third explanation was that the repression was designed to teach the poor a lesson. This position was put forward by Arturo Sosa, director of the Jesuit magazine *SIC*, who stated: "The objective of military aggression on February 27 was to produce visceral fear in the memory of people so that they would realize just how far the dominant elites are willing to go" (quoted in Ellner 1990, 741).

The events of February 27 came to constitute a powerful historical memory in the barrios of major cities and would be given prominence by the Chávez government and movement, which organized annual commemorative activities. The February 27 legacy went beyond the issue of human rights. This was made clear by Sosa's statement: "February 27 was not an 'excess' or a 'bad night.' It was a protest in which people were obliged to utilize extraordinary channels. It was a night that the Venezuelan people should be proud of and remember as an experience in which they were the protagonists" (quoted in Ellner 1990, 741).

Chávez's military supporters belonging to the clandestine Revolutionary Bolivarian Movement–200 (MBR-200), which was formed in 1982, were incensed by the government's decision to call on the armed forces to quell the February 27 disturbances and were repulsed by the excessive use of force. The bitter experience of February 27 swelled the ranks of the clandestine MBR-200 with non-elite officers and convinced the group to take up arms against Pérez. Coup attempts such as the one on February 4, 1992, led by middle-level officers are uncommon in Latin America. But what made Chávez's uprising unique is that the MBR-200 had functioned clandestinely for ten years, an experience that undoubtedly radicalized its members. Although military intelligence knew of the MBR-200's existence, systematic action was not taken against its members. Chávez's explanation that superior officers were held back from taking harsh measures because of the outstanding professional qualifications of MBR-200 members is hardly convincing (Blanco Muñoz 1998, 466). Undoubtedly, complacency had much to do with the inaction on the part of top-ranking officers who accepted the "exceptionalism" notion that Venezuela was exempt from the military disruptions racking other Latin American nations (Naím 1993b, 152). This illusion was heightened at the time by Pérez's overconfidence and faith in his own charisma (Martz 1995, 43; Blanco Muñoz 1998, 216–217).

On February 4, 1992, the MBR-200 rebels took key points in Caracas, Maracaibo, and Maracay, but when it became evident that the expected air-force and extensive civilian participation was not forthcoming and that communication among units had broken down, Chávez called on his comrades in arms to surrender. On November 27 of the same year, navy and air force upper-level officers led a bloodier uprising. Two of the three officers who led the coup attempt were linked to Chávez and would subsequently form part of his government and movement. The third one, Francisco Visconti, was a nonleftist and accused Chávez of disregarding military hierarchy by ignoring the ranks of officers within his movement (Blanco Muñoz 1998, 328–330). Nevertheless, the November 27 uprising received greater popular backing than did the February 4 attempt in large part because the former energized local leftists who were better prepared at the time of the second coup.

The 1992 coup attempts created a groundswell of support for removal of Pérez from office and set off a chain of events that led to congressional action. In an attempt to demonstrate his nonpartisanship and commitment to justice in the wake of the February uprising, Pérez made a number of appointments of independents and others outside of his political circle. The new attorney general, Ramón Escovar Salom, issued a report demonstrating that in 1989 the national executive had speculated with dollars from a Ministry of Interior slush fund and then funneled them into the Office of the President, after which they became unaccounted for. After the Supreme Court recommended bringing Pérez to trial and the Senate authorized it in May 1993, the president stepped down. Congress replaced him with the elderly historian Ramón J. Velásquez, whose interim government lasted until the December presidential elections of that year.

The role of AD in the crisis faced by Pérez is subject to controversy. Certainly AD resented Pérez's appointment of independents to key government posts, his frequent disparagement of the Lusinchi administration, his efforts to establish alliances with new parties, and even his appeal to social movements (Corrales 2000, 135). Some scholars, along with the technocrats who held key cabinet positions, subsequently attributed Pérez's failures on political and economic fronts to the party's staunch resistance to his reform program. Pérez's development minister, Moisés Naím, for instance, argues that lengthy negotiations with AD political and labor leaders slowed down the president's reform program at the same time that the party shelved some of his proposals in Congress and forced him to accept major concessions on others (Naím 1993a, 47, 132; 1993b, 166; see also Weyland 2002, 153; Murillo 2001, 71–72; and Burgess 2004, 136–138). Some of those who adhere to this viewpoint claim that AD "stabbed Pérez in the back" because he had sidestepped the party by appointing independents to key positions in charge of policy formulation.[1] In short, the timid implementation of neoliberalism explained its failure to achieve stated objectives (Corrales 2002, 298). Chávez and other hardline leftists defended a diametrically opposed view, namely that AD congressmen voted to remove Pérez only as a result of a popular clamor that was set off by the 1992 attempted coups (Harnecker 2005, 37–38).

Both Naím and Chávez overstate their cases regarding the relations between Pérez and his party. By blaming AD for Pérez's setbacks, Naím ignores the limitations of the party's resistance to neoliberal reforms. Following the May 1989 strike and worker protests in several cities in February 1990, AD labor leaders refrained from mobilizing their constituency as they threatened to do on numerous occasions. Furthermore, labor leaders in Congress refused to break ranks with fellow party congressmen and thus voted against a motion to censure Pérez's economic program.

Nevertheless, Chávez and other hard-line leftists go to the other extreme. By dismissing internal AD tensions, and specifically those

between AD leaders and the Pérez government, they ignore the importance of congressional resistance to some aspects of the neoliberal
reform program. Indeed, the privatization of social security, the modification of the system of severance payments, and other reforms that
Pérez formulated were held up in Congress, but were subsequently
enacted into law by Caldera. Furthermore, Pérez opposed the Labor Law
of 1990 (drafted by the then anti-neoliberal Caldera) because it held
back the neoliberal-inspired "flexibilization" of the work force, but it
was firmly supported by the CTV and approved by the AD-controlled
Congress. By minimizing internal differences within AD and COPEI,
Chávez and other hard-line leftists pass over an important arena of conflict and struggle, not only in the second Pérez administration but
throughout the entire post-1958 period. Although the left-leaning currents in AD and COPEI lacked ideological consistency and failed to
mobilize the population on behalf of their positions, they nevertheless
articulated viewpoints that reflected the thinking of a large number of
Venezuelans (Ellner 1999d, 130–136). In doing so, left-leaning leaders
maintained the credibility of the state-interventionist model that was
under heavy attack at the time and that Chávez himself would defend
and build upon after 1998.

Chávez and his followers share with many analysts belonging to the
"institutionalist school" of political science a tendency to downplay the
importance of 1989 as a key date that initiated a veritable crisis span-
ning most of the following decade. The institutionalist political scientists who focus mainly on political institutions and who (like Moisés
Naím) attribute the political crisis of the 1990s to extreme centralism
ignore the obvious, namely the dramatic socioeconomic transformations
occurring at this time (see Ellner 2002, 89–91; 2003a, 16–21). In a similar vein, the institutionalist writers downplay or completely pass over
the abruptness and radical nature of Pérez's neoliberal economic model
and its disruptive effects.

Chávez and other fervent leftist critics of post-1958 democracy also
minimized the importance of the changes initiated in 1989. Chávez and
his movement emerged from outside of the existing political system,
rather than as a result of a schism within a ruling party due to its failure to
pursue former goals. By opting for the armed struggle in 1992, Chávez
opposed leftist parties such as MAS, which for two decades had accepted
the rules of the political game and worked within the system. It is not surprising, then, that Chávez put forward an all-encompassing critique of the
political system and its performance since its outset in 1958, thus going
beyond denunciation of the second Pérez government and the policies

first adopted in 1989. Indeed, Chávez alleged that Pérez's corruption was just a continuation of the unethical behavior of his first government and that his "Plan of Disaster" in the 1970s was a prelude to the neoliberal disaster after 1989 (Zago 1998, 182–183; MBR-200 1992, 28). One of Chávez's main political statements that circulated at this time was titled "Thirty Years of Frustrations" (Zago 1998, 72). Writers belonging to Chávez's MBR-200 also passed over the sharp contrast between the state interventionist economic policies prior to 1989 and the neoliberal model adopted by Pérez's second administration. Instead, they dwelled on the new stage of popular resistance and subjective conditions initiated by the *Caracazo*. In short, Chávez and his followers did not consider 1989 a key cutoff point in the formulation of policies during the modern democratic period (Nuñez Tenorio 1998, 15–23; 1993, 20; Ramírez 1991, 83–84).

Nevertheless, contrary to what is stated or implied by Chávez as well as by many political analysts, the changes initiated in 1989 represented a fundamental break with the past and had far-reaching repercussions, including the delegitimization of the political system. The social dislocations and shakeups due to neoliberal policies were aggravated by the suddenness with which they were implemented in the absence of a previous national debate, an approach referred to as the "shock treatment." In spite of the shortcomings of Venezuelan democracy during the previous three decades as discussed in Chapter 3, the major share of the blame for the crisis of the 1990s must be placed on neoliberalism and the socioeconomic transformations associated with it.

▶ The Second Caldera Administration, 1994–1999

The triumph of the left-leaning candidacy of Rafael Caldera in the 1993 presidential elections, at a time when neoliberal thinking had reached a peak, had important implications for Latin America. Caldera, who pledged himself to avoid negotiations with the IMF, was the only president elected on an explicitly anti-neoliberal platform in Latin America prior to Chávez's triumph in 1998. Between Caldera, who received 30 percent of the vote, and the Causa R's Andrés Velásquez, with 22 percent, a majority of votes was cast for candidates on the left of the political spectrum. Pro-neoliberals Claudio Fermín, who belonged to the Pérez faction of AD, and Oswaldo Alvarez Paz of COPEI received 24 percent and 23 percent, respectively.

During its first year and a half, the Caldera administration occupied a center-left position. The government intervened in the economy in the form of controls on interest rates and foreign currency exchange rates at the same time that it resisted price increases on regulated commodities. Top government spokesmen rejected hasty privatization, particularly when it failed to meet national objectives. When the sale of the state airline Aeropostal fell through in May 1994, business representatives attributed the failure to the anti-neoliberal policies of the Investment Fund of Venezuela (FIV), which had fixed the minimum (or "base") price of the company at over 50 percent above its estimated value.

The limits of Caldera's anti-neoliberalism, however, were demonstrated by the president's handling of the banking crisis that broke out shortly after his election. Deregulation under Pérez had unleashed an expansion of banks that left them in control of companies in such diverse sectors as telecommunications, agriculture, tourism, and broadcasting. Predictably, the unbridled growth was followed by the collapse of the Banco Latino, which had maintained close ties with the Pérez administration, and then dozens of other financial institutions. The government took over and administered eighteen of the nation's forty-one private banks representing 70 percent of all deposits

During the crisis, Caldera's failure to face up to powerful financial interests was demonstrated on two fronts. First, the president permitted the foreign takeover of Venezuela's vulnerable banking institutions in accordance with the recently passed General Law of Banks, which lifted restrictions on, and discriminatory treatment against, foreign capital. (The financial crisis of 1994 thus contributed to the weakening of national capital and its subsequent loss of political influence, as would be underscored by FEDECAMARAS's defeats in showdowns with the Chávez government a decade later.) Secondly, Caldera refrained from vigorously pursuing the extradition of Venezuelan bankers who fled to the United States and elsewhere, taking with them capital from the banks they had run into the ground as well as much of the bailout money injected by the Caldera administration. None of the 322 bankers who were subject to government arrest orders were brought to justice in what was (along with the RECADI debacle of the Lusinchi years) the fraud of greatest economic proportions in modern Venezuelan history (Ortiz 2004, 84).

The results of Caldera's initial economic policies were not encouraging. Real wages, which had declined by 3 percent annually following the boom period of the 1970s, decreased by 6 percent in 1994 and again in 1995. Inflation reached 71 percent in 1994 and 57 percent in 1995. Business spokesmen in Venezuela and conservative sectors in the United

States blamed this poor economic showing on the interventionist policies of the Caldera government that held back Venezuela's insertion into
the global economy. The probusiness journalist Carlos Ball, for instance,
attributed the nation's economic woes to Caldera's determination to
"roll back every market-oriented policy implemented to date" (*Wall
Street Journal*, November 10, 1995, A-15). No mention was made of the
disastrous economic effects of the financial collapse of 1994, which was
largely the result of neoliberal-inspired deregulation.

The governing coalition took in Caldera's makeshift Convergence
Party and the left-leaning MAS. In addition, AD reached an informal
arrangement with Caldera in which it agreed to collaborate with his government and accept a fair distribution of congressional committee presidencies in return for a tacit government pledge to refrain from laying off
AD members in public administration positions. At this time, AD leaders organized an "Ideological Congress," which reaffirmed the party's
social democratic commitment in order to differentiate it from the
neoliberalism of the administration of Carlos Andrés Peréz, who was
expelled from the organization.

In 1996, the Caldera administration adopted orthodox economic
policies known as the "Venezuela Agenda," a turnabout that facilitated
an agreement with the IMF. Not only did the IMF grant Venezuela a
$1.4 billion loan to shore up national reserves but it "certified" govern-
ment policies, thus providing an upbeat signal to foreign investors.
Under the influence of neoliberal thinking, the government adopted
plans for the rapid expansion of the oil industry at the same time that it
failed to comply with OPEC-imposed production quotas, thus provoking
the wrath of Saudi Arabia and contributing to the sharp decline of international prices in 1998.

As part of its new economic orientation, the government eased its
demands on foreign capital, privatized the steel company (SIDOR),
attempted to privatize the aluminum industry, and sold the state's
remaining share of the telephone company (CANTV). Shortly prior to
the sale of SIDOR in December 1997, some observers had written off
the possibility of the company's privatization during Caldera's term in
office. Three attempts at auctioning off the nation's aluminum complex-
es fell through in 1998 due in large part to the conditions imposed by
Congress that were more demanding than those formulated by the
Caldera administration. Foreign capital refrained from participating in
the first bidding process because of the requirements established by
Congress, particularly environmental protection, job security for
employees, and special prices granted Venezuelan processing companies

for primary aluminum. In addition, the base price was about 15 percent higher than that recommended by Merrill Lynch.

Modification of the social security system stood out as one of the principal goals of the Venezuela Agenda. In June 1997, Congress reformed the Labor Law in order to gut the severance payment system of its "retroactive" provision whereby the amount of money received by a worker upon leaving a company was pegged to his or her last monthly salary. For decades, Venezuelan business representatives had complained that the calculation of severance pay on the basis of the worker's last salary made it impossible for a company to anticipate costs for the sake of planning. As a way out of the problem, both the private and state sector had begun to pay worker increases in the form of "bonuses" that were not included in the severance pay calculation, a practice that the CTV failed to protest against (Ellner 1999b, 19). Company spokesmen hailed the 1997 labor reform as a sure boon to economic growth and an appropriate response to global exigencies. Subsequently, the health and retirement branches of the social security system were privatized, thus opening up a windfall of opportunities for foreign-owned financial institutions.

Just as Caldera implemented neoliberal social reforms initially proposed by the Pérez administration, he also deepened the partial privatization of the oil industry, known as the "Oil Opening," first implemented by his predecessor. As was the case throughout Latin America, the privatization of Venezuela's main export commodity represented a major challenge for the champions of neoliberalism. In spite of criticism of specific terms, however, the Oil Opening under Pérez at first gained acceptance because its aim was exploitation of unconventional fields requiring large sums of capital and sophisticated technology, which foreign companies could readily supply. Thus, for instance, the "Strategic Associations" created under the Oil Opening were designed for the heavy and extra-heavy oil of the Orinoco Oil Belt area, possibly the largest petroleum reserve in the world. In 1995, however, Caldera sought congressional approval for a new Oil Opening program known as "Shared Profits," which generated greater controversy because it involved light- and medium-weight oil. The arrangement turned over to mixed associations of private and public capital the unexploited fields that had not been thoroughly explored by PDVSA. The state's share of ownership in these companies was limited to between 1 and 35 percent, thus raising fears of loss of national control (Rodríguez Araque 1997, 83–87).

Similar to other Latin American countries under neoliberal presidents, the National Congress stiffened the terms of the Oil Opening in favor of national interests, although it failed to halt the privatization process, nor did it open the issue to public debate (Ellner 2002, 86–87; 1997b, 7–8). Congress, for instance, insisted that representatives of the state—rather than the private sector on the control committees established to run each field—have the final say on all relevant matters. Congress also ensured that the Ministry of Mines, which was considered more responsive to national interests than PDVSA, would designate the committees' chairmen. Finally, Congress included in the Shared Profits legislation an article forbidding PDVSA's foreign partners from taking disputes that arose on the control committees to the international arena for arbitration. Unlike in the case of the state-run aluminum industry, congressional revisions of the terms of oil privatization did not dampen the interest of foreign investors. Bidding in the first round of the Shared Profits program earned the state $260 million, far exceeding general expectations.

Caldera's turn to neoliberalism and specifically privatization found receptivity among PDVSA executives, whose decisionmaking authority exceeded that which was originally envisioned at the time of nationalization in 1976. The Caldera-appointed president of PDVSA, Luis Giusti, called for the sale of minority stock in his company to the private sector. Even more revealing of the attitude of PDVSA heads was an eight-page advertisement in *Time* published on July 21, 1997, entitled "Opening the Door to Foreign Investors: The Venezuelan Oil Opening." The text assured readers that the plans for the foreign exploration of reserves and the private ownership of gas stations and petrochemical operations would bring positive results and pave the way for the private sector's takeover of the entire oil industry, thus constituting the "backdoor route to privatization." Although the piece was run anonymously, it undoubtedly met with the approval of PDVSA's executive leadership.

After the Caldera government's turn to neoliberalism, MAS and AD (and to a certain extent the CTV) followed suit by abandoning their defense of state interventionist policies as well as certain key features of social programs and labor benefits. This sudden turnabout was typical of other Latin American leaders (such as Pérez in Venezuela and Carlos Menem in Argentina) who, feeling the pressure of globalization imperatives and arguments, unexpectedly embraced neoliberal formulas. In the case of MAS, former leftist ideologue Teodoro Petkoff accepted the influential post of planning minister in 1996, but before doing so traveled throughout the country to meet with party members to justify the change of policy from anti- to pro-neoliberalism. Petkoff argued that MAS should be willing to pay the political price of acceptance of the controversial Venezuelan Agenda and enter the cabinet because the nation's democracy was in danger. Not only was inflation reaching an unprecedented 100 percent mark but the aging Caldera lacked an institutionally strong political party to back his rule (a fear shared by AD and other parties). Petkoff also argued that although the Venezuela Agenda formulated the same neoliberal policies put forward by Pérez, Caldera was more astute than his overconfident predecessor and would thus be able to avoid the disruptions of the immediate past. Unlike Pérez's shock treatment, Caldera's approach was gradual and based on widespread consultation.

Caldera's less abrasive style was demonstrated by the creation of the Tripartite Commission of business, labor, and government representatives to draft the new severance payment and social security laws and also study minimum wage increases, a procedure that was hailed as a model for other nations. Whereas under Pérez technocrats drew up economic and social legislation, Caldera chose Petkoff and Luis Raúl Matos Azócar, both of whom were economists and politicians, to reform the severance payment system. Whether the end result of Caldera's more gradual approach was more favorable to the workers and popular sectors in general is open to question. Under the 1997 legislation, the percentage of a worker's monthly salary set aside for severance payment was two to three times greater than under the old system. Nevertheless, the elimination of the calculation based on the worker's last salary was a long-standing goal of the Venezuelan business sector and was generally repudiated by the workers. In effect, the 1997 reform allowed management to grant workers their severance payments as annual bonuses prior to their leaving the company, thus defeating the system's very purpose.

The 1998 presidential campaign reflected the widespread disillusionment toward traditional parties and the belief that necessary political change would only be led by those outside of the political system. The two major candidates had strong credentials as political outsiders and embraced an antiparty discourse. Henrique Salas Römer, as governor of Carabobo after 1989, had gradually broken with COPEI at the same time that he built his own Project Carabobo organization that he then converted into the nationwide Project Venezuela party. Chávez, with his background as a middle-level officer who staged a coup and subsequently called for electoral abstention, was even more of an antisystem candidate. Popular support for a third candidate, Irene Sáez (a former Miss Universe and mayor of a wealthy municipality in Caracas), declined in tandem with her change of image from anti- to proestablishment. In late 1997 Sáez discarded the option of forming slates of members of her makeshift party to run in the upcoming elections, and instead

drew near to COPEI. In the process some loyalists left her organization's fold at the same time that she forfeited the support of parties outside of the mainstream, such as the leftist Causa R, which envisioned a
new broad-based movement to confront AD and COPEI. In the
December elections Chávez received 56 percent of the vote, followed by
Salas Römer with 40 percent and Sáez with 3 percent.

While being "antiestablishment" was an asset in the 1998 campaign,
in the long run genuine commitment to change was defined by opposition to neoliberal economic policies and not by antiparty rhetoric. Thus
following the 1998 elections, the pro-neoliberal Salas Römer was no
longer perceived as a real alternative to AD and COPEI at the same time
that his Project Venezuela party lost popular appeal. In contrast, Chávez
and his Fifth Republic Movement party (MVR) from the outset of the
presidential campaign presented the Bolivarian Alternative Agenda (in
response to Caldera's Venezuela Agenda), which defended state intervention in the economy, state control of the oil industry and other basic
industries, and a negotiated moratorium on the foreign debt.
Nevertheless, during the 1998 campaign and particularly after the moderate MAS endorsed his candidacy, Chávez increasingly emphasized the
holding of a constituent assembly and the political reforms associated
with it at the expense of his economic platform. Indeed, the constituent
assembly proposal would be at the center of the political stage during
Chávez's first year in office. During this moderate stage, however,
Chávez maintained his credentials as an anti-neoliberal by opposing the
privatization of oil and other sectors.

▶ ## Political Response to the
Implementation of Neoliberalism

The turnabouts of those who had previously defended state intervention
in the economy and the deepening of democracy generated a credibility
gap that in turn contributed to the political crisis of the 1990s and the rise
of *Chavismo*. Throughout the 1960s, 1970s, and 1980s, the dissident factions of AD and COPEI, which adamantly supported state interventionism along with the related banners of democratic socialism, social democracy, and (in the case of COPEI) "communitarian property," had provided
an avenue of expression for discontented party members. As discussed in
Chapter 3, the differences regarding economic policy between the left-
leaning factions and parties, on the one hand, and centrist ones, on the
other, were assimilated by a significant number of Venezuelans, even

though these substantive issues were often overshadowed by personality clashes. By the latter part of the Caldera administration, the left-leaning factions of AD and COPEI, as well as left-leaning parties such as MAS and the Causa R, had abandoned support for the state interventionist economic model. During the 1990s, the following parties and factions formerly identified with state interventionism reversed their positions:

• *The Perez faction of AD*. The *Carlosandresista* current of AD did a complete turnabout at the outset of Pérez's second government in 1989 by embracing neoliberalism.

• *The "orthodox" faction of AD*. The anti-Pérez, "orthodox" faction headed by AD's secretary-general Luis Alfaro Ucero inherited the party's traditional support for the interventionist strategy. Alfaro Ucero reached an informal agreement with Caldera following his election in 1993, providing his government tacit support. After 1996 AD backed Caldera's neoliberal Venezuela Agenda while the party's labor leadership in the CTV took part in the drafting of neoliberal social legislation that was enacted in 1997 and 1998.

• *The Caldera faction of COPEI*. Caldera's main political banner during his last years in COPEI and in the 1993 presidential elections was opposition to Pérez's neoliberal policies. In 1996, however, Caldera introduced his Venezuela Agenda embracing the same program and objectives as those of the second Pérez administration.

• *MAS*. MAS formed part of the anti-neoliberal coalition that supported Caldera's presidential candidacy in 1993. Nevertheless, MAS theoretician Teodoro Petkoff entered Caldera's government at the time that his administration turned to neoliberalism in late 1995, and he became an architect of the pro-neoliberal reform of the severance payment system enacted in 1997.

• *The Causa R*. Andrés Velásquez, the Causa R's candidate for the 1993 presidential elections, was at first positioned to the left of Caldera but surprisingly upheld an ambiguous stand on the key issue of privatization. The Causa R then discarded its intransigent approach of rejecting interparty alliances and formed a pact with COPEI and MAS in the National Congress.

In addition to these changes in economic positions, the proleftist dissidents ceased to uphold the banner of internal party democracy, which by the early 1990s became associated with the neoliberals. The pro-neoliberal factions in AD (the followers of Pérez and his protégé Claudio Fermín), COPEI (Eduardo Fernández), and MAS (Petkoff) became the most avid defenders of internal democracy (Ellner 1996, 92–104). The appropriation of the democratic cause by the neoliberals further undermined the credibility of those leaders who represented the more critical and discontented members of the nation's main parties, and who had preferred to work within the existing political party structure to bring about gradual but far-reaching change. Against this backdrop of abandonment of principled and progressive positions by those who were committed to work for change from within the system, the groundswell of antiparty sentiment in Venezuela, which gave an impulse to the rise of *Chavismo,* was to be expected.

Neoliberal defenders attribute the disappointing results of neoliberal policies in Latin America during its heyday in the 1990s to the unwillingness of governments and governing parties to break definitively with the old statist model of centralized control. Venezuelan neoliberals used this argument during the second administrations of Pérez and Caldera. In their writings, Moisés Naím and other technocrats who occupied key positions under Pérez accused AD political leaders of sabotaging the president's program by delaying promulgation of certain reforms and modifying the content of others (see Weyland 2002, 153). Naím ascribed resistance to neoliberalism to the self-serving behavior of party leaders who were unwilling to relinquish their clientelistic privileges and of labor leaders who feared that the private sector in the management of privatized companies would be less flexible and generous to the workers than the state would be. Naím concluded by arguing that Venezuela's crisis of the 1990s was the result of "not too much globalization but too little" (Naím 1993a, 47–48; 2001, 17; see also Ellner 1997a, 210–214).

Nevertheless, the thesis that the neoliberal project was thwarted before it had a chance to prove its viability ignores the significant inroads it made on diverse fronts. Pérez not only deregulated prices, interest rates, and currency exchange rates, but privatized the telephone company and one of the national airlines, and eliminated numerous subsidies as well as the central control of the port system. Caldera sold off the steel industry, closed the second national airline, and implemented the Oil Opening as a strategy to promote the gradual privatization of the oil industry. Pérez's social legislation proposals came to fruition with the privatization of the social security system and the modification of the system of severance payment under Caldera. Neoliberal-inspired state reform passed in 1989 included a complete overhaul of the electoral system, as well as the decentralization law that facilitated the partial transfer of responsibilities in the areas of education and health to the states, and the creation of municipal police forces throughout the nation.

Those writers (Anderson 2000) who argued that neoliberalism worldwide achieved historically unprecedented "hegemony" in the 1990s were telling a half-truth, at least with regard to Latin America (Ellner 2006, 398). Specifically, in the case of Venezuela, it is true that neoliberalism amazingly won over diverse currents of the political elite, including minority factions of establishment parties and the left-leaning MAS. Thus politicians like Carlos Andrés Pérez, Alfaro Ucero, Caldera, and Petkoff, who throughout their entire political careers were committed to different varieties of the state interventionism model, ended up embracing neoliberalism. Nevertheless, mass disturbances beginning with the *Caracazo*, a "wave" of organized protests, two attempted coups, the destitution of Pérez, and finally the 1998 presidential elections monopolized by two antiparty candidates (Chávez and Henrique Salas Römer) all testified to the widespread discontent during the heyday of neoliberalism and its failure to penetrate the popular classes. In short, the use of the term *hegemony*, which implies legitimacy, widespread support, and relative consensus, was inappropriate for Venezuela in the 1990s, and increasingly so since then.

▶ **Note**

1. Some of Pérez's supporters accuse AD leaders who had influence at the community level of initiating the agitation against the government on February 27, 1989, which quickly got out of control and led to widespread looting. Several younger cabinet members including Carlos Blanco (minister of the COPRE) and Pastor Heydra (information minister) personally urged Pérez to take advantage of his popularity among rank-and-file AD members in order to mobilize support for his reform program, but the president rejected the plan (Blanco 2006; see also Corrales 2002, 166).

5

▼

The Four Stages of
the Chávez Presidency

EVER since the election of Hugo Chávez as president in December 1998, political analysts and many Venezuelans in general have tended to focus on his style, discourse, and personality and pass over issues of substance and the long-term implications of the changes under way. There are good reasons for the personality-centered content and superficiality of much of this discussion. Part of it has to do with Chávez himself. Chávez is a charismatic and romantic figure and a didactic leader who thoroughly dominates his movement. These characteristics lend themselves to endless discussion regarding his intentions. Furthermore, for some, Chávez's military background virtually disqualifies him from putting forward serious proposals for the transformation of the nation by democratic means. The opposition's shortcomings, however, also help explain the lack of serious debate on substantive issues. The opposition parties, in an attempt to maintain unity beginning in 1998, have forfeited the formulation of programmatic and ideological positions and instead resort to ongoing personalistic attacks on Chávez and his leading followers.[1]

The rapid unfolding of the stages of the Chávez presidency in the absence of well-defined long-term goals has taken observers by surprise and has frustrated efforts to pinpoint the general direction of the *Chavista* government. Nevertheless, the *Chavista* strategy during these years was characterized by a certain consistency. Policies and legislation, far from consisting of flip-flops, were part of a steady radicalization process. Furthermore, certain positions assumed in one stage led to the next one. Thus, for instance, articles on social security contained in the Constitution of 1999, agrarian reform (Lands Law), and legislation on cooperatives passed in 2001, while not applied at the time, were guideposts for actions taken several years later.

This chapter will describe the three stages of the Chávez presidency: (1) a moderate period (1999–2000) in which socioeconomic objectives were subordinated to political proposals; (2) a more radical stage (2001–2004) in which the government followed an anti-neoliberal course, by ruling out privatization, and at the same time confronted an insurgent opposition that refused to recognize its legitimacy; and (3) the emergence of the outlines of a new economic model (in 2005) made possible by greater political stability as a result of the weakening of the opposition and the windfall in oil revenue. Chávez's resounding victory in the presidential elections of December 2006 and his announcement of economic and organizational changes signal the possible initiation of a fourth stage, which will also be discussed. This overview leads into the examination of the two main strategies adhered to by members of the *Chavista* movement as well as the theoretical framework that focuses on the relationship between the *Chavista* leadership and rank and file (to be dealt with in Chapters 6 and 7, respectively). The discussion on Chávez put forward in this chapter and the following three is in keeping with the main thrust of the book, which stresses transformation, economic issues, resistance, and popular mobilization over style, personality struggles, and intra-elite clashes lacking in substance.

▶ The Moderate Stage, 1999–2000

Chávez's presidential campaign in 1997–1998 emphasized political reforms and set the tone for the first, moderate stage of his presidency in 1999 and 2000. His main electoral pledge was the convocation of a constituent assembly, while more leftist socioeconomic demands, such as the reformulation of the terms of payment of the foreign debt, were toned down. Venezuelan politics in 1999 centered on the elections for the Constituent Assembly, the drafting of the Constitution, and its approval in a national referendum held in December of that year. At the same time, Chávez maintained a dialogue with the private sector and invited numerous businessmen to accompany him on trips abroad. The government's moderate economic course was also indicated by the selection as finance minister of Maritza Izaguirre, who had occupied the same position under the previous neoliberal government of Rafael Caldera. Subsequently, Chávez named MVR congressman Alejandro Armas, who belonged to the soft-line faction of his party led by Luis

Miquilena, to head a presidential subcommittee on social security that would propose the virtual privatization of the pension system.

In spite of Chávez's moderation on economic policy, Venezuelan politics became polarized between the government coalition Patriotic Pole, consisting of the MVR, MAS, Homeland for All (PPT), and the PCV, and the opposition led by AD, COPEI, Project Venezuela, and the newly founded Primero Justicia party. One feature of polarization during the Chávez presidency was the unity of the parties of the opposition and the submergence of differences between them. Polarization dated back to the 1998 presidential elections when Project Venezuela's Salas Römer and AD's candidate Luis Alfaro Ucero concentrated their attacks on Chávez, accusing him of having a secret plan to stage a Fujimori-style auto-coup to centralize executive power. A few days before the elections polarization was intensified when AD and COPEI dropped support for their respective candidates and endorsed Salas Römer in a last-ditch effort to block Chávez's triumph.

In 1999 AD, COPEI, and Project Venezuela, along with the business organization FEDECAMARAS, converged in their opposition to the Constitution but were defeated in three electoral contests held that year. In April Venezuelans voted overwhelmingly in favor of holding a National Constituent Assembly (ANC) to in effect supersede the National Congress, and in elections held three months later 125 Chávez sympathizers were elected to the 131-member ANC. In December the Constitution was ratified in a national referendum with 72 percent of the vote. The opposition criticized the Constitution for reversing the decentralization measures of the 1990s and concentrating power in the national executive at the expense of Congress (now called the National Assembly). Not only did military promotions become the sole responsibility of the national executive without congressional input, but the autonomy of the Central Bank was compromised. Furthermore, the Constitution empowered the president to decree the holding of a constituent assembly, while requiring two-thirds approval of deputies for the National Assembly to be able to do the same (Alvarez 2003, 155).

During the moderate period of 1999 to 2000, members of the opposition tied to the left and organized labor, as well as various political analysts, accused Chávez of promoting neoliberalism and privileging foreign over local capital in spite of his anti-neoliberal discourse (Gómez and Arenas 2001, 122–123; Blanco 2002, 139; Valecillos 2005, 349–350). Some of them pointed out that the Chávez government's preferential treatment toward imports and investments from abroad was designed to deliver a major blow to local capitalists due to their close ties with the opposition (Magdaleno 2003). Additional measures approximating neoliberalism included austere fiscal policies, overvaluation of the local currency, and the retention of the neoliberal-inspired value added tax with the aim of avoiding inflation and shoring up international reserves (Weyland 2001, 79). Furthermore, in mid-2001, the *Chavista* president of the National Assembly's Finance Committee, Alejandro Armas, raised the possibility of applying neoliberal policies such as the reduction of state spending, the reform of the public administration, the partial transference of tax collection to the states, and the modification of the tax system in order to activate the productive sector (Alvarez 2003, 156).

Nevertheless, Chávez's actions during this period hardly fit into the neoliberal mold. Thus, for example, Chávez resisted pressure from the moderate Miquilena wing of his party in favor of the privatization of the social security system and the aluminum industry first slated for sale under the Caldera administration. Similarly, the new Constitution held back privatization by prohibiting the sale of PDVSA stocks. (Undeniably, privatization is much more of a defining characteristic of neoliberalism than are the conservative fiscal policies that Chávez's anti-neoliberal detractors harped on.) In addition, Chávez's national budget substantially increased allocations for social programs beyond the amount that neoliberals would have considered appropriate (Parker 2007, 68–69). Chávez also practically stood alone in raising fundamental objections to the neoliberal-inspired Free Trade Area of the Americas (FTAA) at the Third Summit of the Americas held in Quebec City in April 2001. Indeed, his objections to the FTAA for promoting drastic tariff reduction and his insistence on consulting the general population about any plan for continental integration favored national over multinational capital. Finally, in the 1999 Constitution the *Chavistas* put forward the concept of participatory democracy and radical democracy (to be discussed in Chapter 7), which demonstrated a faith in the political capability of the popular sectors contrary to the more elitist assumptions of neoliberalism.

▶ **The Anti-Neoliberal Stage in the Context of Opposition Insurgency, 2001–2004**

The second stage of Chávez's presidency began in November 2001 when the government enacted a package of forty-nine special laws, which was designed to reverse the neoliberal trends of the 1990s and which signaled a radicalization of the *Chavista* movement. The two most important laws dealt with the oil industry and agrarian reform. The Organic Hydrocarbons Law established majority government ownership of all mixed companies in charge of primary oil operations in order to reverse the neoliberal-inspired Oil Opening program of the previous Caldera administration. Under the Lands Law, idle land was subject to expropriation (article 42) while owners of underutilized land were given two years to grow crops in accordance with a national plan and were obliged to pay a special tax. In addition, the Fisheries Law increased the distance from the shoreline that is off-limits to trawlers from three to six miles. The law was explicitly designed to open opportunities for individual fishermen and to counter the fishing "monopolies," at the same time favoring conservationist objectives. Finally, another law maintained state control of social security, thus discarding attempts to privatize the system undertaken by both the Caldera administration and the Chávez-appointed subcommittee on social security headed by Alejandro Armas.

The second stage, by going beyond the political reforms of the first, added to the importance of the *Chavista* project for Latin America. The passage of the forty-nine laws in 2001 completely disproved the claim that Chávez was a neoliberal disguised as a revolutionary. His political survival put the lie to the Washington Consensus–promoted notion that any deviation from the macroeconomic model in the age of globalization was doomed to failure. Undoubtedly, Chávez's political successes encouraged a shift in the political atmosphere of the continent that contributed to the rise to power of leftists and center-leftists in Brazil, Argentina, Uruguay, Ecuador, and Bolivia, who at least initially stood for anti-neoliberalism and a degree of economic nationalism. These developments took on added significance due to the Bush administration's increasingly hostile stance toward Venezuela.

The radicalization beginning in 2001 intensified political polarization by driving moderates, such as the Movement Toward Socialism (MAS) and the Miquilena wing of the MVR, from the government camp and uniting the opposition around the sole objective of forcing Chávez out of power. The opposition bloc (which eventually called itself the Democratic Coordinator) came to include such newcomers as MAS, Solidarity (consisting of the followers of Miquilena), the Union party (headed by Francisco Arias Cárdenas, the number two man of the February 1992 revolt), as well as various social organizations. By late 2001 the political parties of the opposition played a secondary role to the alliance between FEDECAMARAS and the CTV that led the coup against Chávez in April 2002 and the two-month general strike beginning in December of that year. At this time, the *Chavista* bloc incorporated the Podemos party (a split-off from MAS).

The prolonged alliance between FEDECAMARAS, the CTV, and the parties of the opposition was unprecedented in Venezuelan history. Political scientists had long noted that the Venezuelan business community was more removed from political decisionmaking than their counterparts in the rest of Latin America (Karl 1997; Salgado 1987). FEDECAMARAS's claim to being a nonpolitical organization dated back to 1948 when it rejected a request by Rómulo Betancourt to declare itself against the impending military coup (Moncada 1985, 227), and it refused to condemn human rights violations under Pérez Jiménez with whom it maintained cordial relations until the last months of his rule. Its opposition to the Constitution in 1999, its alliance with the CTV and the political parties of the opposition, and its leading role in the April 2002 coup and the subsequent general strike thus represented a complete rupture with the past.

The radical content of the forty-nine laws spurred FEDECAMA-RAS into breaking with this tradition. Like the Lands Law of 2001, agrarian reforms in 1945 and 1948 preceded military coups by just a few months. Indeed, the expropriation provision of all three laws placed in doubt the sacredness of private property rights and was thus a basic source of concern for the business sector in general (Collier and Collier 1991, 198). The Organic Hydrocarbons Law, which reversed the privatization of the oil industry promoted by top PDVSA leaders, also undermined the interests of powerful economic groups.

FEDECAMARAS spokesmen and the opposition in general claimed that their main objection to the forty-nine laws was the government's use of emergency legislation to rush them through the National Assembly in the absence of public debate. This argument was misleading in that their basic concern had to do with content and not democratic procedures. Specifically in the case of the Hydrocarbons Law, oil-expert politicians, such as the ex-president of Shell of Venezuela Alberto Quirós Corradi and former minister of energy and mines Humberto Calderón Berti, lashed out at Chávez for not sufficiently airing the proposed legislation. Nevertheless, the technocratic and apolitical thesis that oil was too important and technical a matter to open it to public debate had been widely accepted in the industry and among many proestablishment politicians over a period of decades.

Regardless of the opposition's motives, however, its criticism was well founded. Chávez's failure to explain and rally support for the

November legislation left the government in a weaker position in the face of the mobilizations of the opposition that led to the coup. Had it not been for the blunders of the provisional government, headed by Pedro Carmona, in failing to call for immediate elections, Chávez may very well not have returned to power. In this case, one of the main explanations for the coup's success would undoubtedly have been Chávez's failure to galvanize mass support for his socioeconomic reforms.

Several general strikes called by the CTV and backed by the business organization FEDECAMARAS culminated in a violent confrontation in downtown Caracas on April 11, 2002, that resulted in nearly two dozen deaths and hours later gave way to a military coup. FEDECAMARAS president Pedro Carmona headed a provisional government that abolished democratic institutions, abrogated the forty-nine laws of 2001, and pledged to hold elections only within one year. Middle-level officers belonging to the parachutists of the one-thousand-man 42nd Brigade in Maracay refused to recognize Carmona's rule. Supported by several generals, they demanded the release of Chávez, who was being held captive, and threatened armed resistance if their demand was not met (Harnecker 2003, 222–223). They were immediately joined by officers in other bases, which were surrounded by tens of thousands of pro-*Chavista* poor people (as was the presidential palace) in an effort to encourage military rebellion. The concept of a "civilian-military alliance," developed by Chávez in the 1980s, played itself out on April 12 and 13; within forty-eight hours Chávez was back in power.

Contrary to the version of both *Chavista* and opposition spokesmen, differences in economic and political goals among anti-*Chavista* leaders explain the divisions that made possible Chávez's return to power. The opposition was divided between the Carmona government, which sought to reestablish the radical neoliberal policies of the 1990s by delaying the return to democratic rule, and AD and CTV leaders who had an ambivalent attitude toward neoliberalism and insisted on at least a semblance of democratic procedures.

Carmona's appointments privileging the elite created tensions. The navy, for instance, received two key posts in the government, including the Defense Ministry, at the expense of the much larger but less prestigious army, where Chávez had greater backing. The defense minister sought to break up the base of support within the army of the moderate general and coup leader Efraín Vásquez Velasco by transferring some of his key associates to other commands. Furthermore, Carmona appointed two prominent leaders of COPEI—including José Rodríguez Iturbe, a member of the right-wing Opus Dei, as foreign minister—even though that party had been reduced over the recent past to a shadow of its former self. At the same time, he passed over the equally anti-*Chavista* AD, which was by far the largest opposition party but had a populist and clientelistic tradition. Immediately following the coup, Carmona and his leading supporters refrained from meeting with congressional representatives. The Carmona group was reluctant to reach agreements with political parties that would force the government to make concessions regarding top-level appointments and was particularly averse to accepting former anti-*Chavista* Luis Miquilena as an ally (García Ponce 2002, 54–55).

The hard-line neoliberals who were behind the Carmona government obviously wanted to keep parties with any kind of popular following on the sidelines. The neoliberals had learned the "lesson" of the second presidency of Carlos Andrés Pérez, whose drastic neoliberal antipopular measures were opposed by his own party's dominant leadership.

Many of those who supported Chávez's overthrow subsequently claimed that the coup had been "hijacked" by Carmona and a small coterie that surrounded him. Publisher magnate and long-time AD sympathizer Rafael Poleo and his journalist daughter Patricia Poleo systematically put forward this position (Trinkunas 2005, 219). In an interview published by the Poleos, FEDECAMARAS provisional president Carlos Fernández claimed that Carmona cut himself off from his own organization and responded only to a small group "so that there was no way to talk to him, not even by cell phone" (*Zeta*, no. 1363, April 25–May 6, 2002, 14). The Poleos absolved CTV president Carlos Ortega of responsibility for the coup disaster by alleging that he was utilized by Carmona to reach power and was then shunted aside.

This analysis ignores the fact that the neoliberal strategy that Carmona embraced clearly represented the long-standing positions of FEDECAMARAS as well as those of some political leaders of the opposition. Carmona's cabinet consisted of individuals belonging to the nation's dominant institutions and in some cases had held positions in the pro-neoliberal government of Rafael Caldera. Furthermore, Carmona himself was hardly an unknown as he represented the business sector in the Tripartite Commission that reformed the social security and severance payment system in the late 1990s. As president of FEDECAMARAS, it is hard to believe that he acted on his own, as Patricia Poleo alleged.

Throughout the coup attempt, opposition leaders who had misgivings about Carmona's dictatorial and antipopular measures failed to assert themselves by assuming a critical stand toward the provisional government. Thus Ortega, obviously upset that Carmona had largely passed over both AD and the CTV, traveled to the distant state of Falcón in order to avoid being associated with the de facto government. The passive behavior of AD and CTV leaders was in keeping with their ambivalent attitude toward neoliberalism over the past ten years. Indeed, CTV representatives had actually helped draft the neoliberal-inspired social reforms enacted by the Caldera government. Subsequently, AD had concentrated all its efforts on defeating Chávez in the presidential elections of 1998 and in the process further distanced itself from anti-neoliberal positions.

The decisiveness with which Carmona and his closest allies acted on the first day of the coup makes evident the existence of a well-conceived plan to turn the clocks back to the period of neoliberalism. Contrary to what Poleo and others claimed, it is evident that Carmona and those closest to him were not simply interested in a military dictatorship in which they themselves would have wealth and power but rather were determined to bring about a complete break with the populist past. There is nothing to indicate that Carmona was merely stepping in to "fill a vacuum" created by Chávez's loss of control. On the contrary, he and his followers acted decisively to remove all the obstacles to full-fledged neoliberal formulas. The plan to bring Chávez to trial and hold top *Chavista* leaders responsible for distributing the arms that allegedly gunned down demonstrators on April 11 was thus part of a larger strategy. In essence, those closest to Carmona sought to completely discredit Chávez's rule in order to gain support for the radical changes they favored.

Chavista spokesmen failed to distinguish between Carmona and the "shock treatment" neoliberal project he represented, on the one hand, and more moderate sectors that lacked a well-defined position on neoliberal reform but were committed to a democratic outcome, on the other hand. Although politicians of the latter group failed to act decisively during the coup, the moderates in the military led by General Vásquez Velasco played an important role, first by supporting the takeover on April 11 and then by pronouncing against Carmona's measures two days later. The moderate officers prided themselves on defending institutional concerns; Vásquez Velasco and those closest to him insisted that they had broken with the Chávez government as a result of the massacre on April 11 and the breakdown of order. While the hard-liners wanted to bring Chávez to trial for the April 11 deaths, the moderates favored exiling him.[2] The failure of the *Chavistas* to differentiate between the moderate and hard lines was consistent with their analysis of the entire post-1958 period. By condemning all establishment party politicians during the four decades, the *Chavistas* failed to distinguish between AD and COPEI politicians who defended proposals regarding state intervention in the economy, on the one hand, and neoliberals and centrists (such as Betancourt), on the other hand.

Following the coup, Chávez attempted to reduce tensions by moderating his rhetoric and offering the opposition concessions. Thus he created the Presidential Commission for a National Dialogue, which brought opposition and government representatives together in "dialogue tables." At the same time, he announced plans to implement the decentralization provisions of the 1999 Constitution, a proposition that opened opportunities for governors belonging to the opposition (Francia 2002, 106). Finally, Chávez replaced several hard-liners who favored a faster pace of change with *Chavista* moderates. The opposition especially approved of Chávez's decision to name OPEC secretary-general Alí Rodríguez Araque to head PDVSA and rehire seven top oil company executives whom the president had personally fired a few days before the coup. Nevertheless, the opposition's intransigent attitude toward Chávez continued unabated as reflected in its slogan "Prohibited to Forget," which referred to the president's alleged responsibility for the deaths on April 11.

The hard-liners within the Chávez movement pointed to the government's failure to influence the anti-*Chavista* leaders to modify their stance as proof that they would not become a loyal opposition under any circumstance. The most radical among the progovernment hard-liners was a small group of Trotskyists within the labor movement with international ties. Headed by veteran trade unionist Orlando Chirino, the Trotskyists opposed concessions to the opposition on grounds that if the process of radicalization were interrupted all would be lost. The Trotskyists and allied groups on the far left feared that Chávez's concessions after he returned to power on April 13 formed part of a plan of national reconciliation implying austerity policies. They specifically criticized the naming of Felipe Pérez Martí—who they claimed had ties with the International Development Bank and other financial institutions—as planning minister. They also questioned the appointment of Lucas Rincón as defense minister on the grounds that he had betrayed Chávez on April 11 when he publicly announced that the president had resigned (Davis 2005, 141–142).

In December 2002, CTV president Carlos Ortega, FEDECAMARAS head Carlos Fernández, and PDVSA executive Juan Fernández (one of the seven whom Chávez had previously fired), supported by the parties of the opposition, declared an indefinite general strike with the aim of forcing the president out of power. Within a few days, it became clear that the strike's success depended on substantial reduction of oil output. Although a majority of the unionized petroleum workers, including the president of the Federation of Petroleum Workers (FEDEPETROL) and several smaller oil-worker federations, refused to go along with the strike, it was supported by most of the industry's upper-level employees. At a mass rally several days into the strike, when petroleum production had virtually come to a halt, Chávez declared "the hour has arrived to wage the great battle for oil" and he went on to attack the PDVSA executives who masterminded the shutdown saying that "the oil belongs to the entire nation, not just an elite."

The shutdown in the rest of the economy was tantamount to a lockout, in that company owners closed their doors, making employee support largely irrelevant. In contrast, the foreign-owned steel company, SIDOR, and the state-run heavy industries of the Guayana region stayed open and thus the attitude of their workers was put to the test. Production in those companies continued as usual as the vast majority of workers rejected the strike call. Furthermore, in nonaffluent neighborhoods throughout the nation, a majority of commercial establishments remained open.

The eight-week general strike highlighted the shortcomings of the opposition's strategy of concentrating efforts on forcing Chávez out while submerging specific demands and issues that might have undermined the broad unity of the anti-*Chavistas*. Once oil production began to recover, the opposition lacked a fallback strategy of negotiating specific demands as a way to call off the strike and at the same time save face. As a result, during its final weeks the strike simply petered out without any official announcement that it had been called off. The opposition's disregard for concrete issues was demonstrated by the behavior of the oil executives who played a key role in the coup and the general strike. Prior to the April coup, the executives had raised the specter of the politicization of the industry and their replacement by *Chavistas* who were lacking in technical training. However, after the coup, PDVSA's new president, Alí Rodríguez, attempted to placate the company executives, who were even allowed to carry out political activity in preparation for the general strike without reprisals. As a result, the executives dropped the issue of politicization and reduced their entire message to calling for Chávez's removal from office.

The anti-*Chavista* leaders' justification of the coup on grounds that Chávez had lost the support of the people locked them into a position of intransigence in which they subsequently refused to recognize any positive aspect of his rule and denied that he enjoyed popular backing. In early 2004 the opposition launched the Guarimba Plan, consisting of aggressive street tactics including open confrontation with security forces. Armed bands of opposition organizations, including the former leftist guerrilla organization Bandera Roja, hurled Molotov cocktails and attacked the National Guard with objects ranging from stones to bullets. The disruptions mainly occurred in affluent urban areas, which were bastions of opposition support, and consequently those opposed to Chávez were inconvenienced the most. The opposition's *foquista* tactics were undoubtedly a reflection of its diminishing mobilization capacity. Up until the general strike, both sides had been able to count on roughly the same number of followers on the streets, but by 2004 the *Chavistas* were calling marches of hundreds of thousands that were unmatched by the opposition.

Following the general strike, the opposition turned to a new approach to remove Chávez from office through the holding of a recall election. Nevertheless, the government's ambitious social programs known as "missions" in the fields of health and education, which were nurtured by abundant oil revenue, enhanced Chávez's standing. In addition, the failure of opposition leaders to promote specific socioeconomic demands in their all-out effort to force Chávez out took its toll on their popularity. During this time, the sizeable bloc of voters who supported neither Chávez nor the opposition (referred to as *ni-ni*), and whom pro-opposition commentators assumed would vote for the president's removal, swung over to the side of the *Chavistas*. On August 15, 2004, 59 percent of those who went to the polls cast their vote in opposition to Chávez's recall. Just hours after the results were announced, the opposition accused the National Electoral Council (CNE) of committing massive fraud, even though the process was validated by the Carter Center, the Organization of American States, and other international observers. The opposition based its claim on an empirical study, coauthored by former Pérez minister Ricardo Hausmann, that drew on the results of an exit poll conducted by the nongovernmental organization Súmate. The study's objectivity, however, was open to question due to Hausmann's background and the political leanings of Súmate, which received funding from the National Endowment for Democracy and whose vice president, María Corina Machado, had signed the Carmona decree during the April 2002 coup. By discrediting the CNE, the opposition discouraged its own followers from voting in the October 31, 2004, mayoral-gubernatorial elections in which *Chavista* candidates triumphed in all but the states of Zulia and Nueva Esparta. With this round of victories, the stage was set for Chávez to launch a new set of radical policies that would take the "revolutionary process" to a new level.

▶ The Emergence of the Contours of a New Economic Model After 2004

The defeat of the general strike in 2003 and Chávez's triumph in the recall election the following year led to a degree of political stability and eased pressure on the government, providing it with new options. The opposition's decision to boycott the congressional elections of December 2005, on grounds that electoral impartiality could not be guaranteed, further strengthened Chávez's hand. Although the boycott hurt Chávez's reputation abroad (as it undoubtedly was designed to do), it did little to enhance the opposition's standing at home. Opposition leaders who opposed the boycott pointed out that, with absolute control of the National Assembly, the *Chavistas* could reform the Constitution to enable Chávez to run for president in 2012 after his reelection in 2006. The new congressional makeup resulting from the boycott also opened the possibility of far-reaching structural legislation, including the redefinition of the rights of private property. Chávez's reelection as president in December 2006 with 63 percent of the vote also promised to usher in radical changes.

These developments emboldened the Chávez government to go beyond the mere undoing of neoliberal measures. Following the recall election in August 2004, a third stage of the Chávez presidency set in, featuring the application of legislation promulgated in November 2001, which pointed in the direction of a new economic model. By 2004 Chávez began to declare his government "anti-imperialist," and by the following year he called for the definition and construction of a novel brand of "socialism for the twenty-first century." Some of the programs and policies that form part of the new model date back to the aftermath of the 2002–2003 general strike, but their scope was extended after Chávez's victory in the recall election of August 2004. The following government-sponsored activities, while drawing on practices of the past, employ innovative techniques, embody new goals and focuses, and deepen the process of change in the nation:

1. *The mission programs.* In 2003 the government began to establish special programs (called "missions") outside the existing ministerial and

legal structures, mainly in the fields of health and education. Various missions have subsequently gone beyond their original objectives with the initiation of a second, third, and fourth stage. These advances and reformulation of objectives reflect the *Chavista* strategy of constantly deepening the "revolutionary process" by introducing new programs, slogans, and goals.

The antecedent to the Barrio Adentro Mission was the arrival of Cuban doctors in the wake of the devastating floods in December 1999 that particularly affected the coastal state of Vargas. Some of the Cubans remained in Venezuela after the emergency period. Subsequently, twelve thousand Cuban doctors initiated the Barrio Adentro Mission by establishing residences and consultation offices in barrios throughout the country; currently, they are gradually being replaced by young Venezuelan medical personnel. The program provides free medical service and medicine, much of it produced in Cuba. In 2004 the government launched Barrio Adentro II with the aim of constructing 100 diagnostic centers and an equal number of rehabilitation centers located mostly in nonaffluent communities in order to alleviate pressure on public hospitals.

A second set of missions consists of educational programs ranging from literacy classes to university education in which students are given a modest stipend. The literacy program, known as the Robinson Mission, and other programs utilize video cassettes (mainly produced in Cuba) and facilitators in place of classroom teachers. In 2005 the government officially announced that all of the nation's 1.5 million illiterates had been taught basic reading and writing skills. At the same time the government inaugurated the Robinson Mission II to provide those who had completed the program with a primary school education. Similarly, the Vuelvan Caras Mission consists of job-training programs. After the first graduation of 300,000 students in May 2005, the newly founded Ministry of the Popular Economy established the Vuelvan Caras II Mission to provide the graduates with guidance and economic aid to form cooperatives.

2. *Worker cooperatives.* In an initial stage, PDVSA and other state companies, several newly founded state banks such as the Woman's Bank, and various state and municipal governments encouraged the creation of hundreds of cooperatives by providing them with start-up capital and organizing training sessions. The Ministry of the Popular Economy (now called the Ministry of Popular Power for the Community Economy—MPPEC) was designed as a corrective to the dispersion of these efforts. The MPPEC, which is linked to various state banks as well as to the National Superintendency of Cooperatives (SUNACOOP) that

overlooks the terms of credit, provides cooperative members a more thorough and systematic preparation through the Vuelvan Caras II Mission. Under Vuelvan Caras II, MPPEC facilitators, who generally have a university or junior college degree, are assigned two cooperatives each and are in charge of assisting them in dealing with problems that arise and monitoring their activities. In 2005 the Venezuelan state began to follow a policy of giving preferential treatment in the granting of credit to cooperatives formed by Vuelvan Caras graduates. The MPPEC announced that by October 2006 there were 141,000 registered cooperatives, although many of them never got off the ground, with the largest number being in the area of agriculture followed by services, industry, infrastructure, and tourism.

3. *Comanagement.* Labor representation on state company boards in Venezuela dates back to a decree in 1966 that was amplified by the Labor Law of 1990 and the Privatization Law of 1992, which ordered the sale of a percentage of the stocks of privatized companies to workers. Over the years, however, the AD-dominated trade-union leadership selected, as labor representatives for the boards of directors, individuals who had no working or professional experience in the field, and thus their decisionmaking role was insignificant (Ellner 1993, 178). Following the 2002–2003 general strike, the *Chavistas* made efforts to develop more authentic forms of comanagement. At that time, PDVSA chose the presidents of two oil-worker federations (Rafael Rosales and Nelson Nuñez) to represent employees on its board of directors. In 2005 Chávez chose veteran leftist Carlos Lanz to head the state aluminum company ALCASA for the purpose of implementing comanagement arrangements, which were then to be applied to other state companies in the industrial Guayana region. Lanz immediately announced that he would go beyond the token worker representation promoted by the European social democratic movement by allowing ALCASA employees and community members to participate in drawing up the company budget for the year 2006. He also pledged himself to replace the Taylor system, which privileges worker productivity at the expense of humanitarian working conditions. The *Chavista* labor confederation, the National Workers' Union (UNT), particularly its left-wing faction headed by Trotskyist Orlando Chirino, has also rejected token arrangements and insisted on genuine forms of comanagement, such as worker selection and removal of supervisors. Chirino argues that the essence of comanagement is employee decisionmaking power and not the conversion of workers into stockholders, an arrangement that runs the risk of instilling in them the illusion of belonging to the capitalist class.

4. *Worker occupations and government expropriations.* At the time of the 2002–2003 general strike, workers took over several large- and medium-sized companies, alleging that their owners had closed them without paying employees their severance benefits. The government refused to dislodge the workers but also refrained from turning the companies over to worker management and instead deferred to the courts. In some regions, judges and Labor Ministry inspectors were unsympathetic to the worker occupiers. In January 2005, President Chávez expropriated the paper company VENEPAL (which changed its name to the Venezuelan Endogenous Paper Industry—INVEPAL), followed by the valve company Constructora Nacional de Válvulas (CNV) and the tube company SIDEROCA, and announced that he would do the same to all other private companies that shut down. From the beginning of the occupations, the workers of the CNV and SIDEROCA had called on PDVSA to purchase their products. By the end of 2005, INVEPAL, which was run by the workers with minimum participation by the state (even though it held 51 percent of the stock), was the most commercially successful of the expropriated companies. The UNT insists that various enterprises—particularly hotels that faced bankruptcy and are temporarily being administered by the state's Guarantee Fund for Deposits and Bank Protection (FOGADE)—be turned over to the workers rather than to their former owners. The government proceeded to study the cases of 139 failing companies (out of a larger list of nearly 2,000 companies in the same category) and proposed to their owners worker comanagement arrangements in return for state bailout aid as an alternative to expropriation.

5. *Land distribution.* In January 2005, on the anniversary of the death of nineteenth-century peasant leader Ezequiel Zamora, Chávez announced the initiation of an all-out war on *latifundismo*, thus signaling the opening of a new front in the revolutionary process. In doing so, Chávez invoked the 1999 Constitution, whose article 307 declares the system "contrary to social interests" and grants peasants and other agricultural producers "property rights." In subsequent months, the government moved to break up large estates, some of which were owned by powerful Venezuelan and foreign capitalist groups. Far from being chosen arbitrarily or "from above," these estates were targeted for land distribution in response to occupations by peasants who were encouraged by article 307 and the subsequent Lands Law. In April 2005 a reform of the Lands Law authorized the National Land Institute (INTI) to proceed with land takeovers even while cases are in the courts, thus bypassing a decision of the Tribunal Supremo de Justicia

(Supreme Court) several years earlier that had slowed down agrarian reform.

At this time the governor of the state of Cojedes provoked the wrath of Lord Sam Vestey, one of Britain's richest men, by granting land titles to peasants who had invaded one of his ranches. Not only did the INTI support the measure but began to study land distribution on several other estates owned by Vestey. As of late 2005, the government had proceeded to turn over parts of twenty-one large estates to peasants for the purpose of forming cooperatives. The government reached an agreement on indemnification with a tomato processing plant owned by Heinz in the state of Monagas, at the same time that it took over various grain silos belonging to the powerful Polar Group in Barinas, which had been inactive since 2002.

These actions contrast with traditional agrarian reform in Venezuela, which concentrated on the distribution of public land that had always abounded in rural areas. At the same time, the government's negotiating strategy differs from the forceful agrarian breakup of revolutionary governments in Mexico, Bolivia, and Cuba. The INTI has used a carrot-and-stick approach in its negotiations with landowners. On the one hand, the Lands Law provides the government with the means to pressure *latifundistas* into cultivating idle land and turning over some of it to the agricultural work force. Thus the INTI invokes article 107 of the law, which defines *latifundios* as estates with less than 80 percent productivity and subjects "idle estates" to expropriation depending on their size and the quality of the land. The law also levels a tax that is prorated according to productivity and forces unproductive estates to cultivate certain products in accordance with a national agricultural plan devised by the state. In addition, the INTI has presented proof, sometimes dating back to the nineteenth century, contesting the land claims of the owners as well as evidence of the violation of environmental legislation. On the other hand, the INTI has demonstrated a degree of flexibility. The exact amount of land to be taken over and its location, as well as the amount of indemnification, depends on the landowner's willingness to reach an agreement.

6. *Strict enforcement of the tax system.* In another action that undermines business interests, the federal Integrated National Service for Customs and Tax Administration (SENIAT) has made use of new legislation to implement the Evasion Zero and Contraband Zero Plan, which doubled the revenue collected in 2004 over the previous year. In order to set an example, SENIAT fined hundreds of establishments of all sizes— including McDonalds, General Motors, Eastman Kodak, Hewlett-

Packard, and even the state-run petrochemical industry—and enforced two- and three-day closures. In 2005 SENIAT head José Gregorio Vielma Mora threatened twenty-two foreign-owned oil firms with confiscation of assets in case of noncompliance of their tax obligations. SENIAT, which hopes that tax collection will eventually ease the nation's dependence on oil income, has disproved the claim that in Latin America the income tax system can never be effectively implemented due to opposition from powerful business interests (Castañeda 2001, 32; Chávez 2003, 335).

7. *The state's delegation of authority to community organizations.* On February 4, 2002, Chávez issued a decree authorizing urban land committees (CTUs), consisting of residents of individual slums, to undertake surveys, distribute land deeds to longtime residents, and develop public areas for recreational purposes. By mid-2005, six thousand CTUs had been instrumental in the authorization of one hundred thousand land deeds. In addition, commissions of barrio dwellers, such as "water commissions," have participated in the formulation and execution of public works projects in their communities. The practice dates back to the rule of Caracas mayor Aristóbulo Istúriz (future minister of education under Chávez) in the mid-1990s (López Maya 2004, 351). In recent years Chávez and cabinet members in charge of social policy have regularly met in different regions with community and other local leaders (known as the "mobile cabinets") in order to authorize credit to cooperatives and neighborhood organizations for diverse projects.

8. *Rejection of ongoing links with organized business interests.* During the modern democratic period beginning in 1958, the positions of finance minister, development minister, planning minister, and president of the Central Bank were usually reserved for representatives of business interests. Since the resignation of Maritza Izaguirre as finance minister in mid-1999, FEDECAMARAS has gone unrepresented in important government posts. With the radicalization of the Chávez presidency in 2001, the MVR defeated the thesis of its general director, Luis Miquilena, who in internal discussions advocated the cultivation of an alliance with progressive and noncorrupt sectors of the bourgeoisie. Miquilena's MVR critics argued that AD had originally supported a similar strategy and ended up abandoning its popular orientation and appointing business representatives to top ministerial and party positions.

Shortly after his reelection in December 2006, President Chávez announced new radical measures that promised to carry the "revolutionary process" to a new level and thus appeared to initiate a fourth stage in his presidency. Chávez advocated the assertion of state control over strategic sectors of the economy, including the nationalization of companies that had been privatized during the previous decade. Shortly thereafter, the government bought the controlling shares of the telephone company CANTV (from Verizon) and the electricity firm Electricidad de Caracas (from the AES Corporation). While the former company had been privatized in 1991, the latter had always been in private hands. Both AES and Verizon are US corporations, unlike the Latin American consortium consisting mainly of Argentine and Brazilian capital, which owns another key "strategic" company, the steel producer SIDOR, which the state had sold off in 1997. Significantly, the Chávez government did not target SIDOR for takeover in 2007, possibly to avoid friction with allies to the south. The Venezuelan government also assumed greater control over the oil industry by further reversing the neoliberal-inspired Oil Opening policies of the 1990s. Not only were foreign interests forced to accept the Venezuelan state's 60 percent ownership of mixed companies founded in the 1990s, but their employees were transferred to PDVSA's payroll.

Chávez also announced far-reaching organizational changes. Most important, he called for the transformation of the governing coalition into one party called the United Socialist Party of Venezuela (PSUV). The new party was to incorporate social movements and hold internal elections to choose its authorities. Chávez also proposed the holding of an "ideological congress." By June 2007, over five million voters signed up for membership in the PSUV. The *Chavista* parties Podemos, the PPT, and the PCV, however, refused to coalesce into the PSUV, at least for the time being.

The PSUV was designed to overcome several pressing problems facing the *Chavista* movement. The MVR along with the other *Chavista* parties had become election oriented with little formal links with communities and social and labor organizations. Furthermore, large numbers of rank-and-file *Chavistas* resented political parties in general and considered their leaders opportunists. In addition, they were convinced that corruption was rampant, particularly at the local level, and called for a purging process within their movement referred to as a "revolution within the revolution." Indeed, in calling for the formation of the PSUV, Chávez chided the MVR for failing to confront the problem of corruption.

In an additional move designed to deepen the nation's democracy, Chávez promoted the proliferation of small neighborhood councils known as *consejos comunales* (representing between 200 and 400 families) and committed the government to providing each one with about $60,000 to undertake infrastructural and social projects. In addition, he encouraged the creation of organizations representing the community councils at the regional and eventually national levels. By early 2007, about 20,000 *consejos comunales* had been formed.

These measures and other concurrent developments point in the direction of greater centralization and new structures designed to deal with the discontent in the *Chavista* movement and the problems arising in the establishment of a viable economic model. The nationalizations carried out in early 2007 promoted the centralization of the economy under state control. In addition, the PSUV was designed to channel the grievances within the movement along institutional lines. Finally, at this time greater control and restrictions were placed on experimental and decentralized forms of production that had received generous state support. Along these lines, the thesis that the oil industry, the CVG companies (including the aluminum industry, ALCASA), the state-run electricity industry, and other strategic state-controlled sectors should be exempt from arrangements of worker decisionmaking gained widespread acceptance among policymakers. Some *Chavista* leaders also began to express doubts about the efficiency of ALCASA, the paper company INVEPAL, and other worker participation experiences.

Chávez's statement made in mid-2007 that he was not a "Marxist" must also be viewed in the context of apprehension regarding untested models of worker comanagement. In effect, Chávez rejected the notion of the working class as the key agent in the revolutionary process, as he had even before coming to power (Blanco Muñoz 1998, 392–393). Along similar lines, the dominant *Chavista* leadership attempted to block the takeover of the UNT by its most radical current headed by Trotskyist Orlando Chirino (see Chapter 6). Chirino was the most avid supporter of worker participation in decisionmaking in ALCASA, INVEPAL, and other companies.

The fourth stage, like the three previous ones, was ushered in as a result of the defeat of the opposition and its concomitant demoralization. Specifically, Chávez's triumph in the presidential elections of December 2006 with 63 percent of the vote, the highest in any election since 1958, represented one in a series of heavy blows for the opposition. In spite of these setbacks, it failed to embark on a new path or assimilate past errors. The opposition chose as its presidential candidate the governor of Zulia, Manuel Rosales, over the more polished Julio Borges (of the middle-class-based Primero Justicia party) in an effort to overcome its elitist image, even though the latter had greater acceptance among the anti-*Chavistas*. During the campaign, however,

Rosales embraced a neoliberal discourse, which has never resonated among the popular sectors. Furthermore, throughout 2007 the opposition continued to react to Chávez's initiatives rather than put forward its own or attempt to achieve ideological or programmatic clarity. In light of the loss of prestige of the anti-*Chavista* parties, the opposition began to focus its attention on, and provide encouragement to, the anti-*Chavista* university student movement, which developed a mobilization capacity of its own. The anti-*Chavista* students, however, failed to develop a program that would go beyond middle-class concerns. When ten of their leaders were invited to address the National Assembly, with their talks broadcasted live on television and radio, they instead delivered just one statement and defiantly walked out of the meeting, thus forfeiting a golden opportunity to present proposals to the nation. The incident was just one example of the opposition's ongoing failure to attempt to reach the public with a positive message and a program of its own.

In the latter part of 2007, President Chávez and the National Assembly proposed sixty-nine reforms to the 1999 Constitution that were submitted for ratification in a referendum held on December 2. The proposals were designed to promote direct participation by, and benefits for, nonprivileged sectors of the population and strengthen state control of strategic industries in accordance with the general thrust of the fourth stage. Reforms along these lines included allocation of 5 percent of the national ordinary budget to the *consejos comunales* for neighborhood projects; state promotion of national manufacturing and technology, particularly for the exploitation of hydrocarbons; providing students and employees the same weight as professors in the selection of university authorities; reduction of the work week to thirty-six hours; and the creation of a Social Stability Fund, financed both by the state and by workers of the informal economy to provide the latter with social security benefits. In addition, the reform package proposed the elimination of presidential term limits, and referred to Venezuela as the Venezuelan Socialist State. The propositions were defeated by a mere 2 percent of the vote. Immediately after the election, Chávez indicated his intention to seek approval of the reforms at a future date.

▶ The Mixed Results of the New Emerging Model

The new model that began to emerge in the third stage generated problems that the fourth stage was designed to correct. The Chávez government's mistakes in the area of social programs have been particularly costly given the large sums of money and numbers of people involved. Nevertheless, the relative successes and breakthroughs are significant because they have begun to transform the lives of the poorest and marginalized sectors of the population.

More than any other program under Chávez, the balance sheet for the new worker cooperatives is mixed. The cooperatives are heavily dependent on the state. Government incentives include generous amounts of credit with lenient terms of payment and exemption from all taxes. The failure of mass numbers of state-financed cooperatives—due to improvisation or, worse yet, misuse of government funds—has translated itself into the loss of tens or hundreds of millions of dollars. While many cooperatives never got off the ground, in other cases cooperative members ended up pocketing the money received from loans or the down payments for contracts prior to the initiation of work.

Following this initial wave of failures, the MPPEC has attempted to exercise tighter control over the cooperatives in accordance with the general thrust of the fourth stage, but in doing so may have gone to an opposite extreme. The cooperatives are now required every three months to solicit a Certificate of Fulfillment of Responsibilities, which is issued by the ministry's main office in Caracas. The paperwork, which includes a balance sheet signed by a certified accountant, is extremely time consuming. The cooperatives also need to demonstrate solvency with regard to financial obligations to such government agencies as the social security system, the housing authority, and the job training institute known as the National Institute of Educational Cooperation (INCE).

Chávez and his followers generally attribute the problems facing cooperatives to the lack of consciousness of their members, and as a corrective they call for the creation of what Che Guevara called the "New Socialist Man." However, in promoting cooperatives and other social programs, the government faces a practical obstacle that the *Chavista* leaders fail to recognize. Mechanisms have been created to monitor cooperatives, but there are no cases to date of cooperative members who have been penalized for failing to comply with their legal obligations. Although Minister of the Community Economy Pedro Morejón announced in late 2006 that he had taken 300 cases of cooperatives to court, it remains to be seen whether Chávez, who alleges to be the president of the underprivileged, will be willing to jail, or seize the property of, poor people who have misspent public money. In another example of excessive faith in the good will of the people, some *Chavista*-controlled state governments actually provide collateral for cooperatives, thus defeating the system's very purpose (Raby 2006, 180).

On the other hand, those cooperatives that have withstood the test of time may contribute to the transformation of society, particularly because a significant number of their members come from the non-privileged sectors of the population. On the plus side, many cooperative members with the help of the state have learned administrative skills at the same time that their attitude toward cooperation and solidarity may be changing. The cooperatives are obliged by law to engage in work in the communities where they are located, such as carrying out maintenance work in schools and distributing Christmas presents to children. Furthermore, the experience of sharing the profits among fellow workers breaks with the traditional way of doing things. Finally, one positive sign that points in the direction of relative independence is when the cooperative pays off its original loan and goes on to purchase its own equipment. One cooperative member stated at a conference sponsored by the University of Carabobo and the University Centroccidental Lisandro Alvarado: "It gave us great satisfaction to have paid off our loan in seven months. Now it is they [the state bank] who are behind us urging us to apply for new credit" (Rodríguez 2007, 249).

Formal discussion within the *Chavista* movement is essential for detecting and correcting the errors that are inevitable in the trial-and-error road to change called by Chávez "twenty-first-century socialism." During the eight and a half years they have been in power, however, the pro-Chávez parties have failed to establish internal mechanisms of discussion. Furthermore, the status of Chávez as undisputed leader who has the final say on all matters related to his movement—while hardly creating a "caudillo-masses" relationship with his followers, as his adversaries claim—discourages independent thinking within his camp and thus places limits on internal debate. The PSUV, which Chávez claims will be the most "democratic party in Venezuelan history," is designed to overcome the MVR's democratic shortcomings. Nevertheless, the lack of critical internal debate is demonstrated by its failure up to now to analyze the policies toward cooperatives that resulted in massive loss of public funds. With such considerable resources at its disposal, the government's main challenge is not in avoiding mistakes but rather in encouraging formal debate and parlaying frustrating experiences into new, more viable proposals.

▶ The Break with the Neoliberal and Populist Past

Both the second stage, which began in 2001, and the third stage, which followed the recall election in August 2004, helped clarify the general direction of the Chávez phenomenon. The policies of the second stage disproved the opposition's claim that Chávez was a neoliberal disguised as an anti-neoliberal and put in relief the nationalist thrust of his government's foreign policy. The third stage has distanced the Chávez presidency from previous aspects of his rule that resembled the radical brand of populism that characterized such Latin American leaders as Juan Domingo Perón in the 1930s and 1940s.[3] Several key features emerging during the third stage distinguish the Chávez presidency from the Latin American populism of those years.

First, Chávez's ambitious social and economic programs have a marked community focus and are designed to incorporate lower-class neighborhoods (barrios) into the nation's life. Most outlets of the state-run food enterprise Mercado de Alimentos (MERCAL, consisting of stores, storage facilities, and transportation units) are located in lower-class communities, while spokespeople for the program announce that their absence in middle-class areas will be addressed but not in the short-term future. Under the Barrio Adentro Mission, doctors are community-based and work with neighborhood organizations to promote preventive medicine. In the past, few Venezuelan doctors established their offices in the barrios. Furthermore, the Sucre Mission (university-level education) and the "Bolivarian universities" sponsor student participation in community programs. Similarly, most cooperatives operate out of the homes of one of its members, while the government encourages them to act in the spirit of "solidarity" by providing services and programs in the same communities. Finally, the barrio-based "land committees" and water commissions and, more recently, the community councils are innovations of special significance in that they bestow decisionmaking authority for urban planning and land distribution on the collectivity. The collective thrust of land distribution in slum areas contrasts with the practices of populist parties of the past as well as with the prescriptions of neoliberals. Populist governments typically offered urban land titles on an individual basis as a clientelistic transaction with electoral objectives, while neoliberals accepted the authorization of land deeds in order to shore up the system of private ownership and clamp down on squatting (Parker 2007, 68; Soto 1989, 56–57).

Second, Chávez's programs and policies embody a new definition of private property and challenge powerful economic groups in ways that reformist and populist governments never dared to do. Thus the Lands Law and the policy of expropriation of companies reflect the Chávez government's rejection of private property as an absolute right devoid of social responsibilities. The government respects private property ownership under normal circumstances. At the same time it follows a policy of taking over uncultivated land (in accordance with the Lands Law) and companies that have closed down, while paying owners compensation based on market value, after deducting debts owed to the workers and the state. This approach points in the direction of a new definition of private property that stresses social responsibility (Gindin 2005, 81). The concept contrasts with the mass expropriations of socialist revolutions. It also differentiates *Chavismo* from classical populism, which limited expropriation to strategic natural resources.

In addition, the state has promoted diverse types of economic activity that are explicitly designed to challenge oligopoly control. The government-sponsored food chain MERCAL, for instance, competes with privately owned supermarkets, as do state-financed cooperatives with regard to other companies. Thus large economic groups are beginning to be challenged on two fronts: competition from the state sector and from state-supported small- and medium-sized enterprises, including cooperatives.

Third, Venezuelan politics under Chávez has become a zero-sum game at the same time that discourse reflects a clear social bias. Never before in Venezuelan history has the head of state declared that assisting the poor is more important than serving other sectors of the population. Expenditures in the areas of health and education as a percentage of the national budget have increased sharply, while income tax collection has further contributed to the redistribution of wealth. Middle sectors have not been exempt from this shift in priorities. Thus associations of professors and doctors have expressed concern that the mission programs, which benefit the poor, have lowered professional standards and are absorbing resources at the expense of established institutions. This social prioritization contrasts with radical populist regimes in the 1930s and 1940s whose discourse shied away from class conflict as a category (Horowitz 1999, 23) and which promoted alliances linking the business sector with the working class.

Venezuela's emerging socioeconomic model in which new structures (such as the missions) coexist with old ones is costly in that it duplicates bureaucracies. Its success is contingent on continued high oil prices. In the long run, its viability also depends on the eradication of corrupt practices and the development of efficacious mechanisms to ensure that the mass allocation of resources to community and worker ventures are put to good use. Indeed, the left wing of the *Chavista* movement views the struggle against corruption not only as a moral imperative but as a sine qua non for the nation's ongoing socialist transformation, while the moderate wing calls for more effective controls imposed by the state (to be discussed in Chapter 6). As long as the Venezuelan model depends on oil income, its applicability to the rest of

Latin America will be limited. Only by overcoming Venezuela's status as a rentier economy plagued by institutional fragility, inefficiency, and corruption can the nation's *Chavista* experiment develop into a real alternative to neoliberalism and possibly a model to be copied throughout the continent.

▶ ## Analyses of the Chávez Phenomenon that Downplay Socioeconomic Issues

The main thesis of this book is that much political analysis of Venezuela over the years has centered on personalities, style, and political institutions at the expense of socioeconomic conflict and other issues of substance. Nowhere does this tendency manifest itself more than in the writings on the Chávez presidency that largely overlook the political impact of the socioeconomic developments discussed in this chapter. The emphasis on style is not surprising given Chávez's frequent verbal excesses including aggressive remarks that have become front-page news. The shortcoming of these analyses, however, can also be explained by the fact that many of the authors are political actors opposed to Chávez who manifest the opposition's personality-centered discourse and failure to formulate a program of economic change. Writers close to the opposition not only deny the relevance of social cleavages, but accuse Chávez of attempting to stir up both class and racial animosities (see Cannon 2004, 298–300; Herrera Salas 2007, 112–113). Even some *Chavista* writers dwell on Chávez's charismatic qualities and in doing so pass over the central "protagonist" role of the popular classes that is a cornerstone of their movement's doctrine.

As was the case in the past, writers who are closely identified with partisan politics and set the tone for much of the analysis of the current period privilege rhetoric and ignore the substance of the government's novel and experimental strategies and programs. Many of these analysts belong to parties of the opposition and reflect its unnuanced critique of *Chavismo*. Thus AD leaders Carlos Raúl Hernández (formerly of MAS) and Luis Emilio Rondón in the book *La democracia traicionada* (Democracy Betrayed) claim that Chávez has done nothing more than reimplement "old protectionist practices" and conclude by calling him a "populist dinosaur" who has "hibernated for fifty years" (Hernández and Rondón 2005, 308, 312). Others draw on the argument of opposition leaders who claim that Chávez's social and economic policies are a simple reformulation of the policies of the neoliberal period of the 1990s (Petkoff 2000, 102–103). Another ex-MAS*ista* turned AD member,

Andrés Stambouli, calls Chávez a great communicator who "cultivates a sentiment of permanent revolution . . . against internal traitors and foreign aggressors," but for the most part fails to go beyond rhetoric (Stambouli 2002, 217). MAS leader Carlos Tablante in *Venezuela herida* (Venezuela Wounded) argues that Chávez preaches class hatred and struggle devoid of political content. He also calls Chávez "a leftist populist with very little democratic commitment due to his military formation" (Tablante 2003, 61, 119–127). In another book, Carlos Blanco, a former minister of Carlos Andrés Pérez's second administration, labels Chávez a throwback to nineteenth-century caudillo rule with no important programs to show for his widespread popularity (Blanco 2002, 260–262). By writing off the content of the *Chavista* government and movement, these writers prepare the reader for an analysis that centers on style and discourse.

Anti-Chávez writers whose language is less belligerent than those of the hard-line opposition also center their analysis on rhetoric and discourse. Former MAS ideologue Teodoro Petkoff, who is editor of the anti-*Chavista* daily *Tal Cual* (which he founded in 2000), is an example of a prominent political analyst and moderate anti-*Chavista* who stresses style over socioeconomic issues. (Indeed, over several decades MAS exemplified the tendency of much of the Venezuelan left to shy away from social struggle and socioeconomic issues.) Petkoff's central argument places a certain distance between himself and the hard-line opposition to Chávez. He attributes the nation's polarization and political tensions to the intransigence, sectarianism, and aggressive style of both the government and the opposition. Nevertheless, he places most of the blame on Chávez, who, as president, is obliged to unite not divide the nation. Petkoff calls on Chávez to set an example by assuming a conciliatory stance and in doing so take advantage of superior resources and access to the media in order to maintain governability.

In his book *Dos Izquierdas* (Two Lefts), Petkoff claims to represent a responsible left that is at odds with a hard-core left characterized by authoritarian tendencies and the "classical fundamentalism" associated with traditional leftists. Petkoff's critique of Chávez, to his left, and the radical opposition, to his right, is in large part one of style. Thus he accuses Chávez of "verbally gunning down the . . . counterrevolution that he himself generated particularly with his intimidating vocabulary." At the same time he lashes out at the "arrogance" of the private media and others opposed to Chávez (Petkoff 2005, 111–113).

Petkoff attributes the confrontation between both sides to the escalation of verbal attacks. Thus, for instance, Petkoff justifies Chávez's original efforts to refute the distortions of the communications media during the early years of his government, but criticizes the president for reaching an extreme when "he went beyond rational objections and insistence on rectifications by taking the offensive . . . [in the form of] often brutal and intolerant attacks against media owners and reporters." This increasingly hostile posture led into the April 2002 coup (Petkoff 2005, 110–111). A similar process occurred when Chávez traveled in 2000 to OPEC member nations to personally invite heads of state to the organization's Second Summit held that September in Caracas. In Petkoff's opinion Chávez "proceeded correctly" in going to all ten fellow OPEC nations without excluding Iraq, Libya, and Iran, thus defying Washington, which had warned against meeting with terrorists like Saddam Hussein and Muammar Qaddafi. Where Chávez went wrong, however, was in going beyond his original mission. Once in Iraq, Libya, and Iran, Chávez raised the "absurd" banner of "a brotherhood among 'revolutionaries' linking those countries with Venezuela" even though "apart from being fellow members of OPEC we have absolutely nothing in common politically speaking" with those nations (Petkoff 2005, 88). In describing the incident, Petkoff loses sight of the real issue, namely Chávez's efforts to bolster oil prices (as discussed in Chapter 8) that was bound to collide with US policymakers.

Petkoff and other moderate anti-*Chavistas* criticize the hard-core opposition for its exaggerated rhetoric such as its careless use of the term *totalitarianism* and its reference to Chávez as "the dictator," an epithet repeatedly used by CTV president Carlos Ortega during the 2002–2003 general strike (Petkoff 2005, 126). At one point, Petkoff staunchly denied any systematic violation of human rights under Chávez, or that his record in that area was worse than under past governments (asserted in a speech given in Berlin, Germany, October 16, 2003). Petkoff claims that the imprecise evaluation of the Chávez government has led the opposition to turn to insurgency, as in the case of the 2002 coup and the 2002–2003 general strike. In spite of these remarks, Petkoff points to Chávez's intolerance and belligerent rhetoric and his "autocratic temperament" (Petkoff 2005, 126) as proof of the president's lack of a commitment to democracy and of his intention to establish an authoritarian regime.

Along similar lines, analysts and scholars dismiss the Chávez phenomenon as "populist" and in doing so fail to analyze the real issues at stake. According to their thinking, windfall oil revenue has allowed Chávez to combine fiery rhetoric with programs that amount to handouts to the underprivileged without in any way bringing about meaningful change (McCoy 2005, 119–120). These allegations have led some writers to label Chávez a "petropopulist" (Oppenheimer 2006). Writers who call Chávez "populist" also often underline the extreme personalism of his rule that undermines political structures ranging from political parties to the state bureaucracy, as demonstrated by Chávez's constant reshuffling of his cabinet and the incompetence of his ministers (Kornblith 2005, 136; Castañeda 2006a, 39). Other writers draw a connection between the populist-style rule of leaders like Chávez and the "greater concern they show with gaining a firm grip on power than on searching for benefits and progress for the people" (Lepage 2006, 109; Oppenheimer 2005, 223–263). Finally, some writers refer to the cultural dimensions of populism by characterizing Chávez's followers as lacking in political skills, democratic commitment, and experience, which are a sine qua non for democratic stability (Canache 2002, 150; Ratliff 1999, 104–105). Their writing recalls the early works on populism by scholars such as Gino Germani who argued that the urban poor, representing the backbone of *Peronismo* and other populist movements, were first-generation migrants from the countryside with an authoritarian bent at odds with the goals of modern democratic parties (Germani 1978, 153–208).

The simplistic characterization of the *Chavista* movement as demagogic and authoritarian "populist" overlooks considerable scholarly literature on the topic of radical populism. Ernesto Laclau's seminal theoretical study on populism, published in 1977, as well as subsequent studies on populist labor movements in Latin America, such as those of Perón and Vargas, have pointed to the phenomenon's complexity, long-term strategies, and transformational potential (Laclau 1977; 2005; French 1992; James 2000). The four chapters in this book on the *Chavista* presidency and movement focus on these dimensions. The bottom-up methodology that centers on the actions and thinking of *Chavista* social and labor movements, local activists, and the *Chavista* rank and file—as opposed to the rhetoric of national actors—is best suited to place this complexity in proper perspective.

▶ **Notes**

1. The author interviewed sixty-five *Chavista* leaders at all levels of the movement between 2003 and 2006 as part of a research project financed by the Consejo de Investigación of the Universidad de Oriente (Venezuela). The following four chapters and particularly Chapters 6 and 7 draw heavily on these interviews.

2. Vásquez Velasco, a moderate whom Chávez trusted would remain loyal to his government, earned the ire of the different currents in and out of the

armed forces as a result of his actions during the coup. The *Chavistas* condemned him for declaring himself in rebellion against the Chávez government on April 11, while the hard-line anti-*Chavistas* were enraged by his ultimatum against Carmona on April 13, which paved the way for Chávez's return to power. The moderate anti-*Chavistas* in the military criticized him for having turned over power to Carmona on April 11 rather than assuming authority and calling for immediate elections at all levels (Guevara 2005, 134; Harnecker 2005, 84).

3. Latin American populist movements of the 1930s and 1940s, like *Chavismo* during its early years, were characterized by charismatic leadership, support for state intervention in the economy, an anti-elite rhetoric, and the lack of well defined long-term goals. Elsewhere I have argued that important aspects of the Chávez presidency during its early years approximated radical populism more than the "neopopulism" associated with Alberto Fujimori in Peru and Carlos Menem in Argentina in the 1990s (Ellner 2003b). This writing was intended to refute the assertion that as a "neopopulist" Chávez resembled Fujimori in embracing neoliberal economic policies and disdaining political party organization (Ramos Jiménez 2006, 30).

6
▼

Conflicting Currents in
the Chávez Movement

THE PROCESS of radicalization from one stage of the Chávez presidency to the next has influenced the *Chavistas* in their formulation of political strategies. The *Chavistas* took careful note that with each major challenge posed by the opposition, the government and the MVR party emerged victorious, and as a result their position was strengthened and new objectives were defined. In the process, moderates as well as "unreliable" members of the *Chavista* movement and government were shunted aside or left to join the opposition. At the same time, the "enemies of the revolution," such as FEDECAMARAS, the financial sector, the communications media, the hierarchy of the Catholic Church, and the United States government began to openly take sides, thus deepening the struggle and raising the stakes.

This sequence consisting of the intensification of conflict, the exit of moderates, the consolidation of power, and the radicalization of goals has characterized all four stages of the Chávez presidency, as discussed in Chapter 5. Thus during the first stage of 1999–2000 the *Chavistas* obtained ratification of the Constitution in the referendum of December 1999 and went on to win the "megaelections" at national, state, and municipal levels the following year. This success led to the second stage that began with the drafting of forty-nine radical socioeconomic reforms enacted in November 2001, which in turn produced the defection of moderate *Chavista* supporters, specifically MAS and the MVR faction headed by Luis Miquilena.

The coup and the general strike in 2002–2003 allowed Chávez to consolidate his hold over the armed forces and state oil company, PDVSA, with important implications for his rule. Some of Chávez's enemies in the military were identified by their actions in support of the coup and subsequently scores of dissident officers publicly declared themselves in rebellion against the government as part of a strategy to pave the way for the general strike (Harnecker 2003, 119–121; Trinkunas 2005, 221). In July 2002 and 2003, the annual promotions of members of the armed forces favored officers who had demonstrated their loyalty during these events, particularly with regard to positions with command of troops. The consolidation of control of the armed forces by the *Chavistas* ensured the defeat of the opposition's strategy in early 2004 of creating street confrontation and chaos (referred to as the Guarimba Plan) in order to appeal to the military to overthrow Chávez and reestablish order. The *Chavista* control of PDVSA as a result of the general strike facilitated its key role in the "missions," which became the cornerstone of the government's social program.

During the period between the failed coup of April 2002 and the general strike of December, Chávez toned down his rhetoric and made concessions to his adversaries. Thus, for instance, he named various moderates to top government posts, including Alí Rodríguez who became president of PDVSA. These changes underscored the importance of timing in the radicalization process. They demonstrate that the *Chavista* strategy has not ruled out occasional actions to placate the opposition, but that the concessions have been invariably designed to facilitate *Chavismo*'s consolidation of power.

The defeat of the 2002–2003 general strike, more than the coup, greatly weakened the opposition, which was blamed for the hardships that the entire nation endured throughout the protracted conflict. In the aftermath, Chávez introduced anti-imperialist slogans and accused Washington of direct involvement in the coup. The stance contrasted with his more cautious language in his public statements about the United States during and after the electoral campaign of 1998 and even in the months following the 2002 coup.

The triumph in the recall elections of August 2004 and the state-local elections, which the *Chavistas* swept three months later, left Chávez in a stronger position than before and the opposition demoralized, discredited, and absent from spaces it had formerly occupied. Against the backdrop of political stability and a weakened opposition, a third, radical stage ushered in the outlines of a new economic model that denied the absolute sanctity of private property while ruling out arbitrary measures against property holders. Novel policies included the granting of start-up credit for tens of thousands of cooperatives by the recently created the MPPEC, the expropriation of companies that had shut down, and the takeover of idle agricultural property in accordance with the Lands Law. At this time Chávez coined the slogan "On the Path to Twenty-first-century Socialism."

Similarly, a major *Chavista* victory in the form of Chávez's unprecedented vote in the December 2006 presidential elections signaled the initiation of the fourth stage, which further radicalized the "revolutionary process." Leftist measures included the nationalization of key sectors of the economy (which had been a goal incorporated in the 1999 Constitution but then shelved) and the proposed constitutional reform to modify the concept of private property. As in the case of the previous stages, Chávez's sense of timing and insistence on taking advantage of the favorable juncture led him to move quickly by requesting emergency powers from the National Assembly that his movement completely dominated.

▶ **Differentiation of the Two Internal Currents**

This ongoing process of radicalization lay behind the debate within the *Chavista* movement between soft- and hard-line currents. Although formal mechanisms of internal debate are lacking both within the MVR party and the *Chavista* movement as a whole, considerable informal discussion over long-term goals and strategies is not surprising given the leftist backgrounds of most of the movement's activists. Most *Chavista* military officers favor the soft-liners' pragmatic approach, as do the pro-*Chavista* PPT and Podemos parties, which, following the December 2005 congressional elections, announced their intentions of coordinating their activities in the National Assembly. Soft-line military officers assumed governorships in the states of Bolívar, Miranda, Vargas, and Carabobo as a result of the elections of October 2004. A large number of the hard-liners formerly belonged to ex-guerrilla parties (such as the Communist Party, the Liga Socialista, and Ruptura) before joining the MVR (Valencia Ramírez 2007, 137).

The "soft line" considers government advances and successes as ends in themselves, rather than just the beginning of a deepening process. According to this view, the *Chavistas*' overriding task after eight years in power is consolidation of gains rather than further radicalization, which runs the risk of exacerbating polarization and instability and encouraging the international campaign to isolate Venezuela. Most important, the government's reassertion of control over PDVSA as a result of the general strike of 2002–2003 provided the state with sufficient resources to shape the nation's destiny, thus ruling out further internecine political confrontation (B. Alvarez 2006). In spite of its moderate positions, the soft-line current calls the *Chavista* movement "revolutionary" and shares the far-reaching expectations that Chávez has created among the rank and file, even though it lacks a battle plan for deepening the process of change.

The soft-liners view the government's achievements over the last eight years as far reaching and long lasting. The foremost such success is the nation's new Constitution, which embraces fundamental changes on political, social, and economic fronts. For *Chavistas* in general the Constitution symbolizes the essence of *Chavismo* and serves to legitimize the nation's new institutions and policies. In numerous public appearances Chávez holds up a copy of the Constitution, which has also served as a topic of formal and informal discussion among *Chavistas*. Nevertheless, the Constitution is hardly "revolutionary" as it guarantees the rights of private property and an "opportune and just indemnification" in special cases of expropriation when "social interests are at stake" (articles 115 and 116). It also assigns the state the role of promoting "private initiative" (article 112). By spelling out the ideals of the *Chavista* movement while avoiding reference to the specifics of revolutionary socioeconomic change, class struggle, or socialism, the Constitution lends itself to the soft-line view. Indeed, the proposal to reform the Constitution in 2007 in order to radicalize its contents led to the defection of the soft-line Podemos party.

The hard-liners generally favor an immediate and unyielding response to the challenges posed by the opposition, the creation of parallel structures, and a purge of the public sector to enhance efficiency and prevent sabotage. The quick succession of events during the first eight years of Chávez's government supports the hard-line thesis that ongoing change and conflict will inexorably lead to new transformations. The hard-liners argue that the disguised presence of members of the opposition in PDVSA and the public administration in general and the alleged sabotage they carried out, particularly in the oil industry, make necessary mass layoffs of unreliable public employees, as well as the creation of parallel structures to replace old ones. Furthermore, they call on the government to work closely with movements of *Chavista* professionals in areas such as health and education in order to count on reliable allies in the struggle to clean up the bureaucracy. In short, according to the hard-liners, the best defense is an offensive strategy while compromise and fallback positions are a last resort that runs the risk of putting the brakes on the "revolutionary process."

The hard-liners view the creation of parallel structures and the purging of old ones as an essential element of the revolutionary process. Thus, for instance, from the beginning of the Chávez presidency, the hard-liners who dominated the *Chavista* labor leadership favored the creation of parallel worker organizations outside the existing trade union structure. In contrast, the soft-liners, headed by Chávez's right-hand man Luis Miquilena, insisted that the *Chavistas* work within the AD-dominated Workers' Confederation of Venezuela (CTV) and its affiliates. By late 2002 the soft-liners were won over to the proposition of creating a new confederation, but continued to caution against the formation of individual parallel unions in order to avoid the fragmentation of the labor movement. The hard-liners, for their part, insisted on the mass break-off of individual unions from the CTV structure.

In spite of their vision of an eventual complete break with the past, the hard-liners defend their party's commitment to the Constitution, which proclaims respect for private property. The hard-liners insist that changes will occur peacefully in accordance with the Constitution. The *Chavista* strategy of creating parallel structures implies tolerance of and, in the case of the public sphere (such as schools and hospitals), budgetary allocations for the old structures, even though they are allegedly inefficient and penetrated by the opposition. The approach contrasts with the traditional revolutionary concept of an abrupt and thorough break with the past. Indeed those who supported the hard-line approach envision an extended process of revolutionary change that is unprecedented in history and that some claim may take several decades to complete. Nevertheless, in informal discussions, hard-liners raise the possibility of replacing the current capitalist system with a mixed economy that would include state companies (such as CANTV and Electricidad de Caracas, both taken over in early 2007) along with associations of medium-sized cooperatives that would be able to challenge big capitalist groups. The end result would be a complete substitution of old structures in the state sphere and the economy with new structures created by the *Chavista* government and movement. According to the hard-liners, however, the exact makeup of the new society will be determined largely on the basis of experience and not preconceived notions. In accordance with this line of thinking, Chávez, when he publicly embraced socialism in 2005, made it clear that the term had to be reinvented in accordance with new realities.

A small group of Trotskyists share the *Chavista* hard-line emphasis on the intensification of conflict, but occupy a position further to its left. The Trotskyists' visible head is veteran labor leader Orlando Chirino of the UNT, who is backed by an international London-based solidarity group called "Hands Off Venezuela." The Trotskyists argue that the process of change has to move steadily and rapidly to the left and that any hesitation, concession, or retreat will jeopardize the revolutionary project. The hard-line *Chavistas* diverge from the Trotskyists in three basic aspects. First, *Chavista* hard-liners envision a drawn-out process of transformation possibly lasting several decades. Second, they do not rule out occasional retreats, as occurred between the April 2002 coup and the general strike seven months later. They insist on the need to carefully choose targets and resist the temptation of opening too many fronts at the same time, a danger that Chávez has occasionally addressed (Harnecker 2005, 110). Finally, the hard-liners lack explicit long-term goals and believe that the new society will be defined and constructed largely on the basis of experience and not preconceived notions.

The soft- and hard-line currents uphold two distinct positions toward institutions and organizations opposed to the Chávez government. These differences are clearly evident in their attitudes toward the political parties of the opposition. Immediately after the December 2005 elections for the National Assembly, boycotted by most of the opposition, Foreign Minister Alí Rodríguez (who belongs to the PPT party, which is identified with the soft line) "invited" opposition leaders to dialogue with the government as long as it accepted the principle that "in democracy decisions are taken by the majority, not the minority" (*El Universal*, December 6, 2005, 1–11). At the same time, Vice President José Vicente Rangel made a similar conciliatory statement. In effect, Rodríguez and Rangel sought to encourage the opposition to participate in the presidential elections slated for the following December.

The opposite position toward rival political leaders was occasionally expressed by Chávez and more consistently within the MVR by William Lara, who dismissed the possibility that the main traditional parties would ever evolve into a loyal opposition. Lara favored an intransigent stand toward the established anti-*Chavista* parties, and specifically rejection of their demands regarding electoral reform, and at the same time encouragement of the emergence of a new more tractable opposition. Lara's position was premised on the willingness of a small minority of leaders and parties of the opposition to break with the hard-core anti-*Chavistas*, such as AD, COPEI, Project Venezuela, and Primero Justicia, by recognizing Chávez's legitimacy and playing by the rules of the political game. MAS, for instance, decided to take part in the December 2005 elections (although various top party leaders dissented) on grounds that the National Electoral Council had accepted the terms that the opposition had formulated (both publicly and privately to the OAS observers) as a condition for its participation. Furthermore, during the 2006 presidential elections, MAS objected to some of Manuel Rosales's positions such as his pledge to cut off the supply of oil to Cuba.

The *Chavista* movement is also divided between soft- and hard-line currents with regard to FEDECAMARAS and the Catholic Church. Hard-liners point to the leadership role played by FEDECAMARAS in the events of 2002 and argue that new economic structures such as cooperatives will in the long run displace the large monopoly companies that control the business organization. The soft-liners were encouraged by the change of leadership of FEDECAMARAS and the church after Chávez consolidated power as a result of the 2004 recall. Thus José Luis Betancourt, who assumed the presidency of FEDECAMARAS in mid-2005, announced his willingness to accept the government's economic and social policies, although he warned against violation of property rights, such as the breakup of rural landholdings, which he called "political proselytism." Similarly, soft-liners interpreted the appointment of the allegedly moderate cleric Jorge Urosa Savino, first to the position of archbishop of Caracas in 2005 and then as cardinal of Venezuela, as a sign of the intentions of the church hierarchy to seek a modus vivendi with the government. Vice President José Vicente Rangel publicly recognized these developments as conducive to a broad-based dialogue; in mid-2007 he claimed that Pope Benedict XVI favored improving relations with the Venezuelan government.

Differences between the *Chavista* hard and soft lines sometimes manifest themselves in public debate, although not on a regular basis. The positions assumed by leaders of both currents reflect their priorities and strategies. In early 2005, for instance, MVR national deputy Iris Varela, who is identified with the hard line, clashed with the governor of Guárico, Eduardo Manuit (of the PPT), over alleged human rights violations committed by his state's police force. Speaking before the National Assembly, Varela held the Guárico police responsible for the disappearance of 198 people, a claim denied by Manuit. The incident was a reflection of the different social base of the two lines within *Chavismo*. Measures proposed by hard-liners such as Varela against police brutality are a clamor of the poor. In contrast, concern for personal security and support for providing police with sufficient resources cut across class lines, but in general the demand for a stringent and inflexible approach is championed by privileged more than nonprivileged sectors. In effect, by adamantly coming to the defense of the Guárico police force, Manuit was prioritizing the struggle against crime over the issue of human rights.[1]

Podemos's secretary-general, Ismael García, who was president of the National Assembly's ad hoc Committee Against Crime and Violence, also articulated the soft line's uncompromising position on personal security, and its call on President Chávez to emphasize the war on crime. García called for inclusion of the parties of the opposition in a broad front against crime in order to depoliticize the issue and increase the effectiveness of measures taken by the state. García, representing the Committee Against Crime and Violence, met with representatives of the private media in order to enlist their support and convince them to play down violent themes and images that undermined the struggle against crime. García's attitude was contrary to that of hard-line *Chavistas* who considered the media and opposition parties inveterate enemies of the revolutionary process. García also diverged from the hard-line position on human rights. In one public gathering that was organized to air the issue of personal security, García complained that "at times legislation guaranteeing human rights inadvertently detracts from the effort to clamp down on organized criminal activity" (Ismael García, speech, Puerto La Cruz, May 20, 2006).

Another confrontation between hard and soft lines occurred in early 2006 when General Luis Felipe Acosta Carlez, governor of Carabobo, contracted out the administration of a major hospital as a possible first step toward the privatization of the state's health system. Acosta Carlez justified the move by pointing to the inefficient management of the hospital. In contrast, the hard-line MVR leadership in Carabobo, which previously had distanced itself from the governor, joined local UNT trade unionists in harshly criticizing the move on grounds that it violated the Constitution and would generate unemployment. This incident along with the debate over crime and violence revealed the main actors who supported the soft-line approach: the PPT and Podemos, along with military officers.

In the face of these internal differences, the MVR has failed to open itself up to ideological debate for the purpose of achieving greater clarity. Neither of the two currents promotes their positions in organized fashion such as through internal party periodicals or other types of literature. The MVR's Department of Ideological Formation views its role as achieving consensus rather than defending a given ideological model that would run the risk of dividing the party (Morales 2004).

Various factors have held back ideological introspection as well as other urgent tasks, such as an all-out war on corruption within the movement and party electoral democratization. During the early years of government, the *Chavistas* lacked breathing space. Immediate pressing challenges have interfered with efforts at internal renovation, which run the risk of producing internal divisions. Between its founding in 1997 and 2000, the MVR faced seven nationwide electoral contests, and subsequently the opposition attempted to force Chávez out of power by diverse means. In addition, the *Chavista* leadership has appointed military officers to top positions in the movement and also the state as part of the strategy of the civilian-military alliance, which has been essential to the survival of the government. The privileged position reserved for officers impedes internal democracy and ideological debate and may even be conducive to corruption. In addition, *Chavismo* consists of an alliance of political parties as well as social organizations in which the MVR lacks a major presence, and thus mechanisms for formulating positions and channeling them upward within the movement are at best clumsy.

Finally, open ideological debate that reveals the opinions and proposals of hard-liners runs the risk of alarming privileged sectors of the population. Thus, for instance, discussion over the hard-line strategy of prioritizing parallel structures and their eventual displacement of traditional ones would invite protests from those who form part of the latter. More specifically, the prospect of phasing out established institutions of higher education would undoubtedly spur professors and even students in the state universities into action. Similarly, the proposal by hard-line leaders to allocate ample resources to state enterprises and cooperatives in order to allow them to compete with and eventually displace "monopoly" companies would frighten private investors, as would an open discussion regarding the redefinition of private property in "revolutionary" Venezuela. Finally, the airing of plans to purge the state sector of "unreliable" employees tied to opposition parties may set in motion protests by trade unionists of the opposition and accusations of discriminatory hiring practices. In short, the absence of mechanisms to foster ideological and strategic discussion had the advantage of keeping thorny issues from the public arena.

The period following Chávez's resounding victory in the August 2004 recall and the state and municipal elections three months later represented an ideal moment for the renovation of the *Chavista* movement and ideological introspection. As a result of the chain of victories on electoral and nonelectoral fronts, the *Chavistas* found themselves in a comfortable position with an opposition that was highly discredited and demoralized. Nevertheless, Chávez's announced goal of obtaining ten million votes in the December 2006 presidential elections, for which the congressional election of 2005 was to serve as a springboard, once again shifted attention to the electoral arena. Indeed, the *Chavistas* avoided party primaries for the selection of congressional candidates for the 2005 elections. Given Chávez's upper hand, the fixation on electoral battles seemed unfounded, as did the postponement of party primaries, exemplary measures against corruption, and open ideological debate.

Chávez's embracement of socialism in January 2005 at the World Social Forum (WSF) in Porto Alegre, Brazil, appeared to bolster the hard-line current and align *Chavismo* with the hard-line vision of continuous radical transformation. At first glance, Chávez's pronouncement at the WSF was comparable to Fidel Castro's famous speech on December 2, 1961, when he declared himself a life-long Marxist Leninist, a revelation that set his government on an irreversible course. Immediately following Chávez's speech, socialism became an official *Chavista* banner that was fervently defended by everyone in the movement. Support for socialism defined *Chavismo* as a movement that was opposed to the existing capitalist system, but did little to spell out long-term goals. Furthermore, the common acceptance of socialism did not sharpen the differences within *Chavismo*, nor did it discredit or undermine the position of the soft-liners.

Nevertheless, in internal discussion, hard-liners suggest that radicalization, including the transformation of property relations, has to be accompanied by the renovation of the *Chavista* movement. Although rejecting blueprints associated with dogmatic Marxism, hard-liners favor a process of discussion and gradual definition. Thus hard-liner William Lara (ex-president of the National Assembly) expressed support internally for transforming the MVR into an "organic party" with close links to civil society and social movements (Lara 2005, 14–15). Lara viewed Chávez's announcement of an ideological congress to be held following the presidential elections in December 2006 as an ideal opportunity to relaunch the MVR and overcome its ideological ambiguity. In addition, the hard-liners were convinced that various expulsions from the MVR of local- and state-level leaders and the simultaneous decision not to renominate certain national deputies for the 2005 congressional elections formed part of the *Chavistas'* ongoing strategy of purging MVR*istas* of questionable ethical conduct. The hard-liners drew a connection between corruption and a "rightist" faction in the party (which, in effect, was the soft-line current) and viewed the removal of "opportunists" from leadership positions as a necessary first step toward further radicalization.

In spite of the *Chavistas'* ideological vagueness, and the absence of ideologically oriented factions, the hard and soft lines manifest themselves in proposals, arguments, and rhetoric at all levels of the movement. Thus, for instance, the phrase "deepening of the process," which forms part of the *Chavista* lexicon, refers to the radicalization embodied in the hard-line approach. Furthermore, Chávez has never hidden his intentions of engaging in a long, drawn-out struggle that will pass through distinct phases, but he refrains from defining the end results. He has explained the reason for not revealing ultimate goals by invoking the proverb "A preannounced war does not kill soldiers." The phrase indicates that Chávez's support for far-reaching or "revolutionary" change has been left intentionally hazy. Chávez's use of the phrase "revolution within the revolution" also lends itself to the hard-line vision. The term implies the deepening of the process in which leftists (the "hard-liners") replace moderates (or "soft-liners") in leadership positions. Rather than refer to the realm of ideas, however, Chávez indicates that the "revolution within the revolution" will eradicate corruption and self-serving behavior from his government and movement. For hard-liners, the phrase suggests selection of those most committed to far-reaching change to occupy important positions as part of the radicalization process.

On occasion, a third position has emerged that lies between the hard and soft lines, as is the case with the debate over private property. Hard-liners favor the eventual revolutionary transformation in property relations in which new structures replace old ones. Soft-liners envision the ongoing coexistence of old structures and new ones with clearly established rules of the game to minimize tension between them. Until 2005, the *Chavista* leadership accepted the position of the soft-liners by pledging to guarantee private property rights in accordance with the 1999 Constitution. The *Chavistas* refrained from raising slogans in favor of nationalization, at the same time that the government met its foreign debt obligations. Although the opposition claimed that the Lands Law of 2001 was inspired by the Cuban model, it allowed for expropriation only as a last resort. In this sense the Lands Law did not differ from the Venezuelan agrarian reforms of 1945, 1948, and 1960 drafted by non-revolutionary governments. Hard-liners, however, were able to point to specific cases where *Chavismo* questioned the notion of the rights of property as an absolute or sacred principle. This was the case with Chávez's controversial statement made at the outset of his presidency that if his family were starving of hunger he would not hesitate to steal. More important, during and after the general strike of 2002–2003,

Chavista labor leaders encouraged by Chávez threatened to take over various companies that had shut down for political reasons or that had declared bankruptcy without meeting their severance payment obligations. Nevertheless, in the two years following the strike the government refused to recognize worker ownership of occupied companies and left the matter in the hands of the courts.

In early 2005, Chávez modified his stand on property rights. The president announced a new policy of taking over companies that had closed down at the same time that the government took steps to expropriate large estates producing less than 80 percent of capacity in accordance with the Lands Law. In the case of both underutilized rural property and bankrupt companies, the government attempted to reach compromise agreements with the owners. Under these arrangements, the state provided financial assistance to the companies to facilitate their recovery in return for acceptance of worker participation in decision-making (*cogestión*) and their possible ownership of stock. In the case of landowners, the government insisted that they accept the distribution of a portion of their land among the peasants as a condition for retaining ownership of the rest. A third position between the soft and hard lines insists on the social obligations of property holders. At the same time, the third position (like the hard line) rejects absolute property rights and favors extensive land distribution, but (like the soft line) calls for well-defined requirements so that owners who accept the rules of the game will not be threatened by expropriation. In contrast, hard-line labor leaders are skeptical about negotiations between company owners and the government and in private express hope that the talks will fail in order to pave the way for complete worker control and state ownership.

A third position also emerged with regard to Venezuela's close relations with Cuba. Soft-liners deny ideological affinity between the two governments and claim that Chávez's only interest is in demonstrating in no uncertain terms Venezuela's status as a sovereign nation and its unwillingness to submit to the dictates of Washington. In contrast, hard-liners are convinced that the friendly relations reflect ideological convergence and view favorably the eventual eradication of private ownership of large-scale production as occurred in Cuba. The third, less radical position recognizes and praises the influence of Cuba in the development of social programs and particularly the techniques employed in the missions, but denies that Venezuela will ever copy the Cuban statist model.

The government's social programs and its emphasis on "solidarity" have also produced distinct reactions among hard- and soft-liners.

Chávez has pointed out that economic growth does not necessarily translate into material benefits for the underprivileged, and for this reason his government prioritizes social programs. Soft-liners consider these efforts to be temporary measures designed to shake up existing structures in order to reform them without radically changing or eliminating them. In addition, the soft-liners deny that the system of cooperatives will become Venezuela's dominant economic model since the nation lacks a tradition of these types of enterprises and because they will never be in a position to compete with large capital. In contrast, from the outset hard-liners viewed cooperatives and the missions as parallel structures that will eventually displace existing ones, or at least challenge oligopoly control, although more recently they have also attached considerable importance to state-run enterprises.

Chavista leaders stress that the government's social programs are motivated by, and designed to promote, a sense of solidarity. Thus Chávez calls on members of cooperatives that receive government financing to eschew capitalist values and make contributions to the communities where they are based. Furthermore, state companies set aside a significant portion of their budgets for social expenditures, while private enterprises receiving state credit and contracts are expected to do the same. The soft- and hard-line currents have reacted differently to these community programs. The soft-liners view the emphasis on solidarity as evidence that real change consists mainly of a cultural transformation as opposed to a structural one, and as such it is a long, drawn-out process rather than a series of abrupt state-imposed alterations.[2] For the hard-liners, the use of the term *solidarity* points to the paramount importance of confronting the problem of social inequality, which only radical policies and measures can correct.

The government has emphasized socialist values such as solidarity at the expense of practical imperatives, a tendency that in the past the left has called "ultraleftism." At the same time that the Venezuelan government promotes solidarity and appeals to the revolutionary fervor of workers, it has been less systematic and effective in establishing mechanisms to ensure that state resources allotted to cooperatives and other enterprises are put to good use. The slowness of institutionalization and the emphasis on voluntarism are typical of the early stages of revolutionary processes, such as was the case in Cuba in the 1960s.[3]

The differences between the two internal currents are most apparent in four areas: within the MVR party, the *Chavista* labor movement, the state-run oil industry, and discussion over the parallel structures promoted by the state. In these cases, the hard-liners have favored the acceleration of reforms, the strengthening of parallel structures, a confrontation-al approach toward the opposition, and the purge of anti-*Chavistas* in the public sphere. In contrast, soft-liners call for a tolerant attitude toward the legal opposition, a complementary relationship between new and old structures, and, in general, a more gradual approach. The remainder of the chapter examines the debate on these fronts in order to shed further light on the two currents.

▶ The *Chavista* Labor Movement

From the beginning of the Chávez presidency, a group of hard-liners headed by ex–metro workers Nicolás Maduro (a former member of the national committee of MVR's precursor, the MBR-200) and José Khan controlled the *Chavista* labor leadership. The hard-liners called for the creation of a new labor confederation to displace the AD-dominated CTV. They argued that the *Chavistas* should take advantage of their con-trol of the executive and legislative branches of government in order to deliver a decisive blow to the CTV, which was incapable of reforming itself from within. Maduro argued, "[E]ither we construct a force for real transformation or we stay in the CTV" (*El Nacional*, April 30, 2001, D-4). During this period, hard-line labor leaders elected to con-gress and the Constituent Assembly upheld differences with soft-liners over specific labor proposals such as the reduction of the work week and state control of the social security system.

The issue of parallel structures proved to be a major point of con-tention between the hard-line and soft-line currents in the labor move-ment, just as was the case with the hard-liners and soft-liners in general. During Chávez's first three years in office, the *Chavista* soft line headed by Miquilena favored participation in CTV elections rather than risk set-ting off a proliferation of parallel unions. Miquilena, who began his political career as a labor leader in the early 1940s, was aware of the mistake committed by Venezuelan leftists in the 1960s when the CTV isolated them as a result of their decision to form parallel unions. In contrast, the main *Chavista* labor leaders, who belonged to a recent gen-eration and gained prominence after 1998, never assimilated the experi-ences of the 1960s. Soft-liners argued that, notwithstanding the CTV's deviations, a majority of Venezuelan workers identified with the confed-eration, which had had virtually no competitor over the last half-century. They added that the creation of a rival labor confederation would split the entire labor movement to the detriment of workers. Soft-liners were particularly concerned about the accusations formulated from abroad by such organizations as the International Labour Organization that the *Chavistas* were promoting an "official" trade union movement.

Miquilena and his allies used their political influence to block the hard-line strategy of decreeing the abolition of the CTV. In 1999, Miquilena, as president of the National Assembly, refused to proceed with a proposed resolution that would have scheduled elections to unify the labor movement in a new confederation. The following year, soft-line *Chavista* congressmen modified the wording of a proposition for a national referendum (held in December 2000) that would have achieved the same objective. In addition, the soft-liners shelved the proposed Ley de Garantías y Protección de las Libertades Sindicales (Law of Guarantees and Protection of Trade Union Liberties), which implied a labor movement shakeup, and suddenly accepted round-table discussions (*mesas de diálogo*) with CTV leaders under the sponsorship of the Labor Ministry to deal with such issues as social security reform, unemployment, and the unification of the labor movement. The hard-liners reluctantly went along with the meetings but subsequently objected that these encounters failed to meet expectations, and that the CTV leaders disregarded the decisions reached regarding the reorganization of the labor movement.

The results of the national referendum of December 2000 forced CTV leaders at national and state levels to temporarily step down. Maduro argued that while those who replaced them in CTV posts were handpicked, the pro-*Chavista* "regional councils" had greater legitimacy since they were elected in worker assemblies in individual states. In effect, the regional councils were parallel labor organizations at the state level designed to replace old ones, and thus accorded with the hard-line strategy in favor of parallel unionism.

The decision by *Chavista* labor leaders to participate in CTV elections held in October 2001 represented a triumph for the MVR soft-liners, who were opposed to splitting off from the confederation. In another demonstration of flexibility, the *Chavistas* chose as their CTV presidential candidate Aristóbulo Istúriz of the PPT, which had had stormy relations with President Chávez and indeed had refrained from endorsing his presidential reelection the previous year. The MVR described Istúriz as a "consensus candidate," implying a new strategy to reach out beyond stalwart *Chavista* leaders in order to isolate the old-time CTV heads.

The selection of Istúriz over hard-liner Nicolás Maduro also showed the sensitivity of *Chavistas* to the widespread concern among workers about the danger of an "official" labor movement tied to the National Executive. Nevertheless, the *Chavistas* stopped short of choosing Pablo Medina, also of the PPT, who actively campaigned for nomination as the CTV's presidential candidate and accused fellow party member Istúriz of being submissive to the government. Medina pledged himself to lead a campaign against corruption beginning with the social security system. Medina, who accused soft-liner Miquilena of imposing Istúriz's candidacy, soon joined the opposition with a leftist critique of the government.

As part of the *Chavista* "consensus" strategy, Istúriz called for a broad front to block the reelection of Carlos Ortega as president of the Federation of Petroleum Workers (FEDEPETROL), who at the same time was running for the presidency of the CTV. *Chavista* labor leaders thus discarded the sectarian policy of promoting parallel unionism in the petroleum industry that had led to their transformation of an oil workers union in the state of Monagas into a nationwide union named SINU-TRAPETROL to compete with FEDEPETROL. In accordance with their new broad-based strategy, a few weeks before the elections the *Chavistas* switched their support from the president of an oil workers' union in the eastern state of Anzoátegui with little national backing to Rafael Rosales, a former COPEI member and FEDEPETROL treasurer.

The MVR "consensus strategy" was a masterstroke in that it attracted Rosales and other independent trade unionists into the fold of the pro-*Chavista* labor movement. The experience of the October 2001 CTV elections, which were characterized by violence and accusations of widespread fraud, radicalized independents such as Rosales and pitted them against the traditional AD-dominated CTV leadership. Thus AD proclaimed Carlos Ortega's victory as FEDEPETROL president before the federation's electoral commission announced the final tally favorable to Rosales, and subsequently the party refused to recognize the official results. Similar conflicts involving independents occurred in the public employees federation with another ex-*Copeyano*, Franklin Rondón, who was elected president of that organization; steel workers leader Ramón Machuca, who ran for president of the labor federation of the state of Bolívar; and Francisco Torrealba, who became president of the metro workers union. AD's intransigence drew all four labor leaders close to the *Chavista* camp. The four of them went on to assume the leadership of the soft-line position that was opposed to parallel unionism once Miquilena and his followers dropped out of the *Chavista* movement at the time of the April 2002 coup.

In spite of evidence of widespread fraud in the 2001 CTV elections, and the confederation's subsequent support for a series of general strikes designed to overthrow Chávez, the soft-liners led by Machuca (and including Rosales) at first stopped short of calling for separation from the confederation. They favored waiting until the CNE ruled on the validity of the CTV's electoral process in hopes that the council would order a rerun election. The CNE, however, refrained from acting on the matter, undoubtedly due to the presence of Miquilena loyalists (who were by then anti-*Chavista*) on the council.

The CTV's loss of prestige as a result of the eight-week general strike of 2002–2003 strengthened the position of those who favored a new confederation and influenced the thinking of Machuca and his allies. The Machuca group was particularly perplexed and angered by the CTV's prolonged alliance with FEDECAMARAS. Two months before the strike, a conference of *Chavista* trade unionists in Caracas in the presence of President Chávez voted down the proposition to create a new confederation. The soft-liners' thesis that the creation of a new confederation could not be "decreed from above" prevailed at the meeting. However, in contrast to the April 2002 coup, trade unionists played a key role in the effort to defeat the general strike of 2002–2003 by maintaining production in the oil industry, the CVG companies of the Guayana region, and other strategic sectors. This experience as well as the CTV's loss of prestige among rank-and-file workers informed the *Chavistas'* decision to break with the confederation (Chirino 2005, 10).

The Machuca group of soft-liners traveled throughout the country to lay the groundwork for the founding of the National Workers' Union (UNT). At this point, the major difference between Machuca's group and the hard-liners centered on the issue of timing. Soft-liners argued that only through a lengthy process of rank-and-file participation would a truly autonomous confederation be created. The soft-liners added that, until the UNT drafted electoral rules and proceeded to call union elections, confederation leaders should concentrate their efforts on recruiting individual trade unionists. At the same time, the soft-liners cautioned against forcing the issue of affiliation on the large number of unions that were still undecided in order to avoid dividing the entire labor movement into two camps. In contrast, the hard-liners maintained that the political situation in the country, specifically the imminence of another attempted overthrow of the government, required the immediate formation of a pro-*Chavista* workers' confederation with mobilization capacity.

In the weeks prior to the founding meeting of the UNT in April 2003, Machuca actively campaigned for the presidency of the new confederation. He argued that only with an "independent" like himself at the helm of the new confederation could it avoid being labeled an "official" trade union movement. He insisted that the UNT maintain a distance not only from the government and the MVR party, but also the official *Chavista* labor faction, the Bolivarian Workers' Force (FBT). At the UNT's April 2003 meeting, however, the FBT proposed a "horizontal" structure with a twenty-one-member national coordinating committee without a president or secretary-general. FBT leaders argued that such a structure should prevail until UNT elections were held in order to avoid discontent over the naming of a president. In one concession to soft-liners, FBT leaders dropped their insistence on calling Venezuela's new confederation "Bolivariano" (a term associated with Chávez and the MVR) and accepted the nonpartisan-sounding UNT name, which was originally proposed by the Machuca group.

The UNT's first congress held in August 2003 passed far-reaching resolutions that reflected the positions of *Chavista* radical hard-liners. The fledgling UNT advocated the nationalization of banks and rejected payment of the foreign debt. With regard to labor, the UNT called for worker control of companies that had been occupied by employees and the reduction of the work week, a proposal that had been put forward by *Chavista* trade unionists who served as deputies to the National Constituent Assembly in 1999.

In the period after the founding of the UNT, hard-liners split into two factions. A radical group headed by Orlando Chirino (which called itself the United, Revolutionary, Autonomous Class Current) insisted that, although workers wholeheartedly supported the government, political considerations should not hold them back from formulating just economic demands. A second, "political" current had close ties with the MVR and the government, particularly the Ministry of Labor, and followed a more pragmatic line. Indeed, Labor Minister José Ramón Rivero was a fromer trade unionist who was tied to the "political current." Chirino's group labeled the political current as well as the Machuca one "bureaucratic," claiming that their support for the UNT was motivated by thirst for positions within the new trade union structure.

The MVR rewarded the "political current" by naming several of its leading members candidates for national office while maintaining a distance from the Chirino current. Thus the party placed Angel Rodríguez, Maduro, and Khan, members of the "political" camp, on its slate for congressional elections in December 2005, while passing over Chirino (as it had Machuca the previous year in the gubernatorial elections in Bolívar). The MVR also selected Machuca ally Francisco Torrealba as well as UNT coordinator Marcela Máspero (who headed her own current that was situated between the Chirino leftist current and the "political" one) to form part of its congressional slate.

The three-way split also reflected itself in union elections and opened up opportunities for anti-*Chavista* trade unionists. Thus, for instance, in the steel workers' elections in November 2005, Machuca's slate retained control of the president and secretary-general positions, but the fragmentation of the *Chavistas* favored the opposition grouped in "Slate 99" and resulted in a highly divided union executive board.

The refusal of Chirino's group of hard-liners to allow political factors to interfere with the urgent tasks facing the labor movement manifested itself in the UNT in concrete ways. Thus Chirino insisted on the implementation of the old severance payment system as guaranteed by the 1999 Constitution based on the worker's last salary, which neoliberal-inspired legislation in 1997 had scrapped (see Chapter 4). Other *Chavistas* considered the new system a fait accompli that could not be rolled back without seriously straining the economy. Chirino also criticized the Chávez government's "unilateral" style of decreeing wage increases and other worker benefits without consulting labor leaders. Indeed, Chirino objected that the government occasionally conversed with FEDECAMARAS while virtually ignoring the UNT. As a corrective, the Chirino group called for a "social forum" involving the UNT, the peasant movement, and business and government representatives in accordance with the "participatory democracy" embodied in the 1999 Constitution (Corriente 2006). Chirino's followers also criticized the Labor Ministry for delaying legal recognition of the unions they formed while providing preferential treatment to those of the "political current."

In another demonstration of relative independence, the Chirino group was opposed to extending a special treatment to the state in the area of labor relations. On the contrary, Chirino insisted that the public administration set an example for the private sector by fulfilling its contractual and legal obligations and that it immediately negotiate contracts that had expired for state employees. In addition, the Chirino faction called for the elimination of temporary employment in the public administration as well as the use of nonpaid workers or "collaborators," who offered their services in hopes of being hired at a future date. Similarly, it warned against the violation of labor obligations by cooperatives that employ workers for limited periods of time.

The clashes among the *Chavista* factions culminated in a raucous confrontation at the Second UNT Congress held in May 2006 when the Chirino group separated from the rest of the confederation. The showdown was set off by the Chirino group's insistence that elections be held without delay for the UNT leadership. Chirino criticized the "political" current for having held up the electoral process even though the confederation had committed itself at the time of its founding in 2003 to holding elections within one year. At the Second Congress, representatives of the "political" current argued that elections should be put off until the following year so as not to detract from the effort to achieve the goal of ten million votes for Chávez in the December presidential elections. Chirino agreed on the importance of the ten-million-vote banner, but argued that to be politically effective the UNT had to "relegitimate" itself through internal elections. The insistence of Machuca's group that all workers of the formal economy, and not only unionized ones, have the right to vote in UNT elections generated controversy that also contributed to the delay.

After the UNT congress, the Chirino group announced its intentions of calling assemblies of workers in different sectors in order to "discuss and vote on the agreements approved at the Second Congress." In fact, these meetings were designed to force the issue of affiliation with the UNT on individual unions and, in cases in which that objective was not achieved, to create new parallel organizations. At the same time Chirino and his followers lashed out at the Machuca faction for failing to affiliate a single union with the new confederation (Corriente 2006).

Various positions defended by the three main factions within the *Chavista* labor movement correspond to the soft- and hard-line currents within *Chavismo* as a whole. Thus, for instance, Machuca's insistence on opening up the UNT elections to both organized and unorganized workers rather than concentrating on the working class vanguard implies a drawn-out process of winning over the entire working class and enrolling thousands of existing unions in the UNT prior to the new confederation's consolidation. Such a long-term approach coincides with the soft-line strategy within *Chavismo* in which gradual cultural transformation, specifically winning the battle of ideas, had to precede structural changes.

The differences between the Chirino group and the "political" current also fit into a larger context of political strategy. Chirino's insistence on forming new unions affiliated with the UNT coincides with the hard-line of the *Chavista* movement of promoting parallel structures. At the same time, the "political" current's deferment of the UNT's electoral contests in order to focus its efforts on the presidential elections of December 2006 accords with Chávez's strategy of carefully selecting targets rather than striking out on different fronts at the same time.

▶ **The Oil Industry**

The hard- and soft-liners upheld different interpretations of the events surrounding the 2002–2003 general strike in the oil industry and followed distinct approaches. Hard-liners harshly criticized PDVSA president Alí Rodríguez, one of the main soft-liners in the government, for his leniency toward pro-opposition company employees before, during, and after the strike. In the months between the coup and the general strike, Rodríguez refrained from taking measures against PDVSA executives openly identified with the opposition who were planning the December shutdown, and he failed to develop contingency plans for the alleged sabotage perpetrated by the strikers. The hard-liners also pointed out that Rodríguez hesitated to fire company rebels, even after the strike was well underway, and invited them to return to work even when it was evident that the work stoppage had been defeated.

The general strike brought to the fore an issue that had been discussed within the *Chavista* movement from the outset of Chávez's presidency, namely the need to weed out unreliable employees from the public sector. The hard-liners were suspicious of employees who had entered the state sector before 1998, which was imbued with inefficiency and corruption, and claimed that many of them represented a "fifth column" within the public administration under Chávez. Given the sharp polarization in Venezuela, a real possibility existed that some public employees were passing internal information to the media and opposition parties, that they were systematically demoralizing fellow workers, and that they were committing sabotage on the job.

The issue of selection of personnel in the state sector assumed special importance in the oil industry where the stakes were high owing to superior wages, making employment particularly attractive, and due to its strategic importance for the economy. Occasionally, hard-line trade unionists objected to the excess presence of foreigners in the industry, a tendency that had been promoted by the Oil Opening (Apertura Petrolera) of the neoliberal years of the 1990s. As a result of the general strike, PDVSA fired eighteen thousand employees, mostly from its white-collar staff, on grounds that they had engaged in a criminal paralysis of the industry, including sabotage. Hard-line *Chavistas*, however, insisted on the complete purge of the oil industry. They warned that many PDVSA ex-employees were attempting to work their way back into the industry by seeking employment from contractor firms in other locations, a practice that PDVSA's new managers failed to act against. At the same time, the hard-liners raised the specter of another oil workers' strike. In private, hard-liners claimed that theft of key parts of oil installations formed part of a plan to damage the industry for political purposes, a campaign that government spokesmen generally refrained from commenting on.

The publication of the list of those who in late 2003 signed the petition in favor of a presidential recall election unleashed another controversy regarding the presence of anti-*Chavistas* in the public administration. Labor Minister María Cristina Iglesias repudiated the statement by Minister of Health Roger Capella that those who signed the petition should not be working for his ministry. PDVSA president Alí Rodríguez, for his part, denied that the job security of nearly one thousand company employees who had signed against Chávez was in danger. Nevertheless, in many cases PDVSA refused to grant employees who signed the petition and worked for contractor firms permission to enter the premises of its installations. Following the recall election in August 2004, Chávez announced that regardless of whether discrimination against those who had signed against him had been justified in the past, "the list should now be buried" ("Aló Presidente" [TV program], April 17, 2005).

For over fifty years, the oil workers' unions had been given the right to hire a certain percentage of employees in the industry, reaching 80 percent in 1973 and subsequently reduced to 60 percent. The practice of union hiring came under widespread criticism for fostering corruption and clientelism. Under the Chávez presidency, neighborhood groups in surrounding areas became increasingly active in pressuring firms to hire their members and were given a major input after union leaders temporarily relinquished their hiring rights in the collective bargaining agreement of 2000. In succeeding years, some labor and community leaders vociferously asserted their loyalty to the government cause in hopes of being granted hiring privileges. Thus, for instance, a relatively small oil workers' federation, the Federation of Workers of the Hydrocarbons Industry (FETRAHIDROCARBUROS), which for decades had been allied with AD trade unionists, strengthened its hand by switching over to support for the Chávez government. Community groups also saw their positions enhanced as a result of their unyielding efforts to keep the industry open during the 2002–2003 general strike.[4]

Following the general strikes of 2001 to 2003, all with the aim of toppling the government, pro-*Chavista* union and community leaders used three arguments in favor of their participation in the hiring process. The first was pragmatic, namely that those who resisted the general strikes had proved their loyalty to the cause and could thus best be trusted to keep the industry running and avoid another politically inspired strike and sabotage. Second, the *Chavistas* maintained that they should be rewarded for the sacrifice and heroism they displayed during the two-month strike. Third, the participation of pro-*Chavista* union and community representatives in the hiring of employees was viewed as an affirmation of the concept of "participatory democracy" that was enshrined in the 1999 Constitution.

The use of political criteria for employment purposes undoubtedly undermined labor discipline and productivity and lent itself to clientelistic practices. In light of these concerns, the soft line represented by Alí Rodríguez supported a more flexible approach. Soft-liners claimed that many employees had gone along with the strike because they were pressured by their superiors and company executives who warned that those who stayed on the job would be fired once Chávez was removed from office. Furthermore, technical and professional personnel, who represented the bulk of the eighteen thousand who were dismissed, had received extensive training at home and abroad, financed by the Venezuelan state, and thus the industry was about to forfeit considerable skill and experience.

These arguments influenced PDVSA to modify its decision to expel all eighteen thousand workers from the entire industry and instead to accept the employment of some of them by contractor firms. Furthermore, concerned about the decline in productivity, PDVSA adopted the System of Employment Democratization (SISDEM) in early 2005 in an effort to depoliticize the hiring process. The SISDEM created a data bank and used a computer to select employees that best met job description requirements while giving special consideration to residents of surrounding areas. For the second time, PDVSA convinced the unions to give up their right to hire 60 percent of the workers. Worker enrollment in the SISDEM was free of charge and thus eliminated the illegal union practice of charging commissions from those seeking employment in the industry. Under the SISDEM, union and community groups were allowed to monitor the selection process, a practice known as "social controllership" (*contraloría social*), in order to detect abuses. By 2006, the hard-liners identified with Orlando Chirino, who called for a truly autonomous UNT, insisted on the effective activation of the social controllership to correct the new forms of clientelism that the SISDEM had allegedly created.

A second area of differences in the strategies of the hard- and soft-line currents centered on the transformation of the oil industry. The hard-liners claimed that both skilled and unskilled oil workers demonstrated their capacity to run the industry as well as their loyalty to the

Chávez government during the two-month general strike, at a time when most high-ranking PDVSA employees had walked off the job. Taking into consideration this display of capability and commitment, hard-liners advocated the implementation of *cogestión* (or joint decisionmaking) by opening up debate over company policy to the entire work force. Along these lines, they proposed calling an assembly of oil workers, referred to as a *constituyente petrolera* (petroleum constituent assembly), in order to reach major decisions for the industry.

PDVSA rewarded union leaders who had helped keep the industry open during the 2002–2003 general strike by naming Rafael Rosales of FEDEPETROL and Nelson Nuñez of SINUTRAPETROL to seats on the company's board of directors. *Chavista* trade unionists pointed out that these appointments represented an important advance over the previous practice (dating back to 1966) of selecting for state company boards labor representatives who were completely lacking in experience in the respective industry. Nevertheless, the hard-liners insisted that the labor representatives on company boards be elected by the workers and not chosen by the union's top leadership (as occurred after 1966) or by company executives (as was the case with Rosales and Nuñez).

In the immediate aftermath of the 2002–2003 general strike, oil trade unionists pressured PDVSA to grant workers input in decision-making. Subsequently, however, company executives rejected the proposition and began to exert tighter control over the industry. PDVSA heads adhered to a view, which the hard-liners labeled "technocratic," that the oil industry should avoid the types of worker participation being established in other state-controlled sectors due to its overwhelming importance to the nation's economy. One example of the backlash among PDVSA executives was the implementation of the SISDEM, in which management reasserted control over the hiring process. In addition, when Rosales's and Nuñez's terms on PDVSA's board expired, they were replaced by non–trade unionists. PDVSA heads (as well as some MVR leaders) pointed out that Rosales and Nuñez had failed to live up to expectations and instead had used their influence only to benefit individual workers in the form of clientelistic arrangements.

Following the 2002–2003 general strike, industry leaders coined the slogan "PDVSA Now Is Everybody's" to indicate that the company that was formerly a "state within the state" now served national interests and was committed to social programs. The soft-liners pointed to the slogan as evidence that further transformation of the industry was not in order, and that the main challenge now was to consolidate it in order to guarantee stable production and confidence. Consolidation in the wake of the far-reaching changes of the Chávez presidency was the essence of the *Chavista* soft-line strategy in general, which contrasted with the steady deepening of the "revolutionary process" advocated by hard-liners.

▶ The MVR Party

Between the campaign for the presidential elections of 1998 and the radicalization in 2001, Chávez's emphasis on political reforms and the constituent assembly over structural economic change allowed him to attract moderates to his movement. Among them were the allies of MVR's general director Luis Miquilena, who represented the party's soft line, as well as MAS and two of the nation's leading constitutional lawyers.[5] Many of the moderates had campaigned for thorough political transformation over a period of several decades. Thus Miquilena had been a prominent member of the Frente Patriótico (Patriotic Front) founded in 1990, which lobbied for constitutional change, while MAS had stressed political over socioeconomic reforms since the 1970s. In addition, the soft-liners such as MVR*istas* Miquilena and Alejandro Armas opposed the social reforms put forward by party labor leaders. This legislation included the reduction of the work week from forty-four to forty hours and the state's reassertion of control of the social security system (which had been privatized under Caldera). The Miquilena group also denied that the 1999 Constitution mandated the return to the old system of severance payment, in which compensation was calculated on the basis of the worker's last monthly salary. (To this day, the old system of severance payment, which had always been anathema to the business sector, continues to be an explosive issue, as the soft-liners consider it impractical and particularly onerous for small- and medium-size businesses as well as the state.)

In addition to political reforms and economic legislation, a more complex socioeconomic structural issue lay behind the differences between the soft- and hard-line currents, even after the exit of Miquilena and his allies from the MVR in 2002. The soft-liners have favored alliances or understandings with well-established economic groups while the hard-liners would have *Chavismo* eschew any such formal or informal agreement—a strategic dilemma that the left also faces elsewhere in Latin America (Alvarez Béjar 2006, 28). In opposing ties with business interests, the hard-line *Chavistas* point to the example of AD, which following its founding in 1941 was committed to leftist ideals. AD's alliance with the national bourgeoisie and eventual incorporation of representatives of that class in the party leadership and the government led to the abandonment of far-reaching goals and was conducive to widespread corruption.

In contrast, Miquilena, who was closely linked to various economic interest groups, advocated a strategy of establishing party ties with "progressive" or "honest" capitalists (Miquilena 2000). The proposal was one facet of an all-encompassing strategy originally designed by the Communist movement (of which Miquilena had been a prominent dissident member in the 1940s) based on a two-stage revolutionary process for underdeveloped nations. In an initial "anti-imperialist" revolution, the left allied itself with the national or "progressive" bourgeoisie to achieve "national liberation" consisting of independent economic development, democracy, and agrarian reform, which were prerequisites for a second socialist revolution. Although the soft-liners did not explicitly embrace the two-stage thesis, it undoubtedly influenced those *Chavistas* who favored developing close relations with well-established business sectors.

The case of Miquilena appeared to confirm the rightward drift of leftist politicians who maintain ties with the private sector and the tendency of business allies to parlay their political influence into unethical gains. Miquilena, who headed the financial department of Chávez's first presidential campaign, worked closely with a business partner, Tobías Carrero, both before and after leaving the *Chavista* movement. Carrero invested heavily in the *Chavista* electoral campaigns and even provided Chávez with private airplane transportation. In return, Carrero's printing company, Micabú, and the insurance company Multinacional de Seguros (of which he was president) received state contracts that became the center of national scandals implicating Miquilena, who held top government positions at the time. In another revelation, the Argentine branch of Spain's Bilbao Vizcaya Bank made financial contributions to Chávez (as it did the other presidential candidates in 1998) through one of Carrero's companies located in Aruba. Bilbao Vizcaya was undoubtedly intent on benefiting from the plans for the privatization of the social security system supported by the soft-liners.

After radicalization got under way in 2001, the hard-liners rejected formal agreements with the business sector and denied that any of the large economic groups would ever be won over to the process of change currently underway in Venezuela (Pérez Martí 2004). Although local *Chavista* elected officials maintained informal ties with the business sector, they were apparently not as close or of the same proportion as when Miquilena headed the party.

Following the coup attempt of April 2002, retired air force officer and ex–foreign minister Luis Alfonso Dávila succeeded Miquilena as head of the soft-line current. In the MVR's internal elections held the following year, the hard-liners elected fifty-one of the sixty members of the party's amplified national committee (the National Strategic Direction). Even though the pro- and anti-Dávila currents were referred to as "right" and "left," respectively, issues of political substance were not aired, and thus the *Chavista* movement lost the opportunity to engage in a much needed formal ideological debate. In spite of its conclusive victory in the internal elections, the "leftist" current (headed by William Lara) failed to gain control of the MVR's top position of general director, which went to another retired officer, Francisco Ameliach. Chávez persuaded the party's national convention to vote for Ameliach in accordance with the *Chavista* policy of privileging military officers as part of the strategy of the "civilian-military" alliance—a keystone of the movement since its origin in the 1980s. In effect, the approach signifies a disproportionate presence of *Chavista* military officers at the higher levels of the government and movement. The *Chavista* officers are less inclined to support far-reaching social transformation than the hard-liners and insist on obedience and discipline within the movement. The preferential treatment granted to a sector of the MVR holds back clarification of positions through mechanisms of internal debate and rank-and-file decision-making, thus contributing to the *Chavista* movement's ideological vagueness.

Even though the two main successive leaders of the soft-line were clearly defeated within the movement, resulting in the exit of one (Miquilena) and the marginalization of the other (Dávila), that current continues to represent a major point of reference for *Chavismo*. Important leaders both in and outside of the MVR, as well as in the labor movement, defend soft-line positions. Various officers who were elected governors in 2004, led by Diosdado Cabello of Miranda (formerly Chávez's vice president), became identified with the soft-line current, as did the PPT and Podemos. It is natural that the soft line continues to have a following, even with ongoing radicalization and the exit of its most visible leaders, because no consensus has emerged within the party over long-term goals and particularly positions toward private property. Following Dávila's withdrawal from his leadership position in 2003, distinct strategies toward the parallel structures created or supported by the state emerged as the most important issue separating the hard and soft lines.

▶ Parallel Structures Promoted by the State

Chavista hard-liners adamantly defend the creation of parallel structures in the state sector, the economy, civil society, and the communications media. The relations between new and old structures point to an important source of conflict. Soft-liners consider new structures as complementary to old ones and designed to shake them up and revitalize them. In contrast, hard-liners maintain that existing structures have been thoroughly penetrated by clientelistic parties and are riddled by corruption and inefficiency, and thus favor a clean break with the past. They are convinced that in the course of the "revolutionary process" the old structures will become increasingly unviable. Furthermore, hard-liners consider the creation of new structures a strategic necessity in that they are instruments to face insurgency and disruptions generated by the opposition. In spite of this sense of urgency, hard-liners share the general *Chavista* vision of a peaceful democratic revolution that requires toleration and acceptance of existing structures, at least for the time being.

The distinct goals envisioned by soft-liners and hard-liners for the government food retail program MERCAL reveal the differences in positions on parallel structures. Soft-liners, who support the ongoing coexistence of old and new structures and a basically harmonious relationship between them, viewed MERCAL, at least at the time of its initiation, as a simple mechanism to counter price increases. Indeed, the tacit threat of competition from MERCAL has allowed the government to negotiate price agreements with supermarket chains. In contrast, hard-liners emphasize a more ambitious function, namely providing Venezuela with "food security" to counter threats of scarcity, such as occurred during the 2002–2003 general strike when business groups withdrew essential products from the market and throughout 2007 when they attempted to pressure the government into accepting price increases on regulated products. This more far-reaching goal implies aggressive plans to increase capacity and forcefully compete with the private sector. Along these lines, MERCAL claimed by 2005 that over 50 percent of its merchandise was purchased from national companies, nine hundred of which were cooperatives (*Vea* [Caracas], June 17, 2005, 18).

MERCAL's expansion went beyond what soft-liners had envisioned at the time of its creation in 2003. Its diversification of food sources was designed to avoid food dependence on national "oligopolistic" suppliers that could have become a major political liability, according to the thinking of hard-liners. By 2006, MERCAL counted on fifteen thousand food outlets as well as a network of warehouses, silos, and a state food company, CASA, whose products contain labels with political messages and information about Venezuelan history. MERCAL stores are concentrated in lower-class areas, thus guaranteeing food supply in emergency situations to the underprivileged sectors, which represent the government's social base of support. Ironically, diversification of supplies in practice has been achieved through imports from other Latin American countries, as is the case with MERCAL's two most sought-after products: powdered milk, mostly bought from Argentina; and chicken, which at first was largely imported from Brazil, although by 2006 about 50 percent was purchased from local farms. Government policy prioritizes purchases from cooperatives and other small- and medium-sized producers. Nevertheless, MERCAL is heavily dependent on large corporations for packaged items. In short, MERCAL has made important advances in fulfilling the hard-line goal of severing food dependency for security and political reasons, but success is ultimately contingent on the government's ability to promote small-scale agricultural production.

The Chávez government's policy toward national security has also generated discussion within the *Chavista* movement over the role of parallel structures. The concept of the civilian-military alliance, as embodied in the Organic Law of the Armed Forces passed in September 2005, posited civilian input in, and responsibility for, national defense, which was consequently no longer the exclusive preserve of the armed forces. In an attempt to prepare for the perceived threat of a US invasion, Chávez reactivated the national military reserve, which formerly consisted of retired officers but was virtually nonexistent. The newly formed reserve incorporates volunteers from all walks of life between the ages of eighteen and fifty with the aim of reaching a membership of two million. According to the new law, the national reserve answers directly to the president and functions outside the Ministry of Defense. Nevertheless, Chávez named a general to the top position of general director of the reserve, who upon retirement the following year was replaced by another active officer. This link with the armed forces places limits on the reserve's autonomy.

Chavista hard-liners Alberto Müller Rojas and Eliécer Otaiza, both retired army officers and national leaders of *Chavista* political parties, view the national reserve as a counterbalance to the armed forces, which guarantees that another military coup will not occur (*El Universal*, February 6, 2007). Müller Rojas and Otaiza argue that even though the armed forces fulfilled its progressive role at the time of the April 2002 coup, it continues to be intricately tied to the old system and that the institution's "revolutionary faction" represents a minority of its officers. In accordance with the hard-line strategy regarding parallel structures, they consider the national reserve as an important actor in its own right and not a mere complement to the old structure (the armed forces). In April 2005, Otaiza set off public controversy by proposing that anti-US attitudes form part of the doctrinal formation of military personnel.

In an even more polemical statement, Müller Rojas in mid-2007 advocated the right of officers to engage in party politics. Chávez rejected the proposition and called on Müller Rojas, who at the time was an active duty officer and was organizing the PSUV throughout the country, to retire from the army in order to continue his political work. Müller Rojas claimed that large numbers of active officers were already participating in party politics and that Chávez himself favored the legalization of this activity but in a more gradual and "discreet" form (Müller Rojas 2007, 22–23). By favoring the breakdown of distinctions between civilian and military arenas beyond the right of officers to vote (which was established in the Constitution of 1999), Müller Rojas's proposal was seen as intentionally or inadvertently weakening the hierarchical control of the "old structure," namely the armed forces.

Another hard-liner, Iris Varela, called for a purge of the armed forces to rid it of disloyal members (similar to what the hard line favors for the entire public administration). Varela blamed them for the escape of CTV president Carlos Ortega in August 2006 from the military prison in Los Teques, where he was held for having engaged in "civil rebellion" in the form of the general strike of 2002–2003. Varela, who pointed out that the prison was high security, concluded that the escape formed part of a "conspiratorial plan involving military officers well rooted in the armed forces" (from a speech presented to the National Assembly, August 15, 2006).

The conflictive relations and lack of coordination between new and old structures reinforce the hard-line argument on the need to prioritize the former and to work toward the eventual displacement of the latter. Thus, for instance, the Venezuelan medical establishment attempted to prohibit Cuban doctors from practicing medicine on grounds that their university degrees had not been validated by the professional association Colegio de Médicos. Furthermore, many physicians in public hospitals, at least at first, refused to accept patients remitted by Cuban doctors working in the Barrio Adentro Mission. This lack of cooperation convinced the government to expand the mission program by creating a new parallel structure in the form of the popular clinics called Barrio Adentro II, which function alongside the public hospitals.

Similarly, the minister of education has been unable to enlist the support of the autonomous universities in the campaigns sponsored by the educational missions and to implement related policies, such as special admission standards for underprivileged students and outreach programs in poor communities. Tension also exists between the innovative university programs initiated by the Chávez government and established institutions of higher education. New educational undertakings include the Sucre Mission, the training of fifteen thousand Venezuelan medical students in Cuba, and the program for Venezuelan doctors who work in the Barrio Adentro Mission and are expected to enroll in graduate courses taught by Cuban doctors. Students in these programs run the risk of having their newly earned degrees go unrecognized as a result of the stigma in certain circles attached to the education missions, due both to their lower standards and the politically driven resentment against Cuban doctors (Jardim 2005, 37). To overcome this liability, the government has reached agreements with universities under the jurisdiction of the Ministry of Higher Education (particularly the Universidad Rómulo Gallegos) whereby these schools are given a supervisory role in the program (particularly with regard to exams) while permitting the diplomas to be issued in their name. The nation's larger "autonomous" universities, which are politically controlled by the opposition, have refused to participate in these efforts. This intransigence bolsters the hard-line argument on the need to strengthen and extend parallel structures.

The hard-liners argue that the missions and related government programs, rather than representing stopgap measures to ameliorate social problems, form an essential part of the transformation of the economic system. Thus, for instance, Vuelvan Caras (known as the "mission of missions"), with the participation of the Ministry of the Community Economy, provides job training to graduates of other missions. These efforts are aimed at encouraging the formation of cooperatives and other enterprises to perform much needed tasks at the local level. Furthermore, several newly created state lending agencies including the Woman's Bank and the People's Bank have facilitated the formation of thousands of nascent firms by providing start-up credit with special terms for repayment. Finally, PDVSA and other state companies organize training sessions for cooperatives and give them preferential treatment in the bidding of contracts.

The emergence of a bloc of state-aided small- and medium-sized businesses and cooperatives is of fundamental importance due to its implications for the hard-line and soft-line approaches. These nascent enterprises belong to parallel organizations (such as the pro-*Chavista*

Confederation of Agriculturalists and Cattlemen, and the more politically independent Federation of Macro, Small and Medium-sized Businessmen—Fedeindustria), which are at odds with the main business organization, FEDECAMARAS. The *Chavistas* claim that by encouraging the proliferation of companies the anti-FEDECAMARAS bloc contributes to the goal of the "democratization of capital" and points in the direction of a new economic model. They also claim that the competition provided by parallel structures, such as MERCAL and newly created state banks, undermines the monopoly control of the economy and consequently helps combat inflation.

Just as in the case of other parallel structures, hard- and soft-liners uphold distinct views toward the relationship between the emerging enterprises, on the one hand, and large traditional capitalist groups, on the other. Hard-liners deny that the traditional business sector will ever be willing to support or even adapt to the process of change and foresee their eventual replacement by the new bloc. In contrast, soft-liners argue that traditional capitalists are not inveterate enemies of the process of change and that their anti-government behavior is just a temporary reaction to their loss of direct influence over those in power (Barreto 2004).

The differences in attitudes toward the private sector particularly manifest themselves at the state and municipal levels with respect to the granting of contracts for public works and similar activity. Soft-liners support tacit alliances with local interest groups that receive contracts and contribute to *Chavista* political activity, including electoral campaigns. Their basic argument is pragmatic: As long as corrupt practices are avoided, the special relationship with certain economic interests is legitimate and a logical strategy that furthers the interests of the *Chavista* movement. In addition, since 2005 the soft-liners have argued that because the transition to socialism in Venezuela is to be gradual, capitalist and socialist structures have to coexist and the government, while nurturing small non-oligopolistic enterprises, cannot spurn larger capitalist ones.

The hard-liners oppose any strategy that favors select business interests in any way. They view businessmen who have attempted to cement ties with the government as opportunists who will abandon the *Chavista* movement as soon as it appears to be losing strength. Indeed, hard-liners point out that in some cases these same business interests were formerly tied to AD and COPEI. Furthermore, hard-liners argue that the practice of favoring specific economic groups undermines the policy of "democratization of capital," which in effect privileges cooperatives and other small-scale producers. Finally, they view any special relationship with business groups as tantamount to corruption, thus helping explain why many rank-and-file *Chavistas* are convinced that unethical behavior is rampant in the public administration (as discussed in Chapter 7).

Differences in attitudes were also reflected in the cabinet debate over the authorization of dollars at preferential exchange rates to those companies that participated in the two-month general strike. Hard-liners called for discriminatory treatment against local capitalists who had joined the opposition, invoking Chávez's warning "Ni un dolar mas para los golpistas" (Not one more dollar for the coup supporters). In contrast, soft-liners are opposed to taking reprisals against businessmen identified with the opposition. In addition, they point to the possibility that the dialogue occasionally established with capitalist groups such as textile companies (which supported the government's import restrictions) and banks can be transformed into tactical and even strategic agreements at a future date (Pérez Martí 2004). Along these lines, the soft-liners point to the example of Gustavo Cisernos who, having played a major role in the 2002 coup, met with Chávez in a meeting arranged by Jimmy Carter in June 2004, after which the famed Venezuelan capitalist "made his peace" with the government, as evidenced by the even-handed news treatment on the part of his TV channel, Venevisión.

▶ Populism and the Rank and File of the *Chavista* Movement

This chapter has pointed to the paradox of a movement committed to radical change that stops short of any systematic attempt to define its long-term goals. The *Chavistas*, in their ideological vagueness and lack of mechanisms of ideological debate, resemble the radical populism that emerged in Latin America in the 1930s and 1940s. Prominent examples of these movements are *Peronismo* in Argentina, the followers of Getúlio Vargas in Brazil, and AD in Venezuela.

Chavismo converges with radical populism in other respects as well. Similarities include anti-elite discourse, the lack of a well-developed political organization, support for a strong state role in the economy, and stands that set off a harsh reaction from the right resulting in political and social polarization. As in the case of *Chavismo*, some scholars have questioned simplistic notions regarding the caudillo-masses relationship that allegedly characterized radical populist movements. Indeed, over the last several decades, a number of historians have reexamined radical

populism and reached the conclusion that its organizational and ideological weakness and its rejection of class struggle were relative. They
imply or argue that had reaction not set in against the populist-led governments of the 1940s and 1950s, these shortcomings may well have
been addressed and overcome (James 2000; French 1992; for the
Venezuelan *trienio* case see Ellner 1982; 1992; 1999c).

Important aspects of the Chávez phenomenon, even more so than in
the case of the populist experiences of the 1930s and 1940s, disprove
stereotypes of movements characterized as radical populist, particularly
simplistic notions that deny commitment to democracy, ideological clarification, institutionalization, and far-reaching change. Since reaching
power, the *Chavistas* have shown signs of recognizing the importance
of, and have taken steps to promote, ideological clarification and organizational solidification. In 2005, for instance, Chávez raised the banner
of "socialism," a term that, albeit ill-defined, clearly spells out the
movement's rejection of the existing capitalist system and the need to
develop an alternative model.[6] By hosting the World Social Forum in
2006 and announcing an ideological congress for 2007, the *Chavista*
leadership demonstrated that it is aware of the urgency of formal ideological debate. Furthermore, concern for the organizational weakness of
the *Chavista* movement influenced MVR leader William Lara to propose converting the MVR into an "organic party" with links to social
movements and eventually led to the creation of the PSUV. Finally,
while populist movements were generally known to play down class
confrontation and instead appeal to "national unity," Chávez's discourse
has a more conflictive social content. From the outset of his presidency,
both his words and actions have explicitly favored the popular classes at
the expense of privileged sectors and have made clear that politics in
Venezuela has become a zero-sum game that pits one against the other.[7]

The role and attitudes of the *Chavista* movement's rank and file also
diverge from the image of a caudillo-led populist movement. Many of
the rank and file hold a critical attitude toward the parties of the governing coalition and reject vertical forms of control originating from party
leadership. These *Chavista* "independents" see themselves as representing the "will of the people" free of institutional constraints.

The position of the rank-and-file "independents" and Chávez's rhetoric empowering the nonprivileged are conducive to far-reaching
change and would thus seem to coincide with the strategies of the hard-
line current of *Chavismo*. Nevertheless, in practice the rank-and-file
independents reject the political party hegemony defended by both hard-
and soft-liners and instead view social organizations as being the ideal

representatives of the nonprivileged sectors that form the backbone of the *Chavista* movement. Thus any thorough analysis of internal conflict in the *Chavista* movement must situate itself at two levels: soft versus hard lines, and party versus rank-and-file strategies. The following chapter will discuss this second dimension involving party and horizontal approaches. The examination of both sources of internal tension and conflict demonstrates the complexity of the Chávez phenomenon and the superficiality of the writing on *Chavismo* that portrays the movement's rank and file as an uncritical mass.

▶ Notes

1. Chávez himself has been criticized for dwelling on the social cause of delinquency and failing to express sufficient concern for the lack of personal security on the streets, an issue that was exploited by the opposition during the 2006 presidential campaign.

2. The soft-line current in organized labor, for instance, argues that the formation of *Chavista* unions cannot be imposed from above but rather has to await a gradual process of winning over a large majority of the workers to a new style of trade unionism.

3. Another expression of voluntarism in the early stages of socialist revolutions in nations such as Cuba has been the emphasis on moral over material incentives. In addition to voluntarism, Chávez's "ultraleftism" has been exemplified by his aggressive language and threats against various international actors, such as in the case of his confrontation with Peru's Alan García, as will be discussed in Chapter 8.

4. The key role played by local residents who protected oil installations against the threat of sabotage and civil disobedience was demonstrated when PDVSA's anti-*Chavista* employees in some areas demanded their removal as a condition for lifting the strike.

5. Hermann Escarrá and Ricardo Combellas, both constitutional experts and academicians, were elected delegates to the Constituent Assembly on the Chávez ticket, but defected from the movement at the time of the ratification of the Constitution. As head of the Presidential Commission for State Reform (COPRE) under the second Caldera government, Combellas prioritized constitutional reform over other types of legislation.

6. After 2005, Chávez ceased using the term "savage capitalism," a term that implied the possibility of achieving a desirable alternative, namely "humanitarian capitalism."

7. Carles Muntaner (2005) refers to my writing on the *Chavista* movement as an example of a "common apologetic practice . . . to undermine the socialist underpinnings of the Bolivarian process with the 'populist' label." He adds that "following cold war habits, a major concern of the US left is still avoiding any association with regimes that might be labeled 'Communist.'" He concludes by saying: "Given the recent history of interference of our country [the US] with Venezuelan politics . . . writers on the left can help the Bolivarian process with

objective reporting or humble supportive analyses. Or they can leave Venezuelans alone." In fact, by no stretch of the imagination can Venezuela until now be labeled "communist" or "socialist." Comparative analysis that establishes similarities with past governments such as those of Perón and AD during the *trienio* is valid and contributes to an understanding of the challenges facing *Chavismo*. Although populism is sometimes employed pejoratively, political scientists have used the concept to refer to characteristics that have complex implications and indeed overlap with many of the salient features of *Chavismo*, particularly during its early years in power. Finally, Muntaner does little service to the cause of far-reaching change by calling on social scientists to refrain from developing critical analyses of leftist movements in countries other than their own.

7

▼

The Chávez Movement's Top-Down and Grassroots Approaches

AN ANALYSIS of developments in Venezuela under the Chávez presidency sheds light on the viability of policies, movements, and struggles in developing countries designed to bring about far-reaching transformation and to challenge domination from the north. Throughout the third world, these types of political contestation have been initiated from "above" and from "below": by the state and political parties that seek to obtain and retain power (from above) and by social movements and unorganized sectors of the population (from below). The first strategy, traditionally called "anti-imperialist," leads to the assertion of sovereignty by third-world governments and their formation of a bloc of nations around common demands and goals. With this in mind, the traditional Latin American left promoted "revolutions of national liberation" whereby a government linked to an institutionalized political party, a powerful labor movement, and sometimes a progressive national business sector played an interventionist role in the economy and confronted foreign economic interests. Prior to the outset of globalization in the 1980s, nearly all those who supported far-reaching political change defended a statist (or "top-down") strategy along these lines.

A second, grassroots approach centers on horizontal relationships that arise outside of well-established organized structures, often in the form of social movements, which are horizontally connected, internally democratic, and more loosely structured than political parties. The champions of this paradigm have been identified with various related schools of thinking. One of them originating in Europe and then extending to Latin America in the 1980s celebrated loosely structured "new social movements," which they claim have replaced trade unions

175

and political parties as the most effective and transformational interlocutors of the general population in modern (or "postindustrial") society (Evers 1985). A "postmodernist" school also glorifies popular movements and at the same time views broad sectors of the population whose daily lives clash with the logic of the established system (what one work calls the "multitude") as potentially more revolutionary than any political party (Hardt and Negri 2004). These writers rule out forceful government assertion of independence as unfeasible due to global constraints and the danger of international isolation. They also consider statist strategies by nature hierarchical and thus possessing of a limited potential to effect meaningful and far-reaching change (Robinson 2004, 141–142).

The dichotomy between the two approaches within the *Chavista* movement is best defined by the attitudes of its members toward political parties. Those who belong to and closely identify with the main parties of the governing coalition, specifically the MVR, PPT, and Podemos, share the statist approach adhered to by all three political organizations. *Chavistas* who are independent of political parties, and particularly those who are critical of the MVR, PPT, and Podemos, adhere to the grassroots strategy, which spurns vertical political structures. Participation by these independents in *Chavista* social movements or government programs has served as a substitute for party membership as a means of cementing ties and promoting a sense of identification with *Chavismo*.

Unlike the case of other governments committed to revolutionary change, during the eight years of the Chávez presidency those participating in and promoting both approaches have coexisted within the *Chavista* movement with neither one gaining the upper hand. Throughout this period Chávez has given encouragement to both sides at the same time that he has attempted to define the limits of acceptable behavior for the two of them. This chapter will trace the evolution of the two strategies and the actors who defend each one, as well as their discourse, the tension that has arisen between them, and the major issues of contention.

▶ The Two Approaches During the Early Years

One of the salient features of the rank and file of the *Chavista* movement that characterizes those favoring the grassroots approach is the resentment toward local government officials as well as the leaders of the main parties of the governing coalition. These *Chavistas* view their nonmembership in political parties as proof that they are selfless and completely dedicated to the cause, while sometimes expressing the conviction that those in party positions are by definition self-serving and in some cases corrupt. They also insist that their proposals be transmitted directly to state decisionmakers without being held up by intermediary organizations such as political parties.

Distrust of political parties by the *Chavistas* dates back to the early years of the movement. Prior to the 1992 coup, relations between Chávez's MBR-200 and several political parties of the far left were characterized by mutual tensions. Parties such as the Party of the Venezuelan Revolution (PRV), led by Douglas Bravo and the Bandera Roja, were wary of the militarist thrust of the MBR-200, while Chávez resented the strategy promoted by Bravo of utilizing the military rebels to further his party's interests. Following the coup, Chávez criticized the Causa R for taking advantage of his group's prestige by attempting to include the names of various military rebels who were in prison in that party's slates (Raby 2006, 149–155; Harnecker 2005, 38). Chávez embraced an antiparty discourse during the 1998 presidential race when, more than the other candidates, he lashed out at the ruling clique of the nation's political parties and the National Congress that they controlled. Thus, for instance, during the campaign Chávez stated, "[I]f we defeat the political parties, if we defeat [electoral] fraud . . . then a Congress which opposes the call for a constituent assembly . . . should be swept away" (Blanco Muñoz 1998, 545).

The Constitution of 1999 attempted to curb political party hegemony and transfer power to social movements in accordance with the grassroots approach. As a corrective to the inordinate power of party elites, the Constitution promoted the concept of "participatory democracy" and called on the state to "facilitate" popular input in decisionmaking (article 62). It also cut off subsidies to political parties and obliged them to hold internal elections for selection of candidates and for leadership positions (article 67). Finally, participatory democracy was exemplified by the role played by social movements in presenting as many as 624 proposals to the Constituent Assembly, over half of which were incorporated into the new Constitution. The Constituent Assembly was particularly receptive to proposals formulated by human rights organizations (García Guadilla 2003, 186–187, 195; McCaughan 2004, 60).

Although 1999 to 2001 was a moderate stage, the most fervent rank-and-file *Chavistas* defended the concept of "radical democracy," which represents the grassroots approach in its pure form. Radical democracy

not only promotes the creation of mechanisms for direct popular participation. It actually ensures that their decisions are binding and that they
take precedence over or displace representative institutions such as the
Congress and political parties.

This style of democracy was defended by *Chavista* members of the
National Assembly's Citizen Participation Commission, which worked
for legislation of popular assemblies. In addition, since the birth of the
MVR, several national leaders, including Senator William Izarra,
favored conferring basic decisionmaking power for the organization on
party assemblies at the neighborhood level. Luis Miquilena opposed the
proposal on grounds that pressing political tasks made it impractical
(Izarra 2001, 130).

Aspects of the radical version of participatory democracy proved
inoperative in detriment to the grassroots approach. Proposals, for
instance, for holding "assemblies of citizens" whose decisions were to
be binding according to article 70 of the Constitution, were never successfully implemented. At the time, the call for "constituent assemblies"
in the labor movement, the universities, and the oil industry to discuss
the transformation of those institutions became a *Chavista* rallying cry,
but the idea failed to materialize.

At the Universidad Central de Venezuela (UCV) in Caracas, for
instance, students occupied the central administration building for a
month in April 2001, demanding a *proceso constituyente universitario*
(university constituent assembly) as a corrective to the alleged resistance by university authorities to much needed change. President Chávez
expressed sympathy for the students' objectives. Nevertheless, the balance sheet of the incident for the *Chavistas* was negative as the students
failed to gain any concession from the UCV rector. The student protesters were held responsible for violence and the incursion of outside leftist
groups on campus. Another incident occurring almost concurrently in
the labor movement also discredited the banner of radical democracy.
Worker councils chosen in rank-and-file assemblies attempted to run
state-wide labor federations out of anti-Chávez union headquarters they
had seized. The national *Chavista* labor leadership criticized them for
excessive spontaneity and lack of discipline.

During the sharp confrontations with the opposition in succeeding
years, the *Chavistas* refrained from calling for direct participation in the
form of popular assemblies, open city councils (*cabildos abiertos*), or
constituent assemblies (referred to in the Constitution's article 70) as a
way out of the crisis. In future years, the *Chavista* leadership would
view "popular power" as a complement to elected bodies, not as the
supreme source of decisionmaking as embodied in the concept of radical

democracy. Thus the deputies elected to the National Assembly in 2005 promoted *parlamentarismo de la calle* (street parliamentarianism), which consisted of popular assemblies and workshops designed to make recommendations on specific issues of congressional concern.

The intense political polarization that set in with the radicalization process in 2001 was incompatible with the model of civil-society input in decisionmaking in accordance with the grassroots approach. The system established in the 1999 Constitution of participation by social organizations in the nominations for certain posts (members of the CNE, the national controller, defender of the people, and attorney general) was predicated on the nonpartisanship of both those who were doing the nominating and those who were nominated. In the highly charged Venezuelan political setting in which the opposition questions the legitimacy of the Chávez presidency and vice versa, such independence has been highly improbable. Thus, for example, contrary to what the Constitution stipulates, prior to the 2004 recall election, all five members of the CNE were politically identified—three with *Chavismo* and two on the side of the opposition.

Although mechanisms for grassroots participation did not solidify, confrontation politics thrust the rank-and-file *Chavistas* onto the center stage beginning in 2001 and infused them with a sense of empowerment. In the face of the opposition's massive mobilizations calling for Chávez's ouster, the *Chavista* leadership succeeded in calling out equal numbers of its supporters onto the streets. Indeed, the *Chavista* leaders owed their political survival to the rank and file's favorable response to those calls.

Chávez's reaction to the jailing of his controversial firebrand supporter Lina Ron on grounds of engaging in violence provides a glimpse into why popular-class followers responded so positively to the calls for mobilization. The private media had vilified Ron for her participation in a protest outside the United States embassy where a US flag was burned, and then in a violent demonstration at the headquarters of the pro-opposition daily *El Nacional* on December 10, 2001. She also clashed with MVR leaders such as Caracas mayor Freddy Bernal and was expelled from the party. Nevertheless, the rank-and-file *Chavistas* considered Ron one of theirs. In his program *Aló Presidente!* of March 10, 2002, Chávez came to the defense of Ron, and added that "two or three [TV] channels have undertaken a campaign against this woman, who is a fighter organizing on the streets." (Ron 2003, 73).

The rank and file played a central role in the defeat of the April 2002 coup and the general strike that began in December of the same year. Thus, for instance, following the coup on April 11, 2002, large numbers of barrio dwellers, aided by informal networks set in place by social organizations and enhanced by the use of cell-phone text messages, converged on the presidential palace in Caracas and military bases throughout the country to demand Chávez's reinstatement in office. The announcement by Education Minister Aristóbulo Istúriz that Chávez had not resigned but was being held captive, transmitted by community radio stations, incited residents of Caracas's low-income west side to join the protests (Francia 2002, 105).

Just as poor people played a protagonist role in April, the oil workers were essential to the economic recovery that made possible the defeat of the general strike of 2002–2003. With about 80 percent of PDVSA's professional personnel supporting the work stoppage, lower-level employees assumed control of the workplace. Without the use of computers, which depended on secret passwords, workers filled and emptied storage facilities manually. Members of the surrounding communities also contributed to the effort to break the strike by guaranteeing the security of oil installations.

▶ Application of the Grassroots Approach to Politics Since 2004

The *Chavista* model that began to emerge in 2004 stimulated local, community, and worker participation in accordance with the grassroots approach. The creation of tens of thousands of cooperatives, the encouragement of worker input in decisionmaking in both private and public companies, and the formation of community councils (*consejos comunales*) to oversee and in some cases undertake activity ranging from public works to health programs at the neighborhood level embodied the essence of the new model. Furthermore, the MVR was committed to a policy of noninterference in the internal life of *Chavista* social organizations.

These advances, however, have faced major practical obstacles and fall short of the expectations of the grassroots purists who celebrate the absolute autonomy of social movements and distrust the intentions of the central government. Contrary to what those theoreticians advocate, the Venezuelan state has played a central role in giving form to the grassroots approach. The state has created structures conducive to participation, promoted "socialist" values, and financed activity that channel the energy of the large number of *Chavistas* who have a tenuous or nonexistent relationship with the three main parties of the governing coalition (the MVR, PPT, and Podemos) (Gindin 2006, 87–90). In the process, the state has been instrumental in enhancing the sense of empowerment of the rank and file of the *Chavista* movement.

Pro-*Chavista* social organizations and rank-and-file political groups have been short lived. Nevertheless, the continuous creation of new ones demonstrates the tenacity of "grassroots" thinking and behavior. Chávez has often called for the formation of social organizations after which they have sprung up throughout the country outside of the confines of *Chavista* party structures.

This pattern occurred in the case of the Bolivarian Circles (Círculos Bolivarianos), which consisted of seven to eleven members and engaged in political education and community work. Without consulting the *Chavista* political leadership, Chávez delivered a speech on April 25, 2001, in which he pointed to the bureaucracy and lethargy of the MVR and appealed to the rank and file to reestablish the old MBR-200 as a rival organization and to create social movements in the form of Bolivarian Circles. The circles, which were allegedly self-financed, played an important role at the time of the April 2002 coup and in subsequent months proliferated throughout the country (Raby 2006, 166). Nevertheless, neither they nor other *Chavista* social organizations became consolidated or maintained a steady existence throughout these years, nor did they develop a national leadership to articulate rank-and-file positions. Eventually circle members became involved in, and absorbed by, activity sponsored by the state ranging from cooperatives to the missions (both as students and employees). Furthermore, local *Chavista* politicians began to boast that they commanded the loyalty of a specific number of circles, offering to activate them in order to mobilize along political lines.

Many of these same rank-and-file *Chavistas* joined organizations that campaigned for Chávez in the recall election of 2004 (and subsequently the presidential election of 2006). Originally the Ayacucho Command (Comando Ayacucho) led by political party leaders coordinated the campaign in favor of the "No Vote" for the recall as well as the gubernatorial and mayoral elections to be held two months later. The command came under heavy criticism due to its failure to defeat the opposition's efforts to collect enough signatures to hold the recall as well as its error in calculating the number of legitimate signatures. The real objection to the Ayacucho Command, however, was its failure to consult the rank and file in its nomination of gubernatorial and mayoral candidates, some of whom were highly unpopular and were accused of unethical conduct.

Chávez's decision to replace the Ayacucho Command with the Maisanta Command (Comando Maisanta), whose national leadership consisted mainly of nonparty leaders who were to report directly to him, was interpreted as a repudiation of the party elites and thus empowered the rank and file. At the same time, Chávez called for the formation of campaign units known as Electoral Battle Units (UBEs) to canvass in the neighborhoods. As was the case with the Bolivarian Circles, the rank and file of the *Chavista* movement responded positively to Chávez's plea, as UBEs emerged throughout the nation outside the party structure (Hellinger 2007, 162–163). Rank-and-file *Chavistas* were convinced that the UBEs would be retained as a basic unit of the *Chavista* movement and would have an input in the nomination of candidates in future electoral contests. The UBEs, however, also proved to be transient.

The outcome of the elections in 2005 highlighted the standoff between the statist approach, which privileged political parties, and the grassroots approach, which empowered the rank and file. On the one hand, the MVR received an overwhelming majority of the *Chavista* vote both in the August elections for municipal councils and the December elections for the National Assembly. On the other hand, the rank-and-file *Chavista* independents asserted themselves forcefully in various ways. The Communist Party's slate, which privileged unaffiliated social movement activists, scored well in Caracas's all-important 23 de Enero (January 23) district, while the leftist Tupamaros movement, which also ran separate candidates, held militant protests against alleged electoral fraud in the nation's capital. Of greater importance were the 69 percent abstention rate in August and the 75 percent rate in December, indicating that a large number of the *Chavista* "independents" refused to vote in protest against the MVR's failure to reach out sufficiently to the general population.

Rank-and-file units similar to the UBEs were created in the form of "battalions," "platoons," and "squadrons" to campaign at the neighborhood level for Chávez's reelection in December 2006. As was the case with the UBEs, members of these groups were convinced that they would continue to play a central role after the elections. Chávez contributed to this expectation in a speech to campaign workers two weeks after the elections in which he officially launched the United Socialist Party of Venezuela (PSUV). The reelected president insisted that the electoral units be retained and added that they would become the "basic national structure of the PSUV." He called on the activists to update data and draw up a registry of "militants, sympathizers, and friends" in each community where the battalions, platoons, and squadrons were located.

The vulnerability of grassroots structures to interference, particularly from local political figures, was made clear in the case of neighborhood organizations that were designed to deepen decentralization beyond the state and municipal levels. This politicization occurred in the case of the Local Councils of Public Planning (CLPPs). According to legislation passed in May 2002, the CLPPs were to receive 20 percent of the budget of the Intergovernmental Fund for Decentralization (FIDES)—which since the early 1990s had allocated federal money to state and municipal governments for specific projects designed by them. The mayors, however, ended up controlling many of the CLPPs, thus violating the spirit of the *Chavista*-promoted neighborhood legislation (Bonilla-Molina and El Troudi 2005, 232). When a law passed in April 2006 replacing the CLPPs with the community councils, Chávez insisted that the new bodies be led by community leaders free of commitments to political organizations.

"Grassroots" writers underscore the importance of struggles, slogans, and actions that empower the nonprivileged and excluded sectors of the population. The *Chavista* discourse and the activity of community groups and social movements have enhanced the self-confidence, pride, and sense of efficacy of groups such as women, Afro-Venezuelans, and indigenous people. The state has played an important role in this process of transformation of consciousness, even though in the long run the new mentality encourages the assertion of organizational autonomy.

An example of this dynamic is the activity of women of the popular sectors who support Chávez and participate in state-sponsored programs in their neighborhoods, ranging from the health and education missions to popular kitchens. Women who are active in these community programs far outnumber men. They are encouraged and emboldened by official discourse, which emphasizes equality and questions traditional gender roles, as well as by community networks. In their everyday work, these women modify long-standing behavior patterns and embrace new ones such as engagement in collective work and the sharing of responsibilities. The organizational weakness that has been characteristic of the *Chavista* phenomenon as a whole reflects itself on this front as well. The National Institute for Women (INAMUJER) was created in 1999 in order to combat discrimination against women, but is far from being a mass organization as was the case with its counterparts in Nicaragua under the Sandinistas and revolutionary Cuba

(Fernandes 2005; 2007). The lack of a mass-based autonomous women's organization under Chávez and the failure of predominately women-run programs and organizations to embrace well-defined feminist goals and understand "the history of women's struggle in Venezuela" have led some writers to deny the convergence between *Chavista* women's activity and authentic feminism (Rakowski 2003, 400). Nevertheless, the transformation that is underway reflects many of the goals of the Venezuelan feminist movement, albeit in less explicit form.

The Afro-Venezuelan movement is another example of state stimulation of an excluded group, which as a whole goes beyond its original political agenda while remaining unwavering in its support of Chávez. Thus the Network of Afro-Venezuelan Organizations, consisting of thirty groups, has urged the Chávez government to create an Afro-Venezuelan Ministry, include a category for the black population in the national census, incorporate Afro-Venezuelan history in school curricula, and reform the constitution in order to recognize the nation's multi-ethnicity and Afro-Venezuelan rights in particular. In short, movements involving large numbers of Afro-Venezuelans and women, while highly dependent on state initiatives, encourage new patterns of thinking consonant with the grassroots approach.

The *Chavistas* who adhere to the "grassroots" outlook are characterized by their fervent denunciation of *Chavista* politicians for engaging in corruption. In the Venezuelan setting of intense political polarization and a private media closely identified with the opposition, formal accusations of corruption are sometimes met with skepticism. Nevertheless, the rank-and-file *Chavistas* point to cases of local government officials of popular origin who suddenly acquire costly houses and cars as definitive proof of unethical conduct.

Differences between the statist and grassroots camps manifest themselves in the strategies to combat corruption. The independents claim that corruption has reached catastrophic proportions and that the situation requires a "social controllership" in which ad hoc bodies with popular or community participation probe accusations of corrupt dealings. They also warn that corruption may set off a violent reaction on the part of the *Chavista* rank and file. In contrast, party leaders reject the rank and file's pessimistic view that corruption is rampant and favor more institutional means to deal with the problem in accordance with the statist approach. Partial successes in the fight against corruption undermined the rank and file's claim that resistance from the party bureaucracy to efforts against corruption requires a grassroots strategy. Chávez himself has alleged that the private media fails to report government breakthroughs on this front. Successes included the sharp reduction in the money assigned to secret accounts and the employment of Internet procedures that minimize contact between government functionaries and individuals seeking state financial support and other resources (such as in the case of the exchange control system CADIVI and the issuance of passports) (Harnecker 2005, 65).

Beginning in 2006 government initiatives against corruption originated from "above" with specific denunciations formulated by the national executive branch, the state-owned Bank of Economic and Social Development (BANDES), MVR congressmen, and state governors. The most prominent case was the denunciation, by Minister of Interior and Justice Jesse Chacón, of the pro-*Chavista* judge of the Tribunal Supremo de Justicia (Supreme Court) Luis Velásquez Alvaray for illicit enrichment. The *Chavista*-controlled National Assembly voted unanimously to remove Velásquez Alvaray and place him on trial. A second well-publicized case began with the denunciation by the pro-*Chavista* editor of *Ultimas Noticias*, Eleazar Díaz Rangel, of the mismanagement of state allocations for a sugar mill in Barinas, and was followed by imprisonments and a congressional probe that held a former minister of agriculture, a general, and seventeen others responsible and opened the possibility of confiscation of property of those implicated.

In spite of the tension that exists between the two approaches, the programs and proposals associated with each one are to a certain extent complementary rather than contradictory or mutually exclusive. Thus, for instance, those who support the grassroots approach embrace Chávez's call for the creation of "social controllerships" consisting of popular ad hoc committees in the communities and other locations to monitor public programs and probe cases of alleged misuse of state expenditures. In contrast, the statist or top-down approach urges the strengthening of institutional mechanisms, such as SUNACOOP, which is in charge of overseeing worker cooperatives. Both structures designed to combat corruption can function side by side.

Nevertheless, the two approaches manifest widely different concerns and values. Those who favor the grassroots approach, for example, complain that institutional obstacles created by SUNACOOP block or slow down the legal registration of new cooperatives due to the lethargy and inefficiency of government bureaucrats. At the same time, those who adhere to the top-down or statist approach argue that the campaign to promote new "socialist" ways of thinking in accordance with the grassroots approach can hardly be viewed as a panacea for the problem of unethical behavior. They insist that SUNACOOP be provided with sufficient resources to oversee cooperatives that receive state funding and be invested with authority to clamp down on the misuse of funds assigned by the Ministry of the Community Economy.

▶ The Grassroots Approach and the Economy

On the economic front, the most widespread expression of the grassroots approach is the system of worker cooperatives. In contrast to socialist-inspired nationalizations that create vertical structures, cooperatives contribute to horizontal decisionmaking, small-scale production units, and popular empowerment. The *Chavista* government explicitly promotes cooperatives as part of an effort to avoid the pitfalls of vertical socialism associated with the former Soviet Union in hopes that these novel forms of production will gradually lead to a new "socialist" model. Chávez himself has stated that the effort to instill "socialist values" in the members of cooperatives and require them to carry out projects in the communities where they are located is designed to avoid the experience of Yugoslavia, where enterprises of this type ended up becoming veritable capitalist businesses (Lebowitz 2006, 85–118).

In practice, however, the astronomical growth of cooperatives at the time of the founding of the Ministry of the Community Economy in 2004 provided little time to establish effective mechanisms in order to monitor the new enterprises, correct shortcomings, and guarantee that state-allocated start-up capital was put to good use. Frequent accusations against presidents of cooperatives by fellow members for placing personal interests ahead of collective interests have obliged the ministry occasionally to set up "dialogue tables" to resolve disputes. In many cases the government has failed to ensure compliance with the Law of Cooperative Associations (Ley de Cooperativas)—one of the forty-nine laws of the Emergency Legislation (Ley Habilitante) passed in 2001. Ministerial officials recognize that bookkeeping of individual cooperatives has been deficient and auditing conducted by the ministry's superintendency (SUNACOOP) has been infrequent.

Opinions on the state's performance in overseeing cooperatives reflect the differences between the grassroots and statist approaches. Those who defend the former criticize the state for its slowness in approving requests of newly formed cooperatives for legal status. Those who defend the latter attribute the poor, and in some cases dishonest, management of cooperatives to the failure to provide SUNACOOP with sufficient bureaucratic capacity and resources to meet its regulatory duties.

Chavista labor leaders of the UNT are particularly critical of the new system due to their fear that by displacing normal worker-management relations it will eliminate unions. They point out that a large percentage of the new formations are "briefcase cooperatives" (*cooperativas de maletín*), which, in effect, have single owners and hire wage labor for less than six months at a time, as permitted by the Law of Cooperative Associations (Chirino 2005, 21). These businesses are able to take advantage of state financial aid, special programs for raising collateral, exemption from payment of the value added tax and income tax, preferential treatment in bidding for state contracts, and other government measures that privilege cooperatives (Lucena 2007, 77–78).

In spite of these deformations and shortcomings, the system of cooperatives has the potential to develop into a viable sector of the Venezuelan economy. PDVSA, with its superior resources, has been able to demand stricter legal compliance from cooperatives that receive contracts in the oil industry. Many *Chavista* leaders recognize that a large number of cooperatives are poorly and unscrupulously managed and will eventually fail, but argue that those that survive will emerge on a sounder basis and allow the system to consolidate itself and achieve a higher degree of efficiency. Furthermore, even though many of the enterprises that register as cooperatives are essentially small businesses, they have promoted another goal embraced by the *Chavistas*, namely the "democratization of capital." The proliferation of small enterprises, even though many of them may be unworthy of the name "cooperatives," represents a potential challenge to the oligopolistic control of the economy. This phenomenon is particularly pronounced in the countryside, where the application of the Lands Law has given way to thousands of cooperatives on those estates that were subject to land redistribution.

Another system that is in an experimental stage and is compatible with the grassroots approach is worker input in management decision-making (*cogestión*) beyond the token coparticipation arrangements that functioned in Venezuela beginning in 1966. The general strike in the oil sector in 2002–2003, when workers collectively chose their supervisors and took charge of the basic operational facet of the industry, was an important precedent. The workers in the state-owned electricity company CADAFE also ran their firm during the two-month conflict. *Chavista* labor leaders constantly refer to these experiences as proof that *cogestión* in Venezuela is feasible. In an attempt to achieve authentic worker participation, the UNT on May Day of 2005 presented a proposed law that would grant workers 50 percent ownership in companies subject to *cogestión* arrangements. The radical wing of the UNT rejects "static" *cogestión* and insists that the system eventually transform itself into complete worker control, at the same time that it calls on the confederation to lead worker takeovers of failing companies (Chirino 2005, 47–49).

Although only a handful of firms in Venezuela have been expropriated and turned over to the workers, the state's commitment to worker management is greater than in Argentina where two hundred companies have been occupied and run by workers but without firm support from the government, labor movement, and political parties (Ranis 2005, 111–112). In contrast, the Chávez government turned over 49 percent of the stock of INVEPAL (the first company expropriated, formerly called VENEPAL) to the workers who were allowed to select two of the five members of the board of directors. The employees also have the right to choose and remove the company's president, who has to come from their ranks. Given this propitious political climate, the feasibility of the grassroots approach in the industrial sector is being put to the test in the case of INVEPAL and other recently expropriated companies.

▶ Theoretical Implications of the Grassroots Approach

The debate between the traditional statist strategy and the grassroots approach ("movement from below") has taken in a range of major theoretical issues directly related to the transformation of third-world countries in the twenty-first century. Venezuelan political developments under Chávez shed light on this discussion and serve as a corrective to the abstract analysis that has characterized the left's search for new models since the collapse of the Soviet bloc. Chávez himself envisions Venezuela as a laboratory in which a trial-and-error dynamic will lead to the formulation of a new socialist model.

One major issue of debate at the international level that "grassroots" theoreticians address is whether the changes ushered in by globalization are permanent and require a global response on the part of progressive movements in order for their actions to be effective. Writers who champion the grassroots approach do not oppose globalization per se in spite of their critique of the phenomenon, nor do they favor returning to a previous era when the predominance of the nation-state went unquestioned. At the same time that they deny the capacity of US "imperialism" to dominate the world (Hardt 2006, 29), they accept the realities of a new global order in which the enemy is irreversibly transnational. While these analysts point to the limitations of traditional structures such as political parties and the labor movement as vehicles for revolutionary change, they view international alliances and networks of social movements (which they call the "global counterhegemonic movement") as a sine qua non for real transformation (Robinson 2004, 168–173). (This thesis contrasts with the predominately national strategy defended in the past by the traditional left that was influenced by Stalin's dictum of "socialism in one country" in opposition to the "world revolution" course advocated by Leon Trotsky.) In short, the grassroots approach, unlike the anti-imperialism of the traditional left, posits the primacy of strategies of international resistance and denies the feasibility of any national struggle that assigns world solidarity a merely auxiliary role.

Chávez's "Bolivarian" doctrine discards a go-it-alone approach for Venezuela and posits "international solidarity" as a cornerstone of the strategy for Latin America to achieve genuine independence. While Chávez at times appears to embrace "international solidarity" as a moral imperative and an end unto itself, he insists that in today's world Latin American countries have no choice but to promote joint strategies, strengthen ties among themselves, and engage in collective action in order to overcome dependency and underdevelopment. The primacy of international relations under Chávez goes beyond mere discourse, as is reflected in his activism at the world level, his promotion of commercial ventures and other forms of Latin American unity, and the centrality of his foreign policy in national political debate (to be discussed in Chapter 8).[1] Thus, for example, on the all-important issue of payment of the foreign debt, Chávez rules out individual action and indicates that Venezuela will continue to pay it off until the entire continent is ready to act collectively to face the unjust terms of payment (Harnecker 2005, 109–110).[2]

Chávez's diplomatic initiatives, however, diverge from the grassroots strategy in one fundamental way. In its pure form, the grassroots approach has a local and global focus that passes over the nation-state (an orientation sometimes referred to as "postmodern"). In its practical application, the approach attempts to establish links to people's struggles throughout the world while paying less attention to relations with other governments. The approach is exemplified by Chávez's fiery rhetoric and popular stands, which appeal to the general population in Latin

America while straining relations with some heads of state. Nevertheless, foreign policy under Chávez has prioritized alliances and agreements with other third-world governments on diverse fronts, an objective that bypasses ideological and political differences.

A second issue that the debate on the grassroots approach has raised at the international level is the feasibility of proposed revolutionary models. In its pure form the grassroots approach, like classical anarchist thinking, borders on utopianism, as demonstrated by its rejection of well-structured organizations and minimization of the importance of the state. All revolutionary movements at one time or another—particularly during their early years in power—manifest romanticism and quixotic notions while relegating practical considerations to a secondary plane. In the case of Venezuela, leftists have in different contexts justified historical decisions that were taken against all odds. Chávez, for instance, has stated that days prior to February 4, 1992, the coup leaders realized that the probability of success was negligible, but decided to proceed anyway.[3]

The ongoing tension between a realistic perspective conducive to the construction of a workable model, on the one hand, and social and humanitarian concerns along with support for cultural transformation, on the other, has characterized the *Chavista* movement throughout the Chávez presidency. The grassroots approach prioritizes the latter objectives. It is imbued with idealism and distrust of authority. Its adherents in the rank and file of the *Chavista* movement exhibit a faith in the capacity of the general population grouped in rudimentary organizations (in large part neighborhood ones) and a wariness of institutions, particularly political parties and the government (specifically at the local and state level). Those who adhere to the grassroots approach distrust the "institutionalization" of the revolutionary process, which would lock initial changes in place and hold back the continuous transformation based on experience, as Chávez has called for.

These tendencies are evident in the government's ambitious program of cooperatives, which is designed to democratize capital and eliminate hierarchical structures in accordance with the vision of grassroots theoreticians.[4] Since the founding of the Ministry of the Community Economy in 2004, state promotion of cooperatives has taken on the form of a social program generating employment, more than the seeds of an economically productive and self-sustaining model that would form an integral part of the nation's economy. At the level of discourse, both Chávez and the literature of the ministry stress the goal of solidarity among the members of the cooperatives and toward the community where they are located. This focus is designed to avoid submitting cooperatives to the logic of the capitalist system based on exploitation and perpetual reinvestment. The rhetoric also deprecates the "profit motive" for individual cooperative members even though socialist thinking has long considered material incentives a valid form of stimulation.[5] In keeping with these priorities, the ministry requires cooperatives to invest in community programs. At the same time, the expansion of the ministry's superintendency (SUNACOOP), which is in charge of monitoring cooperatives and ensuring that state funds are put to proper use, at least at first failed to keep pace with the sharp increase in the number of cooperatives throughout the country. In short, the goal of transforming "capitalist"-promoted values and solving social problems eclipsed practical considerations necessary to ensure the viability of a new economic model.[6]

On the political front, the grassroots approach in its pure form proved inoperative and out of tune with Venezuelan political reality. During the early years of Chávez's presidency, the prospects for a paradigm that extols autonomous social movements and predicts their transformation into the cornerstone of a new type of democracy in accordance with the grassroots approach appeared promising. Not only did social organizations play a constructive role in formulating proposals, which were incorporated in the 1999 Constitution, but the Bolivarian Circles proliferated throughout the nation at the time of the 2002 coup. Nevertheless, the circles and other organizations of the *Chavista* movement proved short lived as their members enlisted in the missions, cooperatives, and other state-sponsored activities that provided them with personal opportunities. Some writers who defend the grassroots approach have failed to recognize this hard reality and claim that the growth of autonomous social movements in the barrios is "the most powerful and novel element in Venezuela's Bolivarian revolution" and not its "anti-imperialist stance" (Hardt 2006, 29).

Another political paradigm that is compatible with the grassroots approach and at first appeared propitious is "radical democracy," in which the direct participation of the people displaces representative institutions. The abolition of the National Congress, the nation's maximum "representative" institution, as a result of the referendum in April 1999 and its replacement by a National Constituent Assembly committed to participatory democracy pointed in the direction of this novel democratic model. Nevertheless, the intense political polarization and confrontations that set in during the early years of the Chávez presidency impeded the development of independent organizations and autonomous decisionmaking structures that are basic to radical democracy. Thus the mechanisms established by the Constitution to name judges, members of the National Electoral Council, and the "Poder Ciudadano" (which includes the National Controller and the Attorney General) required the creation of nonpartisan commissions, an unlikely development given the intensity of the political atmosphere in the country. Furthermore, the provisions of the Constitution that subordinated representative institutions to the direct input of the people, such as the convocation of popular assemblies with binding decisionmaking power, failed to translate themselves into workable procedures.

Nevertheless, in the course of the eight years of the Chávez presidency, the discourse, assertiveness, and self-identification of the rank-and-file *Chavistas* who are unaffiliated with any political party and who adhere to the grassroots approach have not diminished in intensity. Their perception of "us" versus "them" with reference to their relations with *Chavista* party leaders is typical of their ongoing resentment toward hierarchical structures. Many of these *Chavistas* dropped out of the Bolivarian Circles and other social groups to join state-financed programs such as the missions. Participation in state-initiated programs is a far cry from membership in autonomous social movements extolled by grassroots theoreticians. Nevertheless, their involvement in the missions is significant from a political viewpoint in that it cements identification with *Chavismo*, just as membership in a *Chavista* social organization, party, or union would have done. In spite of their migration from social organization to state-sponsored program, their critical attitudes toward the party and local government and support for the grassroots approach has remained unaltered. In addition to the independent thinking of rank-and-file *Chavistas*, the grassroots approach expresses itself in aspects of government policy on the international front and social policy that subordinates realistic considerations regarding the construction of a viable economic model to the promotion of new values and the achievement of social equality.

The uneven existence and short duration of social organizations and programs are in large part due to circumstantial factors and thus do not necessarily represent a fatal flaw in the grassroots approach. The exceptionally high prices of oil during the Chávez presidency, for example, has contributed to the cooptation of social movement activists by the government and the transfer of rank-and-file *Chavistas* from social organizations to state-financed social programs. In addition, organizational instability is largely the result of the frequent change in priorities that has characterized the Venezuelan process under Chávez. Shifting tactics and priorities, for their part, are natural given the "experimental" road to socialism embraced by Chávez and his movement. Between 2003 and 2005, for instance, the Chávez government focused attention on cooperatives, but they were subsequently eclipsed by the community councils, twenty thousand of which sprung up throughout the country in 2006 and 2007.

The coexistence of support for both grassroots and statist strategies within the *Chavista* movement over such an extended period of time, and Chávez's own endorsement of elements of both, suggest the necessity of a synthesis. Such a combination is feasible because those who identify with both approaches do not uphold a rigid or theoretically consistent position, as do many theoreticians whose idealistic and dogmatic mentalities preclude the possibility of crossing the lines of the paradigms they have created. Thus, for instance, even though the grassroots *Chavistas* are distrustful and resentful of political party leaders and state bureaucracies, they avidly support the anti-imperialist strategy in which third-world states assert national sovereignty (statist approach). Paradigms formulated over the last quarter of a century play a valuable role in framing issues. The everyday practice of the *Chavista* government and movement, however, is what will determine the outcome of Venezuela's incipient model, which is certain to become an important point of reference for analysts throughout the world for years to come.

The logical starting point for achieving the proposed synthesis is the democratization of the *Chavista* party to create mechanisms for the rank and file to participate in decisionmaking in accordance with the grassroots approach, while maintaining a centralized command and enforcing internal discipline. Proposals formulated over the recent past in favor of party reorganization were designed to generate formal debate in such arenas as ideological conferences, internal elections, and party publications, which would open opportunities for different *Chavista* political currents (as defined in Chapter 6) to formulate positions. Indeed, internal democratization without ideological clarification leads eventually to vacuous factionalism based on personality differences, as was demonstrated by the experience of Venezuelan parties in the 1990s, discussed in Chapter 4 (Ellner 1996, 104–107). The coalescence of *Chavista* parties and social organizations into the United Socialist Party of Venezuela (PSUV) proposed in December 2006 provides a golden opportunity to achieve organizational renovation and to deepen democracy along these lines, but at the same time runs the risk of suppressing diversity within the movement in the name of ill-defined long-term goals.

▶ **Notes**

1. Chávez's ambitious continental strategy of promoting economic agreements refutes the criticism that his regime is a "dinosaur" in that it is attempting to go back in time to the "development from within" strategy associated with import substitution policies or, worse yet, the autarky associated with Mao Zedong in China (Hernández and Rondón 2005, 312–320).

2. In contrast, Alan García's go-it-alone approach to the payment of the Peruvian foreign debt proved catastrophic for the nation's economy during his first administration in the 1980s.

3. Similarly, members of the Venezuelan left have argued that on the days prior to the Soviet revolution of 1917, the possibility of success of the Bolshevik plan to seize power was remote, but it was a chance worth taking, as was the case with Fidel Castro's armed attack on July 26, 1953, initiating the Cuban revolution and the decision of the Venezuelan left to take up arms in the 1960s (Ellner 1988, 47–48; 2004, 29).

4. Grassroots writers envision the emergence of an economic system in which cooperatives, the informal economy, and other types of low-profit activity occupy spaces left by global capital and eventually "coalesce" into a new class of producers united by a sense of solidarity (Burbach, Nuñez, and Kagarlitsky 1997, 155–158).

5. Thus Marx defined socialism as a system in which workers are remunerated according to their productivity ("to each according to his/her work").

6. The tension between social and economic objectives has always manifested itself in the decisions taken by state companies in Venezuela, particularly in the case of PDVSA. The executives of the "New PDVSA" that emerged after the general strike of 2002–2003 claimed to have repudiated the "technocratic" approach, which had prevailed until then and had submerged social concerns to market criteria. In its place, they committed themselves to dealing with problems facing neighboring communities and social issues in general.

8

▼

The Chávez Government in the International Arena

POLITICAL adversaries and critics of President Chávez have put forward two interpretations of the motives behind his government's foreign policy. Some writers characterize Chávez's fiery rhetoric and confrontational style as demagogic and "populist" in that it is exclusively designed to gain support among Venezuelans by appealing to nationalist sentiment. In doing so, these analysts implicitly or explicitly dismiss the relevance of substantive issues. They also argue that for all of Chávez's pronouncements on a new world order, his grandiose international schemes, and his challenges to the United States, his international initiatives have achieved nothing for the nation or for transformations at the world level (Corrales 2006, 39–40).

A second group of anti-*Chavista* writers point to power for power's sake as the motivation behind Chávez's actions abroad. These writers emphasize Chávez's ambitions and eagerness to spread revolution, while stating or implying that the changes he stands for lack substance. According to them, "petrodollars" made possible by oil price hikes have allowed Chávez to pursue geopolitical ambitions by subsidizing Latin American leftist movements and governments and buying support from nations throughout the world (Falcoff 2004, 38–40; Castañeda 2006a, 38–40; 2006b; Gunson 2006, 63). Thus, for instance, the agreements with Latin American and Caribbean nations that provide oil at special discounts and terms of credit are designed to win over governments to Chávez's diplomatic stands, which in no way further national interests.

These two analyses of foreign policy focusing on rhetoric and power are typical of much of the literature on Venezuelan politics and history that has been the central concern of this book. Over the years,

195

much political writing has centered on style and personalities, on the one hand, and the quest for power, on the other. In the process it has passed over concrete issues directly affecting national interests and the class interests of distinct sectors of the population.

The following discussion of President Chávez's foreign policy also reinforces the book's previous three chapters by adding to their analysis of the basic trends of the *Chavista* government and movement. Venezuelan relations with the United States, for example, is the most graphic illustration of the dynamic discussed in Chapter 6 whereby intensification of conflict produces an ongoing process of escalation of rhetoric and positions. During its early years the Chávez government's dealings with Washington were relatively cordial even though the *Chavistas* clashed head-on with the Venezuelan opposition. The dynamic of the escalation of mutual hostility between the two governments began at the time of the 2002–2003 general strike and quickly reached a threshold of daily confrontation, which led Chávez to declare the US government his principal adversary. The abrupt escalation of conflict has at times produced overreactions on the part of the Venezuelan government in the form of certain actions and rhetoric that Chapter 7 labels "ultra leftist." An example was Chávez's threat in 2006 to sever diplomatic relations with Peru if Alan García, who Caracas labeled a "lackey of US imperialism," were to win the upcoming elections in that nation.

Finally, the simultaneous application of the grassroots and statist approaches and the tensions between them, as discussed in Chapter 7, clearly manifest themselves in foreign policy. The statist approach has been conducive to cordial relations with governments of diverse ideological tendencies including that of neighboring Colombia. In contrast, the grassroots approach appeals directly to people throughout the world, and specifically to leftists, who in some cases are confronting the governing leaders of their respective nations (Kozloff 2007, 133–144). It also explains the friendly informal relations that the Chávez government maintains with nearly all the important social movements in Latin America (Dieterich 2005, 193–194).

▶ Relations with the United States

Until the general strike in 2002–2003, the Chávez government employed cautious language in its dealings with the United States. Chávez's discretion became evident during the presidential campaign in 1998 when he refrained from criticizing the Clinton administration for its decision on two occasions to deny his request for a visa. At the same time he raised the possibility of maintaining a dialogue with the IMF and pledged to respect existing agreements with foreign capital. In September 1999 Chávez addressed the UN General Assembly, met with President Clinton (for the second time), and spoke to the US Chamber of Commerce, where his remarks were considered positive and encouraging. On the same trip Chávez promised the Inter-American Press Association to pass on its concerns regarding the persecution of independent Cuban journalists to Fidel Castro. The following year Chávez traveled to Puerto Rico where he avoided reference to Puerto Rican independence and largely skirted the disruptive issue of the US military presence on the island of Vieques (Romero 2004, 141).

Nevertheless, during its early years, the Chávez government assumed nationalist and independent positions, although in some cases indicating a willingness to accommodate US interests. Following heavy flooding in December 1999, Chavez snubbed a US offer to send Marine Corps engineers and bulldozers to repair devastated areas and at the same time removed Minister of Defense Raúl Salazar who had previously ratified the proposal, and who subsequently joined the opposition (Arenas and Calcaño 2006, 90). Chávez feared that the presence of as many as one thousand US military personnel on Venezuelan soil would set a dangerous precedent and would undermine his credentials as a nationalist (Toro Jiménez 2006c). The Chávez administration also turned down repeated requests from Washington to allow US surveillance planes to use Venezuelan airspace to combat drug trafficking on the Colombian border. Similarly, after promising to consider the idea, Chávez refrained from acting on a proposal made by General Charles Wilhelm, chief of the US Southern Command, to set up a base that would house US military advisers and high-tech equipment on Venezuela's Colombian border to block the movement of guerrillas (Guevara 2005, 44). Many other issues separated the two countries: Chávez's neutral position on the Colombia guerrilla conflict and his initiatives to mediate the dispute; his denunciation of NATO for its air attacks on Yugoslavia; Venezuela's vote in the UN's Human Rights Commission in opposition to the censorship of Cuba and China and the claim by the Chávez government that the US ambassador in Caracas had pressured it to endorse the resolution; and refusal to approve the final resolution of the Summit of the Americas held in Quebec City in April 2001 due to Venezuela's critical position toward the Washington-promoted Free Trade Area of the Americas (FTAA).

The moderate line of the Clinton administration was formulated by US Ambassador John Maisto, who argued that Chávez's overwhelming electoral triumph obliged Washington to take a tolerant approach and that economic constraints would most likely force him to moderate his positions. An opposing view was defended by hard-liners who eventually included Undersecretary of State for Western Hemisphere Affairs Peter Romero, who at one point warned Chávez against pushing the limits of acceptable action. In a remark that made international news, Romero indirectly referred to Maisto's strategy toward Chávez: "They tell us 'wait,' but we gringos are not exactly known for our patience." The outspokenly critical Venezuelan political scientists Anibal Romero and Moisés Naím ascribed US passivity to its lack of interest in Venezuela and blamed Washington for evaluating Chávez's credentials as a democrat solely on the basis of electoral politics while ignoring other indicators such as democratic liberties (Ellsworth 2003, 11).

Nearly from its outset, the Bush administration hardened the US stand toward the Chávez government by consistently criticizing its policies and statements. Following the September 11, 2001, attacks, Chávez's actions clashed with Bush's "with us or against us" approach to fighting terrorism. The State Department characterized as "totally inappropriate" Chávez's televised appearance in which he held up photos of victims of the US bombing of Afghanistan and called it "a slaughter of innocents." In response to the incident, Washington temporarily recalled US Ambassador Donna Hrinak. Subsequently, Secretary of State Colin Powell expressed doubts about Chávez's "understanding of what the democratic system is all about" (Arvelaiz and Porras Ponceleon 2003, 25).

The Bush administration supported the April 2002 coup on different fronts. During the weeks prior to April 11, administration officials and those tied to the government-financed National Endowment for Democracy (NED) met with numerous Venezuelan opposition leaders in Washington without in any way attempting to discourage them from carrying out the coup (Corn 2003, 128–129, 131). The CIA knew of the details of their plans, which included (in the words of one document dated April 6 that the agency sent to the State Department) efforts "to try to exploit unrest stemming from opposition demonstrations" to serve as the justification for the coup and the arrest of Chávez along with ten government officials (Golinger 2005, 104, 247). The day after Chávez's removal, White House Press Secretary Ari Fleischer justified the coup by referring to the April 11 shootings: "We know that the action encouraged by the Chavez government provoked this crisis." The statement was deceptive because the White House had known that the coup was in the making at least several days prior to April 11. At the same time, Undersecretary of State for Western Hemisphere Affairs Otto Reich summoned Latin American ambassadors to his office in an effort to convince them to follow the US lead by extending diplomatic relations to the Carmona regime. Indeed, Washington's immediate recognition of Carmona, and the meeting between US Ambassador Charles Shapiro and the provisional Venezuelan president after he decreed the abolition of congress, broke with traditional US policy.

Finally, the United States provided material support for the opposition and possibly logistical support for the coup plotters. Between 2000 and 2001, Venezuela went from the tenth to the first largest recipient of NED funds in the region, much of which was allotted to opposition groups that participated in the mobilizations leading to the coup and then supported Carmona (Clement 2007, 194–195). Chávez claims that US military ships and helicopters were stationed off the Venezuelan coast at the time of his overthrow and passed logistical information to the coup leaders.

In the interim between the April coup and the general strike in December 2002, Chávez toned down his aggressive rhetoric toward the Venezuelan opposition at the same time that he refrained from lashing out at the United States for its role in the overthrow of his government. This moderation was demonstrated by Chávez's bland reaction to the decision of the US Agency for International Development (USAID) to install an "Office of Transition Initiatives" in the US embassy in Caracas, which was to generously fund opposition activity in Venezuela. Chávez responded to the announcement by saying, "[W]e ought to watch it closely and pay attention calmly and patiently" (Harnecker 2005, 134).

The Chávez government's harsh attacks against the Bush administration beginning in 2003 was a reaction to Washington's hardened stand over the previous two years that broke with Clinton's more tolerant line. In 2003 Chávez began to employ the term *imperialism* to describe the role of Washington in world affairs, and subsequently accused it of committing genocide in the Mideast and warned of a possible US invasion of Venezuela. Chávez singled out Washington as his principal enemy that overshadowed his internal adversaries and stood in contrast with Venezuela's good relations with nearly all other governments throughout the world. In addition, Chávez responded to verbal aggression against him by the United States with personal attacks against Bush and other members of his administration. Chávez sometimes resorted to name-calling, such as when he labeled Bush a "mad man," "the greatest terrorist in the world," and (at his UN appearance in September 2006) a "devil."

Bush responded to Chávez's denunciations by accusing the Venezuelan government of supporting guerrilla movements in Colombia and elsewhere, flagrantly violating human rights, and refusing to coop-erate in the wars on drugs and terrorism. Secretary of State Condoleezza Rice called Chávez a "challenge to democracy" and a "negative force in the region." In order to underline Chávez's authoritarianism (as well as that of several other countries), Bush employed the same tactic as President Ronald Reagan when he met with Soviet dissidents, encoun-ters that left the opposition open to the charge of subservience to Washington. In May 2005, in one of a series of well-publicized meetings with opposition leaders of nations throughout the world, Bush met in the White House for fifty minutes with anti-*Chavista* NGO leader María Corina Machado, who had signed the Carmona decree. Machado later told reporters that the meeting was a "recognition and signal that the world does care about what is happening" in Venezuela (*Washington Post*, June 15, 2005, 1).

The Bush administration's opposition to Chávez went beyond ver-bal attacks and symbolic actions. Not since the US intervention in Chile under Salvador Allende in the early 1970s and in Nicaragua against the Sandinistas in the 1980s had Washington carried out such an intensive campaign on diverse fronts against a democratically elected government. Following the coup, the US government funneled money through the Office of Transition Initiatives (OTI) in order to support the Venezuelan opposition's initiatives, such as the campaign for the recall election. The OTI allotted five times more money than the National Endowment for Democracy, which had played an important role prior to the coup. The OTI was more secretive than the NED and, in the words of an author who researched democracy promotion in Venezuela, was "a more efficacious instrument to infiltrate civil society" (Golinger 2005, 132).

In a particularly delicate area, the United States attempted to block the sale of military equipment to Venezuela that was designed to diversi-fy the nation's military relations. The Chávez government alleged that the weapons were mainly defensive and denied the US claim that they significantly enhanced the nation's offensive capacity while threatening to set off an armaments race in the region. The deals included one hun-dred thousand Kalashnikov assault rifles from Russia (and their possible fabrication along with munitions in two plants in Venezuela); about two dozen Supertucano fighter planes from Brazil; and twelve surveillance and transport planes from Spain (a plan that fell through after the Spaniards were unable to substitute US-produced parts, which Washington had refused to supply). Venezuela's efforts to establish ties with new manufacturers of military equipment was partly a response to the US refusal to supply parts on a regular basis for Venezuela's fleet of F-16 planes (which had been sold to the nation two decades earlier).

The United States and Venezuela also clashed as a result of electoral processes in the UN and affiliated organizations. Thus in 2005 the United States originally reacted to Venezuela's endorsement of the candidacy of Chile's José Miguel Insulza as secretary-general of the Organization of American States (OAS) by throwing its support behind Mexico's foreign affairs minister Luis Ernesto Derbez (*New York Times*, May 3, 2005). The following year, the United States opposed Venezuela's bid for a nonpermanent seat on the UN Security Council by actively campaigning in favor of Guatemala. Washington argued that Venezuela would politicize debate in the UN and in doing so would break with the tradition of reaching decisions on the basis of consensus.

The intensification of political conflict that led to new thresholds of confrontation forms part of the radicalization of the Chávez presidency, as discussed in Chapter 6. In the case of foreign relations, the process of escalation beginning in 2003 was preceded by the Bush administration's ongoing criticism of Venezuela's positions over the previous two years, its support of the April 2001 coup, and its installation of the Office of Transition Initiatives in the US embassy in Caracas. Once the Chávez government adopted an offensive stance in 2003, escalation soon led to a state of continuous hostility between the two nations. Indeed, the process was accelerated by Chávez's impromptu remarks and his tendency to react aggressively to statements against him and actions taken against his government.

Nevertheless, focusing on this dynamic as the root cause for the deterioration in relations overlooks the clash of national interests and the real issues at stake. Regardless of the overreaction on the part of the United States and the rhetorical excesses on the part of Chávez, diametrically opposed international strategies underpinned by different long-term goals and interests were the motor force of the escalation. As stated in the opening paragraphs of this chapter, many analysts writing on foreign policy under Chávez have ignored these substantive issues. Most important, Venezuela's attempt to promote a multipolar world and its OPEC policy, designed to stabilize oil prices at upper levels, placed the two countries on a collision course. The chapter will now turn to these two sources of conflict.

▶ A Multipolar World

From the beginning of his presidency, Chávez advocated a "multipolar world" as a corrective to the "single-polar world" based on the hegemony of one nation. In doing so, the Venezuelan president envisioned the transformation of groups of nations bound together by alliances into powerful political blocs. In the case of Venezuela, the blocs included OPEC, the Caribbean community of nations, and MERCOSUR (the Common Market of the South), in which Chávez solicited membership during the early months of his government. Although defense of national sovereignty was a cornerstone of his political thinking, Chávez was influenced by the goal of Latin American solidarity and unity preached by Simón Bolívar as well as the notion of interdependency in the modern world. Chávez was thus keenly aware that overcoming dependency and underdevelopment required a collective strategy (Lander 2005, 31).

The term "single-polar world" was a euphemism for US hegemony, to which Chávez refrained from directly referring before 2003. The outset of Chávez's presidency in 1999 was an ideal moment to raise the "multipolar world" banner. US political power at the international level had peaked in the years following the collapse of the Soviet Union in 1991, and the widespread acceptance of the US-promoted model based on macroeconomic formulas also declined by the late 1990s. Furthermore, Chávez's denunciations of US imperialism after 2003 coincided with the widespread recognition of the fragility and vulnerability of US economic power, the loss of US prestige as a result of the invasion of Iraq, and the Bush administration's subordination of pressing worldwide economic problems to the war on terrorism.

Underlying the "multipolar world" concept was the goal of economic diversification in order to overcome dependency on the United States. As an oil-exporting country, Venezuela was more of a single-commodity exporter and more dependent on the US market than other Latin American countries. In 1997, the year before Chávez came to power, Venezuela exported 67 percent of its oil production to the US market (Ministerio de Energia y Minas, *Memoria y Cuenta*, 2002, table 38). The decline in oil exports to the US was modest throughout the Chávez presidency but reached 8 percent in the years 2005 and 2006.

The Chávez government's initiatives in favor of a multipolar world—as is the case with its internal socioeconomic programs—obey two sets of stated objectives, one economic and the other humanitarian. On the one hand, Venezuelan diplomacy is designed to promote the diversification and transformation of the nation's economy and specifically its oil industry in order to overcome dependency and underdevelopment. Agreements providing oil to other countries under special terms as well as bilateral hydrocarbon ventures form part of a commercial and technological strategy of diversification. The Venezuelan government points out that the special credit provisions conceded to neighboring countries is a normal commercial practice in any competitive market. In addition, government-to-government commercial arrangements for oil eliminate middlemen and thus save considerable money that partly compensates for the generous terms of payment.

On the other hand, Chávez justifies the agreements on humanitarian grounds in support of underprivileged nations and individuals. As discussed in Chapter 7 with regard to programs such as the creation of worker cooperatives, the second (humanitarian) objective has taken priority over the first (economic) one at the level of discourse and, to a certain extent, implementation. Chávez's emotional rhetoric in favor of international solidarity and his failure to emphasize the economic advantages of the programs make them susceptible to misunderstanding and controversy. Not surprisingly, Chávez's adversaries have harped on the costliness of the humanitarian and political sides of Venezuelan diplomacy, which they claim represent a heavy burden for the nation and a betrayal of national interests.

In June 2005, Venezuela signed an agreement with Cuba, Jamaica, the Dominican Republic, and ten other Caribbean nations creating PetroCaribe, which is the most ambitious program involving the sale of oil. Under the deal Venezuela allows between 30 and 50 percent of the going price of oil to be paid off in twenty-five years (depending on international prices) with a two-year grace period and 1 percent interest rate, and leaves open the possibility that the debt would be paid off in products such as rice, bananas, and sugar. The accord amounts to 198,000 barrels a day, a sharp increase in the amount of oil Venezuela provided in previous years under special terms. Jamaica's share of twenty-one thousand barrels a day, for instance, represented a threefold increase.

Venezuelan oil diplomacy also includes cooperation in infrastructural projects related to the industry. By late 2007, for instance, PDVSA was to complete work on the oil refinery in Cienfuegos, Cuba, which had been initially undertaken by the former Soviet Union but then paralyzed in 1991. According to this arrangement, Venezuela is to supply the refinery with oil and will own 49 percent of the installation. A similar arrangement with Brazil for the construction of a refinery in Pernambuco is in the planning stage, as is the gas line that is to reach Argentina, while another one that goes to Colombia (and eventually Panama) was completed in 2007.

PDVSA's sale of discounted heating oil in poor neighborhoods in the Bronx and Boston in 2005 was an easy target for the Venezuelan opposition because it provided the nation with no commercial benefits and represented a form of charity for a developed nation bankrolled by an underdeveloped one. As in the case of other oil initiatives, Chávez justified the arrangement by appealing to humanitarian sentiment. In doing so he failed to emphasize pragmatic arguments, specifically that nonprofit community organizations administered the program thus partly offsetting the reduction of profits as a result of discounts. By 2006 the program, which offered discounts of 40 percent (and in some cases up to 60 percent), was extended to other northeastern states as well as to homeless shelters free of charge. In the same year, PDVSA announced its intention of selling discounted heating oil to the poor in London (whose leftist mayor, Ken Livingstone, was a staunch Chávez supporter).

The sale of discounted heating oil had mixed political results. The program began as a response to the requests of fourteen Democratic Party senators (including Hillary Clinton) that oil companies use their exceptionally high profits to subsidize heating oil for the poor and it was enthusiastically defended by politicians in those states where it was implemented. In addition, the program received remarkably favorable local press coverage in the usually hostile US media. In contrast to the United States, Chávez's initiative was a political liability in Venezuela. The Venezuelan government expanded the program in 2006 even though the opposition seized upon it as a major campaign issue in the presidential elections of that year. Indeed, the slogan of presidential candidate Manuel Rosales, "*El petroleo no se regala!*" (The oil shall not be given away), was misleading: it conflated the sale of discounted heating oil in the United States, which was devoid of commercial advantages, with PetroCaribe and PetroSur, which formed part of a commercial strategy and was profitable even with the special terms of payment that were offered.

The Venezuelan government declared that PetroCaribe, PetroSur, and other oil initiatives formed part of a plan to unify and integrate Latin America, known as the Bolivarian Alternative for America (ALBA). Cuba and Venezuela launched ALBA in Havana in 2005, with forty-nine trade and cooperation agreements signed by both countries, including the training of thirty thousand Venezuelan medical students and free cataract operations for one hundred thousand Venezuelans on the island. In 2006 Ecuador announced its intentions of forming part of ALBA, while shortly thereafter several Caribbean nations expressed interest in participating in ALBA-sponsored cooperative agreements. ALBA was conceived of as a new model for Latin American integration, as well as a mechanism to promote international solidarity in response to the individualism and intense competition associated with globalization. In underlining Latin American cooperation, ALBA exposes a major shortcoming of the Washington-promoted Free Trade Area of the Americas, whose cornerstone is the promotion of commercial competition. The FTAA has made no effort to redress the barriers on immigration and in general lacks the spirit of continental unity and solidarity that are stated objectives of the European Union.

In its critique of globalization, ALBA views asymmetric relations between developed and underdeveloped countries as a major obstacle to free trade. As a corrective, it proposes preferential treatment for underdeveloped nations and nonprivileged sectors of the population. While ALBA opposes the protectionist measures of developed countries and particularly the United States, it defends the right of poor countries to protect their peasant population. Its statement of fundamental principles affirms that "in these countries agriculture is a way of life and cannot be treated as just any form of economic activity." ALBA also rules out the participation of the World Bank and other multinational institutions in the formulation of integration plans and proposes the creation of "compensation funds" to aid those displaced as a result of commercial agreements. Other ALBA proposals represent the antithesis of neoliberal formulas. The program calls for priority treatment for national companies and cooperatives and exempting state companies from antimonopoly legislation. ALBA also insists on the retention of workers' historical gains and respect for existing legislation. Finally, legal disputes with foreign corporations are to be resolved in national courts, and only after all instances have been exhausted can the matter be brought to international tribunals.

Venezuela's creation of ALBA, PetroCaribe, and PetroSur and its membership in MERCOSUR all represent important statements of intent, but their concrete effect on the Venezuelan economy in the short- and medium-term future is less clear. Venezuela's strategy of Latin American economic integration confronts the reality of the nation's extreme dependence on a single commodity and its lack of comparative advantages. Over a lengthy period of time, oil-derived revenue encouraged imports and undermined efforts to deepen the process of import substitution. This structural weakness limits the economic advantages for Venezuela in continental trade agreements. In essence, integration opens opportunities only for the diversification of the sale of oil and related products and services as well as imports, and in doing so helps sever commercial dependence. In addition, government spokesmen point to tourism and the export of steel, aluminum, and commodities produced by small- and medium-sized Venezuelan businesses and cooperatives as sources of revenue for the nation over a longer period of time.

▶ **Venezuela's OPEC Strategy**

From the outset of the Chávez presidency, the term "multipolar world" was more than an abstract slogan, particularly because the concept was applicable to Venezuela's OPEC strategy and was thus certain to have an impact on the world economy. Multipolarism implies the strengthening of organizations representing blocs of nations, the most important of which in the third world is OPEC. Under the influence of neoliberal thinking in the 1990s, the Venezuelan government had undermined OPEC by promoting ambitious plans for increasing the nation's oil capacity at the same time that it violated the production quotas assigned it by the organization. This practice contributed to a price war in 1998 with Saudi Arabia and other Gulf countries. As a corrective, Chávez, during his first presidential campaign, pledged to reduce oil investments by 15 percent and to work to strengthen OPEC. Immediately following his election, Chávez carried through with these promises and cut oil production in order to abide by OPEC quotas, a move that won the respect of organization members, including the conservative Saudi Arabia.

The new Venezuelan government under Chávez played a major role in OPEC's recuperation after two decades of declining influence in the world oil market. A newly radicalized leadership in Iran was in close contact with Venezuela as well as Saudi Arabia (thus overcoming the tense relations between the two Middle East countries) in order to lay the groundwork for OPEC's March 1999 meeting. These political developments enhanced the prospects of OPEC's decision to withdraw 2.1 million barrels per day from the market, unlike in previous years when member nations failed to comply with similar agreements. In Venezuela, longtime oil experts such as Humberto Calderón Berti and Leonardo Montiel Ortega, who were associated with proestablishment parties, criticized the accord on grounds that sharp cutbacks were detrimental from a technical viewpoint and would be compensated for by exports from non-OPEC oil-producing nations (*El Universal*, May 31, 1999, 1–2).

Venezuela's proposal to systematically stabilize oil prices at higher levels and its hosting of OPEC's Second Summit in September 2000 catapulted Chávez onto the center stage of the organization. During the previous month, Chávez traveled to all ten fellow OPEC member nations to invite personally the head of state of each one to the conference. Chávez was the first top political figure to visit Iraq since the Gulf War, and he was particularly well received by Saddam Hussein, who proposed that Venezuela occupy the leading OPEC position of secretary-general. The US State Department criticized Chávez for traveling to Iraq as well as to Libya and Iran and insinuated that Venezuelan-US relations might be affected. In response, Chávez alleged that his discussions with Saddam were limited to issues related to OPEC and oil arrangements between the two countries, although during his tour the Venezuelan president called for the lifting of UN trade sanctions against Iraq.

At the Second Summit, Venezuela gained ratification for its proposal to maintain oil prices between twenty-two and twenty-eight dollars. According to the plan, when oil exceeded the twenty-eight-dollar limit for more than twenty work days, OPEC nations would inject five hundred thousand barrels per day into the world market, and vice versa in the case of prices inferior to twenty-two dollars. In his address at the summit, Chávez called for "the relaunching of OPEC" in the form of a new strategy that "goes beyond the defense of the barrel of crude." His plea found expression in the summit's final Declaration of Caracas, which among other proposals committed the organization to creating an OPEC Bank.

Important members of the Venezuelan opposition criticized Chávez's efforts to organize the Second Summit. In an article titled "Foreign Policy: Irresponsibility and Messianism" in *El Universal*, Fernando Ochoa Antich, who had been minister of defense at the time of the April 1992 coup and then foreign minister, argued that the internal divisions in the Middle East would doom the summit to failure and that the meeting would only further politicize the organization. Furthermore, given the recovery of international oil prices over the recent past, the holding of an OPEC summit was uncalled for, at least at this time. Finally, Ochoa Antich argued that the United States had a perfect right to take reprisals against Venezuela as a result of Chávez's meetings with Washington's enemies, such as Saddam and Muammar Qaddafi (Ochoa Antich 2000, 1–6). As he had done before, Humberto

Calderón Berti (who was a national leader of COPEI) criticized Chávez's OPEC initiatives for cutting back on investment and production in the industry.

By failing to rally behind Chávez in the face of US criticism and to back the oil price stabilization plan, the Venezuelan opposition set the stage for the extreme polarization that set in the following year. Polarization was aggravated by the opposition's failure to back any of Chávez's policies and actions, and its denial of his legitimacy as president. Support for Chávez's OPEC policy, which of all his actions appeared to be the most successful in that it facilitated the recovery of oil prices, may have enhanced the opposition's credibility and the plausibility of its criticisms of more controversial government policies. Furthermore, the refusal of opposition leaders to distance themselves from the US State Department over its disapproval of Chávez's OPEC-nation tour (coupled with their support for Washington's request to use Venezuelan space to track down drug traffickers [El Universal, August 21, 2000, 1–13]), set the tone for their ongoing convergence with US positions that became graphically evident at the time of the 2002 coup. Indeed, both the head of the coup, Pedro Carmona, in April 2002, and opposition candidate Manuel Rosales, during the 2006 presidential elections, followed the US line by announcing their intention to suspend the export of oil to Cuba.

In recent years, the Chávez government has continued to play an important role in the reduction of OPEC oil production in order to maintain prices at higher levels. In doing so, Chávez has departed from Venezuela's traditional stand as an OPEC moderate, which over various decades had attempted to reconcile the position of the hard-line wing of the organization (consisting of Iraq, Libya, Algeria, and, since the late 1970s, Iran) and that of the conservatives (headed by Saudi Arabia). In his fiery rhetoric, Chávez (along with the government of Iran) has cushioned Saudi Arabia from Washington's outcry against OPEC for high oil prices. The Saudis are thus able to discreetly go along with price hikes, which are attributed to the OPEC "radicals," without having to pay a political price in the form of strained relations with the United States (Mohamedi 2006).

▶ **Foreign Policy and the Grassroots Strategy**

Two basic aspects of Chávez's foreign policy that are sometimes fraught with tension correspond to the "statist" and "grassroots" approaches discussed in Chapter 7. On the one hand, the Chávez government has scored important diplomatic victories that are made possible by its tolerance toward, and friendly relations with, heads of state who adhere to widely diverse ideological positions (the statist approach). On the other hand, Chávez's zealous rhetoric in favor of revolutionary change and his glorification of Che Guevara and other revolutionary icons have generated widespread fervent support among social movements and leftist activists and the general population throughout Latin America in accordance with the grassroots strategy. The diplomatic, "statist" strategy sought to avoid the error committed by the Castro regime in the 1960s when it aided revolutionary movements throughout the continent and in doing so forfeited the possibility of winning over or neutralizing democratic governments, which ended up supporting OAS-sponsored measures against the island. Indeed, Castro, who in more recent years has prioritized the diplomatic, statist strategy, evidently advised Chávez to follow a realistic approach to foreign relations by avoiding actions that would alienate neighboring governments (Spenser 2005).

One of the Chávez government's most important diplomatic successes stemming from the statist approach was the decision of MERCOSUR to admit Venezuela as a regular member of the organization. At different international encounters, MERCOSUR governments have defended uniform positions, thus opening the possibility that they would act as a "bloc" of nations in accordance with the "multipolar world" concept advocated by Chávez. The MERCOSUR nations, for instance, supported Venezuela's request to occupy a nonpermanent seat on the UN Security Council, which the organization's General Assembly voted on in October 2006. More important, the MERCOSUR governments defeated President George W. Bush's effort to reactivate discussion on the FTAA at the Fourth Summit of the Americas held in Mar del Plata, Argentina, in November 2005.

Chávez's rhetoric and actions have placed him to the left of the center-leftist Luiz Inácio Lula da Silva (Brazil), Néstor Kirchner (Argentina), and Tabaré Vásquez (Uruguay). Nevertheless, Venezuela shares with the other MERCOSUR nations critical positions toward unilateral intervention and domination from the "North," at the same time that all of them maintain friendly relations with Cuba. Furthermore, Chávez has refused to allow ideological differences to get in the way of his close relations with his counterparts to the south even though various leftist movements were strongly opposed to those same governments. Chávez's pragmatic, "statist" approach was demonstrated by his speech at the 2005 World Social Forum in Porto Alegre, Brazil, in which he proclaimed his adherence to socialism. Chávez responded to heckling in the audience directed at Lula by pointing out that each revolution has to choose its own pace, and went on to say, "I like Lula, I appreciate him, he is a good man with a great heart."[1] A pragmatic approach has also enabled Chávez to maintain cordial relations with Colombian president Álvaro Uribe even though they occupy opposite extremes on the political spectrum.

After Chávez consolidated political control in Venezuela, as a result of the recall election in August 2004, the Venezuelan government assumed a more audacious stance in its relations with various countries and began to place greater emphasis on the "bottom-up" approach at the expense of diplomatic considerations. Until then, Chávez's statement rang true that it was only with the Bush administration that Venezuela had tense relations. Chávez's harsh verbal exchange with Mexican president Vicente Fox at the Summit of the Americas in November 2005 signaled a political shift in which the Venezuelan government occasionally spurned the diplomatic or "statist" approach. At the summit, Chávez clashed with Fox's effort to place the issue of the FTAA on the agenda for discussion and ended up calling the Mexican president a "puppy dog of the [US] empire."[2]

Chávez's collision with Peruvian presidential candidate Alan García on the eve of the runoff election in June 2006 was even more intense. In the first round of the elections, the centrist García had come in second place behind leftist candidate Ollanta Humala, whom Chávez supported. In response to García's claim that Chávez was "trying to impose his candidate" on Peruvian voters, the Venezuelan president called him a "bandit" and "Peru's Carlos Andrés Pérez." Chávez went on to threaten to sever diplomatic relations with Peru in the event that García was elected president. In fact, García may have deliberately provoked Chávez, in which case the Peruvian politician's scheme was a master stroke. In the campaign for the second round, García attempted to draw votes from former candidate Lourdes Flores (who had been eliminated in the first round), who was to his right, even though many of her followers considered García a radical populist and a demagogue, stemming from his first presidency in the late 1980s. García capitalized on Chávez's remarks by claiming they were intended to intimidate voters, an accusation that became an important campaign issue. García, undoubtedly with a large percentage of the votes of Flores's supporters, defeated Humala in the second round.

The main arguments Chávez employed to justify Venezuela's withdrawal from the Andean Community of Nations (CAN) in April 2006 also put in evidence the Venezuelan president's occasional rejection of pragmatism, which is the cornerstone of the diplomatic, statist approach. Chávez's surprising announcement of the decision, which put an end to Venezuela's thirty-three-year membership in the organization, was a response to bilateral free-trade agreements signed by both Peru and Colombia with the United States. Chávez pointed out that neither government had previously consulted with CAN members as they were obliged to by the organization's statutes, and he added that those accords "favor the elites and the transnationals, but do not serve the interests of indigenous people, blacks, or the poor." Chávez and other government spokesmen, however, failed to explain emphatically why Venezuela would be better off outside of the CAN from a commercial viewpoint. Specifically, Venezuela ran the risk of being inundated by US products that entered Colombia under the terms of the new trade agreement. The way Chávez presented his case in Manichean emotional terms, while largely passing over concrete economic concerns, illustrated the idealistic, nonpragmatic tendency characteristic of the grassroots approach.

In another example of Chávez's confrontational style that undermines diplomatic objectives, the Venezuelan president in mid-2007 blamed the right in Brazil and Paraguay for delays in congressional ratification of Venezuela's request for membership in MERCOSUR. Chávez went on to announce that his government would withdraw its request to enter the organization if the two congresses did not reach a decision within three months. In another statement that hurt Venezuela's case for membership, Chávez criticized the organization's largest nation, Brazil, for failing to lend a helping hand to tiny Uruguay and Paraguay.

The grassroots approach in Venezuela has been conducive to the excesses in both rhetoric and action that have sometimes been labeled "ultraleftism," as discussed in Chapter 7. Most important, the *Chavista* leadership has evinced a sense of voluntarism and optimism that has proved to be a poor predictor of events. This lack of realism recalls the Cuban government's foreign involvements in the 1960s as illustrated by Che Guevara's famous slogan, "To Create One, Two, Three Vietnams," and his quixotic Bolivian venture that cost him his life. In the case of Chávez, the assumption that leftists Humala in Peru and Andrés Manuel López Obrador in Mexico would be elected presidents in 2006 led Chávez to confront Alan García and Vicente Fox, respectively. Similarly, Chávez's insulting remarks against Bush made in his New York appearances just days before the vote on Venezuela's request for a seat on the UN Security Council swayed various delegates to vote against Caracas out of fear that it intended to use its sought-for position to promote highly controversial stands (*New York Times*, October 25, 2006, 6).

The grassroots strategy, which spurns existing political structures, has long been defended by fringe political movements on the far left. The age of globalization, however, gave the approach a special boost. Both activists and scholars began to question the relevance of the state and centralized institutions, such as political parties, and in their place have argued for the viability of local decisionmaking and autonomous social movements. More recently, the upsurge of leftist forces in Latin America has encouraged Chávez to appeal directly to the people on the basis of an emotional discourse in accordance with the grassroots approach.

There is no fundamental incompatibility between the two approaches, however, and the Chávez government could have strived for a happy medium between the two. Nevertheless, as in the case of internal policies, discussed in the previous chapter, the grassroots approach seeks to maximize the enthusiasm and commitment of the popular sectors of the population, which pragmatic politics associated with the statist approach tends to dampen. The dynamic of direct emotional appeal to the general population is particularly important because it parlays passive (or electoral) support to active support among Chávez's followers.

In the area of foreign policy, the growth and assertiveness of social movements, such as those that racked Bolivia, Ecuador, and Peru in recent years, have increased the attractiveness of the grassroots approach. At the same time, however, the independent positions pursued by other Latin American governments and their ideological shift to the left encourage the pursuance of the statist approach. Specifically, unity among center-leftist and leftist governments that have come to power since 1998, and are grouped in MERCOSUR and ALBA, open possibilities for the emergence of a bloc of nations in the continent, with Venezuela playing a pivotal role. These developments lend themselves to Chávez's multipolar strategy that is conducive to the statist, diplomatic approach to foreign policy.

▶ **Notes**

1. The extreme expression of the grassroots approach that writes off the state and the struggle for state power was associated with the World Social Forum (WSF) following its initiation in 2001. A shift, however, took place at the Sixth Forum held in Caracas in 2006. A major thematic category of discus-

sion at the gathering was "power, politics, and social emancipation." In addition, the proposal to authorize the WSF organization to assume positions on specific issues gained ground, even though grassroots activists feared that the proposition ran the risk of infringing on the autonomy of individual social movements. The Venezuelan hosts, along with various prominent leftist intellectuals, including WSF founders Emir Sader of Brazil and Samir Amin of Egypt, contributed to the support for this reorientation.

2. In addition, the discounted heating oil program in poor communities of the northeastern United States was designed to appeal directly to the general population of that nation in accordance with the grassroots approach.

9

▼

Conclusion

THIS book has addressed the need to differentiate issues and changes of paramount importance from secondary ones in order to understand the main political developments throughout Venezuelan history and particularly over the recent past. Much of the writing on Hugo Chávez, and to a certain extent previous historical periods, focuses on personalities, discourse unconnected to concrete policy, and changes of political and state institutions, while paying less attention to social and economic dimensions. The book argues that these non-socioeconomic factors in themselves are incapable of explaining the dramatic events that have shaped Venezuelan history, such as the military coups of the 1940s and 1950s, the schisms in the nation's two major political parties after 1958, the popular outbursts of 1989, the subsequent political crisis of the 1990s, and the Chávez phenomenon.

One of the key questions that need to be addressed in order to differentiate fundamental from relatively superficial factors during critical periods is why leading members of powerful groups such as the armed forces, business organizations, the church hierarchy, and the US government have acted decisively to block certain changes that have been initiated. The relevance of this issue is evident in the case of the unrelenting hostility of the different sectors opposed to the Chávez government. Had FEDECAMARAS played a less central role in the April 2002 coup, and had it modified its stand immediately afterward, or had Washington sought reconciliation with the Venezuelan government following the incident, then their behavior could have been attributed to circumstantial factors or exaggerated fears. The intense hostility, which continued unabated in spite of Chávez's triumphs, indicates that fundamental interests have been at stake.

Political analysts and historians over a considerable period of time have generally downplayed class interests. These writers, for instance, have for the most part focused on two causes for the 1948 and 2001 coups that are unrelated to class. In the first place, they stress the fiery rhetoric and exclusionary discourse of AD leaders during the *trienio* and Chávez from the outset of his presidency. In the second place, they emphasize the hegemonic designs of those in power who spurned the system of checks and balances and consequently alienated minority political organizations and institutions.

Political scientists writing on the political crisis of the 1990s also centered on institutions, and thus crucial factors, such as the social unrest highlighted by the *Caracazo*, were underestimated. The institutional approach was highly critical of the centralism of the state and political parties, specifically the concentration of authority in the hands of the executive branch, and in doing so coincided with the neoliberal critique of the political system that was widely accepted at the time. The implication of this analysis was that if only decentralization and state reform had proceeded apace, the crisis would have been avoided and Chávez never would have reached power.

The sharpened class tensions and polarization, the zero-sum-game politics that pits the interests of the poor against privileged sectors, and the class content of official discourse under the Chávez presidency have left an indelible mark on the thinking of many writers, as well as on the Venezuelan people as a whole. Specifically, the new setting is conducive to reexamining the notion that Venezuelan politics for the most part does not reflect social conflict and differences. Thus, for instance, a number of social scientists have recently undertaken studies in the barrios, an area that had failed to attract significant scholarly attention in the past (Ellner 2003b, 161–162).

The approach advocated in this book, unlike much political analysis up until now, attaches particular significance to economic issues. The paramount importance of economic interests became starkly clear in late 2001 with the promulgation of a package of socioeconomic laws, including agrarian reform and legislation halting the gradual privatization of the oil industry and the social security system, as well as measures favoring small-scale fishing, microcompanies and cooperatives. Overnight, militant protests by the middle- and upper-class opposition broke out and soon called for the ouster of President Chávez. The cause-and-effect relationship between popular and nationalist measures of an economic nature, on the one hand, and the belligerent reaction of privileged sectors, on the other hand, was anything but subtle.

Immediate economic interests alone, however, cannot explain the confrontations unleashed under Chávez, just as they could not in other historical contexts. Several examples unrelated to Venezuela will suffice to illustrate the obvious shortcoming of economistic explanations. As one example, the interests of armament manufacturers, in themselves, cannot explain the US decision to enter World War I, contrary to the writings of economic determinist historians. Similarly, the extraordinary profits of Halliburton and Bechtel, with their close ties to the Bush administration, are not the main reason for the US invasion of Iraq. In a similar vein, immediate economic interests are hurt by the US embargo of Cuba and thus cannot explain why it has lasted nearly half a century.

In addition to economic factors, this book has emphasized the long-term political effect of struggles over concrete demands and the resultant phenomenon of popular empowerment. The approach advocated here highlights empowerment as an ongoing process, which opens a window of opportunity for far-reaching change, and a historical memory that keeps alive struggles over time. Such subjective factors play a key role during critical junctures when political fluidity and power vacuums, or the lack of consolidation of power, are conducive to radical change. Defeated struggles and unsuccessful movements in Venezuela, which were written off by political actors at the time and subsequently by many historians and political scientists, have often weighed heavily on future developments.

The book points to several examples of the importance of political consciousness over a period of time that found expression at key junctures. Thus it traces nineteenth-century struggles, beginning with agrarian and political movements prior to the Federal War, which failed to achieve their principal goals of democracy and social justice. In addition, the assertions of nationalist positions by Cipriano Castro seemed futile in light of his overthrow by his trusted lieutenant, Juan Vicente Gómez, with the backing of the United States. Traditional political historiography plays down the importance of this heritage and dates the movement for democracy and transformation to the generation of 1928, which allegedly exerted overwhelming influence in the struggle for progressive change following Gómez's death. Nevertheless, the students of 1928 represented an inchoate middle class and did not by themselves account for the radically new political environment in 1936—violent disturbances with nationalist overtones that broke out just hours after the announcement of Gómez's death and the subsequent political turbulence culminating with the oil workers' strike, which reflected anti-imperialist sentiment (Bergquist 1986, 232–242) and received support across class lines. In short, century-long struggles for democracy, social change, and nationalist demands were important antecedents to the goals formulated and achieved after 1936.

A second example of the ongoing importance of struggle that has often been dismissed as lacking in political content is the factionalism within the dominant AD and COPEI parties. Despite changes in personalities and political contexts, leftist factions originating from the early years of AD in the mid-1940s (Ellner 1979, 183–184; 1982, 147) continued through the first administration of Carlos Andrés Pérez in the 1970s, but never gained control of the organization due in part to the undemocratic practices of the party machine. AD leaders such as Rómulo Betancourt attributed these internal conflicts (with the exception of the MIR split of 1960, which was overtly ideological) to personal ambitions, a view echoed by many historians and political scientists. Nevertheless, the leftist dissidents defended positions ranging from the defense of democratic procedures to the promotion of nationalist political and economic goals. In spite of the turnabouts of many of the dissident leaders who ended up returning to the AD fold, these factions kept alive critical and leftist positions within the political mainstream.

Similar to the changes ushered in after Gómez's death, the *Chavista* movement in power cannot be seen as occurring in a vacuum or resulting exclusively from events of the immediate past. Indeed, the *Chavistas* have always invoked historical symbols and have highlighted the political struggles of the past that raised banners such as social equality, nationalism, and radical change. Thus the *Chavistas* have exalted leaders such as leftist martyrs Argimiro Gabaldón, Fabricio Ojeda, Jorge Rodríguez, and Alberto Lovera by naming streets, plazas, health centers, and production units after them and presenting information about their lives in the state- and *Chavista*-supported media and publishing outlets.

Popular empowerment has historically been given a major impulse by radical governments that forcefully express support for social justice and nationalist ideals. Discourse, however, that fails to go beyond empty rhetoric has little impact. The radicals in power need to tie their style and rhetoric to concrete policies and reforms in order to maintain their credibility. The radical governments of AD during the *trienio* of 1945–1948 and Chávez since 1998 are prime examples of this dynamic. Both governments helped bring about a change in political culture as a result of the mobilization of politically excluded sectors of the population that produced important gains. In the case of the *trienio*, the most important type of mobilization was the massive unionization of agricultural and urban workers. The social base of the Chávez presidency at its outset was the marginalized sectors, specifically the workers of the informal economy and the nonunionized ones of the formal economy, which participated in the marches and other demonstrations that were essential to Chávez's political survival from 2001 to 2004. In both periods mobilization and radical discourse were accompanied by concrete reforms, the essential ingredients for infusing the popular movement with a sense of empowerment. Furthermore, some of the reforms pointed in the direction of far-reaching structural change. Thus, for example, the decision of the Gallegos government in 1948 to sell one-fourth of oil royalties on the international market opened the possibility of state competition with the multinationals at a future date, even though this was not the government's intention at the time.

In both periods, powerful proestablishment groups rejected the government's reformist impulse, but they undoubtedly could have tolerated it and assumed a position of loyal opposition had it not been for other circumstances. Their unyielding intransigence was in response to what was for them a dangerous combination of factors: popular and nationalist reforms and policies, on the one hand, and the mobilization and concomitant sense of empowerment on the part of the popular classes on the other. Indeed, both periods represented critical junctures. Given the political incorporation and empowerment of nonprivileged sectors, as well as the government's lack of well-defined, long-term goals, and the weakening of traditional organizations, the nation's political future was highly uncertain. One possible scenario was a revolutionary chain of events leading to far-reaching socioeconomic transformations.

The Bush administration's position toward Chávez resembled that of the Venezuelan elite and was motivated by a similar preoccupation with the larger implications of his government's actions. Indeed, US opposition to Chávez went beyond occasional criticisms of specific stands or policies and came to reflect a virtual obsession on the part of the Bush administration. This attitude was made blatantly evident by the announcement made in mid-2002 that Washington had decided to set up an "office of transition" in Caracas and the subsequent preposterous statement by Secretary of Defense Donald Rumsfeld comparing Chávez with Adolph Hitler.

What most preoccupied Washington was the prospect that Venezuelan policies would serve as an example for the rest of the continent. This "demonstration effect," and not the unproven allegations that Chávez was financing revolutionary movements with "petrodollars," accounted for Washington's intense hostility toward Venezuela. When the Chávez government implemented anti-neoliberal reforms in 2001, it was defying the premise of the Washington Consensus that any strategy other than macroeconomic formulas was doomed to failure. Chávez's survival in power increasingly undermined the validity of this dictum. The challenge Chávez posed to the hegemony of the US-promoted neoliberal project in Latin America reached a new threshold when his presidency entered the third stage after 2004 (as discussed in Chapter 5) and a new economic model began to emerge at the same time that Chávez incorporated the term *socialism* into his discourse. In addition, the election of center-leftist and leftist presidents in Brazil, Argentina, Uruguay, Bolivia, Ecuador, and Nicaragua increased the regional influence of Chávez, who played a key diplomatic role in defeating US initiatives on the FTAA and other issues. The possibility that a cohesive bloc would emerge and assume radical positions on issues such as payment of the foreign debt and integration of Cuba into the community of nations loomed large.

Writers who focus on major political party leaders while minimizing the importance of political and social actors at lower levels tend to skirt the larger issues addressed in this book. These analysts write off the relatively autonomous role of social and political movements and the challenge posed by those in AD and COPEI who defied their party's national leadership. In essence, these accounts view the dominant leaders of the traditional parties as having successfully straight-jacketed their own rank and file, as well as organized labor and social movements.

As a corrective, this book has emphasized expressions of relative autonomy during key junctures beginning with the appearance of the first modern parties following the death of Juan Vicente Gómez. The popular struggles that broke out in 1936 cannot be seen as responding to orders from party leaders, as some scholars have stated or implied. At another critical juncture, the nascent CTV favored calling a general strike to face the impending coup in November 1948. The proposal was vetoed by AD political leaders who pursued a negotiation strategy, producing internal frictions that persisted for years and led into the party schisms of the 1960s. At a third critical juncture, in 1958, students, workers, and others took power into their hands by occupying the streets in order to thwart several coup attempts and in the process demanded that the government assume a hard line toward pro–Pérez Jiménez officers. The Junta Patriótica and other organizations that promoted unity in favor of democracy, and in which the Communist Party and the left wings of the nation's three other parties were well represented, clashed with traditional leaders who ended up launching separate candidacies for the 1958 presidential election. Betancourt, who realized that independent loci of influence competed with national party leaderships, insisted on the dissolution of the Junta Patriótica on grounds that it had completed its mission with the overthrow of the dictatorship.

Scholars who ignore these sources of tension credit the multiclass parties and particularly AD with having created mechanisms to contain social conflicts by channeling them internally, thus avoiding open confrontations between labor and capital (Fagen 1977, 189–192). They overlook the fact that AD trade unionists for many years considered the multiclass status of their party as temporary and embraced the goal of transforming it into a "labor party" (Ellner 1993, 98–99). A similar vision was upheld by labor leaders in Perón's Partido Justicialista at the party's outset (James 2000).

The need for analysts to go beyond dominant political leaderships to examine expressions of political diversity and popular influence is particularly evident in the case of the Chávez presidency, as discussed in Chapter 7. Much of the discussion about *Chavismo* at all levels, including published works by political analysts, dwells on Chávez himself and, to a lesser extent, the positions adopted by his MVR party. Nevertheless, contrary to the claims of Chávez's adversaries, who reduce the *Chavista* phenomenon to *caudillismo*, a large block of rank-and-file *Chavistas* are not beholden to any political line and view themselves as the backbone of the movement. These "independents" are particularly assertive within the *Chavista* labor confederation, the UNT, and take stands that do not always coincide with the official positions of MVR politicians. Events during the coup of April 11, 2002, underscore the crucial role played by the *Chavistas* who are independent of political parties. At a time when the MVR leadership had gone into hiding, hundreds of thousands of independents marched to military bases to exhort officers to declare themselves in open rebellion against the Carmona government. Subsequently, the independents were further empowered by their successful campaign under the direction of the Maisanta Command in favor of the "No Vote" for the recall election of August 2004. The independents considered Chávez's decision to create the Maisanta Command a rebuke to political party leaders, who, having controlled the Ayacucho Command, had failed to block the opposition's attempt to collect enough signatures to hold the recall.

Political analysts need to place the independents in a central position in any theoretical analysis designed to understand the inner workings of *Chavismo*. Chapter 7 examined the role of both the "independents" and political party leaders, the two principal components of the

Chavista movement, which embody two distinct ways of doing politics that are often in conflict with one another. Those in both camps point to certain statements made by Chávez as vindicating their respective positions. Considerable literature on leftist and social-movement theory over the past three decades has examined and defended the two approaches in contexts ranging from the Zapatista struggles in Mexico to the Workers Party of Brazil.

The independents stand for a grassroots or "horizontal" approach, which favors maximizing the input of rank-and-file *Chavistas* and social movements in decisionmaking including the naming of candidates to run for office. They are critical of party leaders for tolerating corruption and promoting bureaucratic behavior that dampens the movement's enthusiasm and blocks the unfolding of the revolutionary process. At the Constituent Assembly in 1999 the grassroots approach underpinned the thesis that direct democracy would eventually displace (rather than complement) representative democracy. Those who identify with the grassroots approach were encouraged when in April 2001 Chávez harshly criticized the MVR for failing to represent and harness the zeal of the movement's popular base, and as a corrective called for the activation of social and political movements, including the Bolivarian Circles and the old MBR-200. Beginning in early 2004 Chávez again invoked the grassroots vision by calling for a "revolution in the revolution" to shake up bureaucratic structures and unleash an all-out war on corruption.

Party leaders in general favor a "vertical" or statist approach that views the MVR as essential to the revolutionary process and calls for the maintenance of the movement's unity at all costs. The "verticalists" are wary of the undisciplined and occasionally disruptive behavior of the *Chavista* rank and file. Like those who champion the grassroots approach, those who support the vertical approach can draw on important aspects of the *Chavista* experience as well as remarks by Chávez himself. Thus, for instance, shortly after his release from prison in 1994, Chávez disparaged the participation of some of his followers in electoral campaigns to reach office at the state and municipal levels, which some grassroots theoreticians consider a major arena of contestation. Chávez viewed these campaigns as a diversion from the basic goal of gaining power at the national level. Even though Chávez occasionally criticizes the *Chavista* political parties and state bureaucracies for being out of touch with the people, he recognizes the MVR's outstanding legislative role beginning with the activity of party representatives in the Constituent Assembly in 1999 (Harnecker 2005, 161). Furthermore, Chávez's insistence on the overriding importance of the unity of his movement runs counter to the grassroots approach of waging an internal struggle against vertical forms of control.

The ongoing friction between a large number of independents who actively support Chávez, on the one hand, and the main governing parties, on the other, is a unique feature of the *Chavista* process requiring novel political and theoretical formulations. The failure of both groups and their respective strategies to gain the upper hand during such a protracted period of intense political conflict undermines the argument that one of the two approaches is unviable and irrelevant as a strategy for revolutionary change in the modern political setting. The coexistence of the two approaches would suggest the need to develop a synthesis that links the two sets of actors in ways that would break down the barriers and distrust between them. A logical starting point is the renovation of the MVR in order to ensure a two-way flow between the party and autonomous social movements and establish internal elections for party candidates and authorities.[1] It is unclear at the time of this writing whether the PSUV is well positioned to achieve such an objective.

The general thrust of this book draws on two Marxist traditions, as is particularly evident in the discussion of the grassroots and statist approaches in Chapter 7. The book's emphasis on empowerment and historical memory is informed by the historiography and methodologies associated with such historians as E. P. Thompson and Herbert Gutman, sometimes referred to as "people's history" or "bottom-up history." This school values the importance of the banners of defeated struggles and traces their reemergence and reformulation often in the distant future (Roberts 2005, 550–551; for Latin America, see Nash 1979). Along these lines, this book has viewed the nineteenth-century struggles and those throughout the Castro and Gómez regimes as important antecedents to post-1936 political developments. Similarly, an examination of the progressive banners of the 1945–1948 *trienio* and those emerging from the factional struggle in AD and COPEI after 1958 is essential to understanding the Chávez phenomenon.

The second Marxist tradition focuses on state power. This book has pointed to the centrality of the state for achieving far-reaching change, a proposition that some grassroots theoreticians dismiss as unfeasible for Latin America in the age of globalization (Holloway 2005b). Thus, for instance, the book highlights the volatility and unpredictability of the critical junctures of 1945–1948, 1958, and 1998 when those committed to radical change but lacking in ideological definition were in, or close to, the seats of power. The prospect of structural transformation carried out by a revolutionary state lay behind the support of powerful groups for the coups of 1948 and 2001, and the concerted efforts by traditional political leaders to isolate and neutralize the left and social organizations during the turbulence of 1958. Finally, under Chávez, the state, through official discourse, programs, and policies, has played a major role in promoting rank-and-file mobilization and organization that point in the direction of structural transformations.

The pragmatic dimension of Chávez's foreign policy provides another example of the state-centered approach. Chapter 8 highlighted the Venezuelan government's efforts to create a Latin American bloc and reach out to governments worldwide in order to overcome dependence on the United States and to lessen Washington's influence. Intergovernmental alliances above ideological considerations were designed to achieve a "multipolar world," a concept that placed the state at the center of the process of far-reaching change.

Marxism has sometimes been accused of putting forward all-encompassing formulations and spurning the uniqueness of individual countries. This book in no way denies the specificity of Venezuelan politics and class behavior, which historically was devoid of the bloody confrontations that traumatized countries such as Chile, Argentina, and Colombia. In spite of the book's systematic criticism of "exceptionalism" thesis writers, it recognizes the veracity of their statements differentiating the Venezuelan case from these tragic and sanguinary historical experiences occurring elsewhere.

Nevertheless, the absence of extensive political violence in Venezuela that is highlighted by exceptionalism writers does not signify long-lasting social harmony or the existence of viable mechanisms for the resolution of class differences. Indeed, the exceptionalism thesis passes over Venezuela's status as a dependent, third-world nation that implies political and social instability. In any analysis of concrete socioeconomic issues, whose importance this book has underlined, as well as political and institutional ones, Venezuela cannot be taken out of the Latin American context. As is typical elsewhere in the continent, sharp political and social tension in Venezuela has never been easily contained. A large part of the social conflict in post-1958 Venezuela was expressed outside of the political mainstream and was not subject to existing political and legal mechanisms, nor did it receive fair coverage in the communications media. In this sense, the political system was more exclusionary than those who defended the exceptionalism thesis recognized at the time.

Violence for the most part did not manifest itself in the political arena in Venezuela until more recent years. Not surprisingly, the violence that broke out in 1989 (in the form of mass national disturbances), 1992 (two coup attempts), and 2002 (another coup) put the nails in the coffin of the exceptionalism thesis. Thus Venezuela's "exceptional" status during the years that the exceptionalism thesis was widely accepted consisted, in effect, of low levels of violent political confrontation, but not low levels of intense conflict stemming from concrete political and social demands.

The same combination of features that are specific to Venezuela and those characteristic of the entire region lay behind the Chávez phenomenon. Unique aspects include the participation of the armed forces and the overriding importance of oil revenue. At the same time, however, the Chávez experience debunks the myth of Venezuela as devoid of the acute social and racial tensions characteristic of the rest of Latin America and their ongoing expressions on the political front. In short, the achievement of a balance between factors shared by neighboring Latin American nations such as class conflict and foreign dependency, on the one hand, and unique qualities mainly related to Venezuela's oil producing status, on the other, is a major challenge facing the revisionist approach to history and politics outlined in this book.

▶ **Note**

1. Some social scientists in recent years have proposed such a synthesis based on a symbiotic relationship between parties and social movements (Hellman 1992; Schönwälder 2002). In doing so, they are reacting against the formulations dating back to the 1980s that celebrated the emergence of "new social movements" as an alternative to party politics. Significantly, John Holloway, who is a foremost advocate of the grassroots approach in its pure form, has viewed Venezuelan developments as pointing in the direction of a combination of the two strategies (Holloway 2005a, 123).

Acronyms

AD	Acción Democrática (Democratic Action)
AFL	American Federation of Labor
ALBA	Alternativa Bolivariana para la America (Bolivian Alternative for America)
ANC	Asamblea Nacional Constituyente (National Constituent Assembly)
APRA	Alianza Popular Revolucionara Americana (Popular American Revolutionary Alliance)
BANDES	Banco de Desarrollo Económico y Social (Bank of Economic and Social Development)
CAN	Comunidad Andina de Naciones (Andean Community of Nations)
CANTV	Compañía Anónima Nacional de Teléfonos de Venezuela (Anonymous National Telephone Company of Venezuela)
CDN	Comité Directivo Nacional (National Directive Committee)
CEN	Comité Ejecutivo Nacional (National Executive Committee)
CIT	Confederación Interamericana de Trabajadores (Interamerican Confederation of Workers)
CLPP	Consejos Locales de Planificación Pública (Local Councils of Public Planning)
CNE	Consejo Nacional Electoral (National Electoral Council)
COFAVIC	Committee of the Families of the Victims of February–March 1989
CONACOPRESA	Comisión sobre Costos, Precios, y Salarios (Commission on Costs, Prices, and Salaries)
COPEI	Comité de Organización Política Electoral Independiente (Committee of Independent Political Electoral Organization)
COPRE	Comisión Presidencial para la Reforma del Estado (Presidential Commission for State Reform)

227

CSUN	Comité Sindical Unificado Nacional (National Unified Union Committee)
CTAL	Confederación de Trabajadores de América Latina (Workers' Confederation of Latin America)
CTU	Comité de Tierra Urbana (urban land committee)
CTV	Confederación de Trabajadores de Venezuela (Venezuelan Workers' Confederation)
CVG	Corporación Venezolana de Guayana (Venezuelan Corporation of Guayana)
CVP	Corporación Venezolana de Petróleo (Venezuelan Petroleum Corporation)
DIGEPOL	Dirección General de Policía (General Office of Police)
DISIP	Dirección de Servicio de Inteligencia Policial (Office of the Police Intelligence Services)
FBT	Fuerza Bolivariana de Trabajadores (Bolivarian Workers' Force)
FEDECAMARAS	Federación Venezolana de Cámaras y Asociaciones de Comercio y Producción (Venezuelan Federation of Chambers and Associations of Commerce and Production)
FEDEPETROL	Federación de Trabajadores Petroleros (Federation of Petroleum Workers)
FETRAHIDROCARBUROS	Federación de Trabajadores de la Industria de Hidrocarburos (Federation of Workers of the Hydrocarbons Industry)
FIDES	Fondo Intergubernamental para la Descentralización (Intergovernmental Fund for Decentralization)
FIV	Fondo de Inversiones de Venezuela (Investment Fund of Venezuela)
FOGADE	Fondo de Garantía de Depósitos y Protección Bancaria (Guarantee Fund for Deposits and Bank Protection)
FTAA	Free Trade Area of the Americas
IMF	International Monetary Fund
INAMUJER	Instituto Nacional de la Mujer (National Institute for Women)
INCE	Instituto Nacional de Cooperación Educativa (National Institute of Educational Cooperation)
INTEVEP	Instituto Tecnológico Venezolano del Petróleo (Venezuelan Technological Institute of Petroleum)
INTI	Instituto Nacional de Tierras (National Land Institute)
INVEPAL	Industria Venezolana Endógena del Papel (Venezuelan Endogenous Paper Industry)
LOD	Ley Orgánica de Descentralización (Organic Law of Decentralization)
MAS	Movimiento al Socialismo (Movement Toward Socialism)

MBR-200	Movimiento Bolivariano Revolucionario–200 (Revolutionary Bolivarian Movement–200)
MEP	Movimiento Electoral del Pueblo (People's Electoral Movement)
MERCAL	Mercado de Alimentos (food market)
MERCOSUR	Mercado Común del Sur (Common Market of the South)
MIR	Movimiento de la Izquierda Revolucionaria (Movement of the Revolutionary Left)
MPPEC	Ministerio del Poder Popular para la Economía Comunal (Ministry of Popular Power for the Community Economy)
MVR	Movimiento Quinta República (Fifth Republic Movement)
NED	National Endowment for Democracy
OAS	Organization of American States
OPEC	Organization of Petroleum Exporting Countries
OTI	Office of Transition Initiatives
PCV	Partido Comunista de Venezuela (Communist Party of Venezuela)
PCVU	Partido Comunista Venezolano Unitario (United Venezuelan Communist Party)
PDV	Partido Democrático Venezolano (Venezuelan Democratic Party)
PDVSA	Petróleos de Venezuela, Sociedad Anónima (Petroleum of Venezuela, Joint Stock Company)
PPI	Programa de Promoción del Investigador (Program of Researcher Promotion)
PPT	Patria para Todos (Homeland for All)
PRV	Partido de la Revolución Venezolana (Party of the Venezuelan Revolution)
PSUV	Partido Socialista Unido de Venezuela (United Socialist Party of Venezuela)
RECADI	Régimen de Cambio Diferencial (Differential Exchange Regime)
SELA	Sistema Económico Latinoamericano (Latin American Economic System)
SENIAT	Servicio Nacional Integrado de Administración Aduanera y Tributaria (Integrated National Service for Customs and Tax Administration)
SI	Socialisto International
SIDOR	Siderúrgica de Orinoco (Orinoco Steel Company)
SINUTRAPETROL	Sindicato Único Nacional de Trabajadores Petroleros (Sole National Union of Petroleum Workers)
SISDEM	Sistema de Democratización del Empleo (System of Employment Democratization)

SUNACOOP	Superintendencia Nacional de Cooperativas (National Superintendency of Cooperatives)
UBE	Unidades de Batalla Electoral (Electoral Battle Units)
UCV	Universidad Central de Venezuela (Central University of Venezuela)
UNT	Unión Nacional de Trabajadores (National Workers' Union)
URD	Unión Republicana Democrática (Republican Democratic Union)
USAID	US Agency for International Development

References

Agee, Philip (1982). *White Paper Whitewash*. New York: Deep Cover Books.

Alexander, Robert Jackson (1962). *Prophets of the Revolution: Profiles of Latin American Leaders*. New York: Macmillan.

—— (1964). *The Venezuelan Democratic Revolution: A Profile of the Regime of Rómulo Betancourt*. New Brunswick, NJ: Rutgers University Press.

—— (1969). *The Communist Party of Venezuela*. Stanford: Hoover Institution Press.

—— (1973). *Aprismo: The Ideas and Doctrines of Victor Raúl Haya de la Torre*. Kent, OH: Kent State University Press.

—— (1982). *Rómulo Betancourt and the Transformation of Venezuela*. New Brunswick, NJ: Transaction Books.

Alvarez, Angel E. (2003). "State Reform Before and After Chávez' Election." In *Venezuelan Politics in the Chávez Era: Class, Polarization, and Conflict*, ed. S. Ellner and D. Hellinger, 147–160. Boulder, CO: Lynne Rienner Publishers.

Alvarez, Bernardo (2006). Author interview with Venezuelan ambassador to Washington and PPT member. August 25. Washington, DC.

Alvarez, Federico (1994). "Deciphering the National Elections." *NACLA Report on the Americas* 27, no. 5: 16–22.

Alvarez Béjar, Alejandro (2006). "Mexico's 2006 Elections: The Rise of Populism and the End of Neoliberalism?" *Latin American Perspectives* 33, no. 2: 17–32.

Anderson, Perry (2000). "Renewals." *New Left Review* 1 (January-February): 5–24.

Arenas, Nelly, and Luis Gómez Calcaño (2006). *Populismo autoritario: Venezuela 1999–2005*. Caracas: CENDES.

Arias Amaro, Alberto (1985?). *Historia de Venezuela*. N.C.: Editorial Romor.

Arvelaiz, Maximilien, and Temir Porras Ponceleon (2003). "U.S. Pushing for a Coup D'Etat." In *Coup Against Chávez in Venezuela: The Best International Reports of What Really Happened in April 2002*, ed. Gregory Wilpert, 25–33. Caracas: Fundación por un Mundo Multipolar.

Baily, Samuel L. (1967). *Labor, Nationalism, and Politics in Argentina*. New Brunswick, NJ: Rutgers University Press.

Baloyra, Enrique A. (1977). "Public Attitudes Toward the Democratic Regime." In *Venezuela: The Democratic Experience*, ed. John D. Martz and David J. Myers, 47–63. New York: Praeger.

Barreto, Juan (2004). Author interview with future mayor of Caracas. March 24. Caracas, Venezuela.

Barrios, Gonzalo (1963). *Los días y la política*. Caracas: Editorial Arte.

Battaglini, Oscar (1993). *Legitimación del poder y lucha política en Venezuela, 1936–1941*. Caracas: UCV.

———(1997). *El medinismo*. Caracas: Monte Avila.

———(2001). *La democracia en Venezuela: una historia de potencialidades no realizadas*. Caracas: UCV.

Berger, Mark T. (1995). *Under Northern Eyes: Latin American Studies and US Hegemony in the Americas, 1898–1990*. Bloomington: Indiana University Press.

Bergquist, Charles (1986). *Labor in Latin America: Comparative Essays on Chile, Argentina, Venezuela, and Colombia*. Stanford: Stanford University Press.

Betancourt, Rómulo (1959). *Posición y doctrina*. Caracas: Editorial Cordillera.

——— (1979) [1956]. *Venezuela: política y petróleo*. Barcelona, Spain: Seix Barral.

Blanco, Carlos (1993). "The Reform of the State in Latin American Perspective." In *Venezuela in the Wake of Radical Reform*, ed. Joseph S. Tulchin and Gary Bland, 97–104. Boulder: Lynne Rienner Publishers.

——— (2002). *Revolución y desilusión: Venezuela de Hugo Chávez*. Madrid: Catarata.

———(2006). Author interview. October 31. Boston, MA.

Blanco Muñoz, Agustín [interviewer] (1998). *Habla el comandante*. Caracas: UCV.

Bonilla-Molina, Luis, and Haiman El Troudi (2005). *Historia de la revolución bolivariana: pequeña crónica, 1948–2004*. Caracas: Impresos Publigráfica.

Brito Figueroa, Federico (1960). *Ensayos de historia social venezolana*. Caracas: Imprenta Universitaria.

———(1973). *La victoria en la historia de Venezuela*. Caracas.

——— (1985). *El problema tierra y esclavos en la historia de Venezuela*. Caracas: UCV.

Burbach, Roger, Orlando Nuñez, and Boris Kagarlitsky (1997). *Globalization and Its Discontents: The Rise of Postmodern Socialisms*. London: Pluto Press.

Burgess, Katrina (2004). *Parties and Unions in the New Global Economy*. Pittsburgh: University of Pittsburgh Press.

Burggraaff, Winfield J., and Richard L. Millett (1995). "The Crisis in Venezuela's Civil-Military Relations." In *Lessons of the Venezuelan Experience*, ed. Louis W. Goodman et al., 54–78. Baltimore: Johns Hopkins University Press.

Bustamante, Nora (1985). *Isaías Medina Angarita: aspectos históricos de su gobierno*. Caracas: Fondo Editorial Lola de Fuenmayor.

Caballero, Manuel (1993). *Gómez: el tirano liberal*. Caracas: Monte Avila Editores.

———(1998). *La crisis de la Venezuela contemporánea (1903–1992)*. Caracas: Monte Avila.

————(2002). *Revolución, reacción, y falsificación.* Caracas: Alfadil.
Canache, Damarys (2002). *Venezuela: Public Opinion and Protest in a Fragile Democracy.* Coral Gables: North-South Center, University of Miami.
———— (2004). "Urban Poor and Political Order." In *The Unraveling of Representative Democracy in Venezuela*, ed. Jennifer L. McCoy and David J. Myers, 33–49. Baltimore: Johns Hopkins University Press.
Cannon, Barry (2004). "Venezuela, April 2002: Coup or Popular Rebellion: The Myth of a United Venezuela." *Bulletin of Latin American Research* 3, no. 23: 285–302.
Carnevali de Toro, Dinorah (1992). *Araguatos, Avanzados, y Astronautas. COPEI: conflicto ideológico y crisis política en los años sesenta.* Caracas: Panapo.
Carrera Damas, Germán (1969). *El culto a Bolívar.* Caracas: UCV.
———— (1972). *Boves: aspectos socioeconómicos de la Guerra de Independencia.* Caracas: UCV.
———— (1984). *Una nación llamada Venezuela: proceso sociohistórico (1810–1974).* Caracas: Monte Avila.
———— (1988). *Formulación definitiva del proyecto nacional: 1870–1990.* Caracas: Cuaderno Lagoven.
———— (1995). *La disputa de la independencia y otras peripecias del método crítico en historia de ayer y de hoy.* Caracas: Ediciones Ge.
———— (2000). *Búsqueda: nuevas rutas para la histora de Venezuela (ponencias y conferencias).* Caracas: Contraloría General de la República.
Castañeda, Jorge (2001). "Mexico: Permuting Power." *New Left Review* 7 (January-February): 17–41.
———— (2006a). "Latin America's Left Turn." *Foreign Affairs* 85, no. 3 (May-June): 28–43.
———— (2006b). "Latin America's New Proxy War." *Newsweek* [international edition], September 25.
Castillo D'Imperio, Ocarina (1990). *Los años del buldozer: ideología y política, 1948–1958.* Caracas: Tropykos.
Chávez, Hugo (2003). *El Golpe fascista contra Venezuela.* Habana: Ediciones Plaza.
Chirino, Orlando (2005). *Orlando Chirino responde.* Caracas: Instituto Municipal de Publicaciones.
Clement, Christopher I. (2007). "Confronting Hugo Chávez: United States 'Democracy Promotion' in Latin America." In *Venezuela: Hugo Chávez and the Decline of an "Exceptional" Democracy*, ed. Steve Ellner and Miguel Tinker Salas, 185–204. Lanham, MD: Rowman & Littlefield.
Collier, Ruth Berins (1999). *Paths Toward Democracy: The Working Class and Elites in Western Europe and South America.* Cambridge, UK: Cambridge University Press.
Collier, Ruth Berins, and David Collier (1991). *Shaping the Political Arena: Critical Junctures, the Labor Movement, and Regime Dynamics in Latin America.* Princeton: Princeton University Press.
Collin, Richard H. (1990). *Theodore Roosevelt's Caribbean: The Panama Canal, the Monroe Doctrine, and the Latin American Context.* Baton Rouge, LA: Louisiana State University.
Colomina, Marta (2000). "En defensa de los partidos políticos." *El Universal*, August 20, 2000, 1–4.

Consalvi, Simón (1979). "Introducción: antecedents y consecuencias del 18 de octubre." In *18 de octubre de 1945*, ed. Rómulo Betancourt, 9–19. Barcelona, Spain: Editorial Seix Barral.

Coppedge, Michael (1994). *Strong Parties and Lame Ducks: Presidential Partyarchy and Factionalism in Venezuela.* Stanford: Stanford University Press.

Corn, David (2003). "Our Gang in Venezuela?" In *Coup Against Chávez in Venezuela: The Best International Reports of What Really Happened in April 2002*, ed. Gregory Wilpert, 127–135. Caracas: Fundación por un Mundo Multipolar.

Corrales, Javier (2000). "Presidents, Ruling Parties, and Party Rules: A Theory of Economic Reform in Latin America." *Comparative Politics* 32, no. 2 (January): 127–149.

——— (2002). *Presidents Without Parties: The Politics of Economic Reform in Argentina and Venezuela in the 1990s.* University Park, PA: Penn State University.

——— (2006). "Hugo Boss." *Foreign Policy* 152 (January-February): 32–40.

Corriente, Clasista (2006). "Las bases se impusieron: Congreso UNT." Pamphlet, May 28.

Davis, Roland [interviewee] (2005). "Venezuela: Inside the Bolivarian Revolution." *International Socialism* 106 (Spring): 135–143.

de la Plaza, Salvador (1973). *Venezuela: país privilegiado.* Caracas: UCV.

——— (1993). *Diario 1917/1918.* Mérida, Venezuela: Universidad de los Andes.

de la Plaza, Salvador, and Jacques Duclos (1973). *Antecedentes del revisionismo en Venezuela* [documents]. Caracas: Fondo Editorial Salvador de la Plaza.

Del Valle, María (2005). "Una revisión necesaria del pasado." Paper presented at the *Jornadas de Investigación y Docencia en la Ciencia de la Historia.* Barquisimeto, July.

Dieterich, Heinz (2005). *Hugo Chávez y el socialismo del siglo XXI.* Barquisimeto, Venezuela: Horizonte.

Duno, Pedro (1975). *Los doce apostoles: proceso a la degradación política.* Valencia, Venezuela: Vadell Hermanos.

Duverger, Maurice (1954). *Political Parties, Their Organization and Activity in the Modern State.* New York: John Wiley and Sons.

Ellner, Steve (1979). "The Venezuelan Left in the Era of the Popular Front, 1936–45." *Journal of Latin American Studies* 11, no. 1 (February): 169–184.

——— (1980). "Political Party Dynamics and the Outbreak of Guerrilla Warfare in Venezuela." *Inter-American Economic Affairs* 34, no. 2: 3–24.

——— (1982). "Populism in Venezuela, 1935–1948: Betancourt and Acción Democrática." In *Latin American Populism in Comparative Perspective*, ed. Michael L. Conniff, 135–149. Albuquerque: University of New Mexico Press.

——— (1987). *The Venezuelan Petroleum Corporation and the Debate over Government Policy in Basic Industry.* Occasional Paper 47: University of Glasgow.

——— (1988). *Venezuela's Movimiento al Socialismo: From Guerrilla Defeat to Innovative Politics.* Durham, NC: Duke University Press.

——— (1989). "Generational Identification and Political Fragmentation in

Venezuelan Politics in the Late 1960s." *Latin American Issues*, no. 7.

——— (1990). "Memories of February 27: Uncovering the Deadly Truth." *Commonweal* (December 21): 740–741.

——— (1992). "Venezuela." In *Latin America Between the Second World War and the Cold War, 1944–1948*, ed. Leslie Bethell and Ian Roxborough, 147–169. Cambridge, UK: University of Cambridge Press.

——— (1993). *Organized Labor in Venezuela, 1958–1991: Behavior and Concerns in a Democratic Setting*. Wilmington, DE: Scholarly Resources.

——— (1995). "Venezuelan Revisionist Political History, 1908–1958: New Motives and Criteria for Analyzing the Past." *Latin American Research Review* 2: 91–121.

——— (1996). "Political Party Factionalism and Democracy in Venezuela." *Latin American Perspectives* 23, no. 3 (Summer): 87–109.

——— (1997a). "Recent Venezuelan Political Studies: A Return to Third World Realities." *Latin American Research Review* 32, no. 2: 201–218.

——— (1997b). "Venezuela: The Politics of Privatization." *NACLA: Report on the Americas* 31, no. 3 (November-December): 6–9.

——— (1999a). "Obstacles to the Consolidation of the Venezuelan Neighbourhood Movement: National and Local Cleavages." *Journal of Latin American Studies* 31, no. 1 (February): 75–97.

——— (1999b). "The Assault on Benefits in Venezuela." *NACLA: Report on the Americas* 32, no. 4: 18–19.

——— (1999c). "The Heyday of Radical Populism in Venezuela and Its Aftermath." In *Populism in Latin America*, ed. Michael L. Conniff, 117–137. Tuscaloosa, AL: University of Alabama Press.

——— (1999d). "The Impact of Privatization on Labor in Venezuela: Radical Reorganization or Moderate Adjustment?" *Political Power and Social Theory* 13: 109–145.

——— (2002). "The Tenuous Credentials of Latin American Democracy in the Age of Neoliberalism." *Rethinking Marxism* 3, no. 14 (Fall): 76–93.

——— (2003a). "Introduction: The Search for Explanations." In *Venezuelan Politics in the Chávez Era: Class, Polarization, and Conflict*, ed. Steve Ellner and Daniel Hellinger, 7–26. Boulder, CO: Lynne Rienner Publishers.

——— (2003b). "The Contrasting Variants of the Populism of Hugo Chávez and Alberto Fujimori." *Journal of Latin American Studies* 35 (February): 139–162.

——— (2004). "Leftist Goals and Debate over Anti-Neoliberal Strategy in Latin America." *Science and Society* 68, no. 1 (Spring): 10–32.

——— (2006). "The Defensive Strategy on the Left in Latin America: Objective and Subjective Conditions in the Age of Globalization." *Science and Society* 70, no. 3 (July): 397–410.

Ellner, Steve, and Daniel Hellinger (2003). "Conclusion: The Democratic and Authoritarian Directions of the *Chavista* Movement." In *Venezuelan Politics in the Chávez Era: Class, Polarization, and Conflict*, ed. Steve Ellner and Daniel Hellinger, 215–226. Boulder, CO: Lynne Rienner Publishers.

Ellsworth, Brian (2003). "Política de EEUU hacia Venezuela: dormida al volante." *VenEconomía* 20, no. 6 (March): 10–12.

Evers, T. (1985). "Identity: The Hidden Side of New Social Movements in Latin

America." In *New Social Movements and the State in Latin America*, ed. David Slater, 43–71. Amsterdam: CEDLA.

Ewell, Judith (1984). *Venezuela: A Century of Change.* Stanford: Stanford University Press.

——— (1996). *Venezuela and the United States: From Monroe's Hemisphere to Petroleum's Empire.* Athens: University of Georgia Press.

Fagen, Stuart I. (1977). "Unionism and Democracy." In *Venezuela: The Democratic Experience*, ed. John D. Martz and David J. Myers. New York: Praeger.

Fajardo, Victor (1992). "Colapso del paquete económico: causas, efectos y perspectives, Venezuela 1989–1992." *Cuadernos del CENDES*, no. 20.

Falcoff, Mark (2004). "Latin American Crack-up?" *Commentary* 118, no. 1 (July-August): 36–41.

Fergusson, Erna (1939). *Venezuela.* New York: Alfred A. Knopf.

Fernandes, Sujatha (2005). "Gender, Populism, and Women's Participation in Popular Politics in the Barrios of Caracas." Paper presented at the annual meeting of the American Political Science Association, Washington, DC.

——— (2007). "Barrio Women and Popular Politics in Chávez's Venezuela." *Latin American Politics and Society* 49, no. 3: 97–127.

Fernández Avello, Manuel (1974). *Bobes: Mariscal Asturiano para la historia.* Oviedo: Instituto de Estudiois Asturianos.

Ferry, Robert J. (1989). *The Colonial Elite of Early Caracas: Formation and Crisis, 1567–1767.* Berkeley: University of California Press.

Francia, Néstor (2002). *Abril rojo—el rescate de Chávez: crónicas, análisis, documentos, entrevistas.* Caracas: Imprenta Nacional.

Frank, Andre Gunder (1967). *Capitalism and Underdevelopment in Latin America: Historical Studies of Chile and Brazil.* New York: Monthly Review Press.

French, John D. (1992). *The Brazilian Workers' ABC: Class Conflict and Alliances in Modern São Paulo.* Chapel Hill: University of North Carolina Press.

——— (2004). "The Robert J. Alexander Interview Collection." *Hispanic American Historical Review* 84, no. 2: 315–326.

Fuenmayor, Juan Bautista (1969). *1928–1948: Veinte años de política.* Caracas: Miguel Angel García e Hijo.

——— (1978). *Historia de la Venezuela política contemporánea, 1899–1969.* Vol. 1. Caracas: Miguel Angel García e Hijo.

——— (1981). *Historia de la Venezuela política contemporánea, 1899–1969: acentuación del neocolonialismo bajo un gobierno de dictadura castrense, 1948–1958.* Vol. 8. Caracas: Miguel Angel García e Hijo.

Gall, Norman (1973). "Carnival in Caracas." *New York Review of Books* 20, no. 18 (November 15).

García Guadilla, María Pilar (2003). "Civil Society: Institutionalization, Fragmentation, Autonomy." In *Venezuelan Politics in the Chávez Era: Class, Polarization, and Conflict*, ed. Steve Ellner and Daniel Hellinger, 179–196. Boulder, CO: Lynne Rienner Publishers.

García Márquez, Gabriel (1990). *The General in His Labyrinth.* New York: Alfred A. Knopf.

García Ponce, Guillermo (2002). *El golpe de estado del 11 de abril*. Caracas: Imprenta Nacional.

Germani, Gino (1978). *Authoritarianism, Fascism, and National Populism*. New Brunswick, NJ: Transaction Books.

Gindin, Jonah (2005). "Made in Venezuela: The Struggle to Reinvent Venezuelan Labor." *Monthly Review* (June): 73–87.

——— (2006). "Chavistas in the Halls of Power: Chavistas in the Streets." In *Dispatches from Latin America: On the Frontlines Against Neoliberalism*, ed. Vijay Prashad and Teo Ballavé, 86–92. Cambridge, MA: South End Press.

Godio, Julio (1982). Interviews with the author. April 13 and 19. Caracas, Venezuela.

Golinger, Eva (2005). *El Código Chávez: Descifrando la intervención de los EE.UU. en Venezuela*. Caracas: Editorial Questión.

Gómez, Luis, and Nelly Arenas (2001). "Modernización autoritaria o actualización del populismo? La transición política en Venezuela." *Cuestiones Políticas* 26 (January-June): 85–126.

González, Asdrúbal (1979). *Manuel Piar*. Valencia, Venezuela: Vadell Hermanos.

Granier, Marcel [director] (1987). *Mas y mejor democracia*. Caracas: Grupo Roraima.

Guerón, Carlos (1993). "Introduction." In *Venezuela in the Wake of Radical Reform*, ed. Joseph S. Tulchin and Gary Bland, 1–18. Boulder, CO: Lynne Rienner Publishers.

Guevara, Aleida [interviewer] (2005). *Chávez: Venezuela and the New Latin America*. Melbourne, Australia: Ocean Press.

Gunson, Phil (2006). "Chávez's Venezuela." *Current History* 105, no. 688 (February): 58–63.

Hansen, David R., Kirk A. Hawkins, and Jason Seawright (2004). "Dependent Civil Society: The Círculos Bolivarianos in Venezuela." Paper presented at the Twenty-fifth Congress of the Latin American Studies Association (LASA), Las Vegas, NV.

Hardt, Michael (2006). "From Imperialism to Empire." *The Nation* (July 31–August 7): 26–29.

Hardt, Michael, and Antonio Negri (2004). *Multitude: War and Democracy in the Age of Empire*. New York: Penguin Press.

Harnecker, Marta (2003). *Militares junto al pueblo: entrevistas a nueve comandantes venezolanos que protagonizaron la gesta de abril de 2002*. Caracas: Vadell Hermanos.

——— [interviewer] (2005). *Understanding the Venezuelan Revolution: Hugo Chávez Talks to Marta Harnecker*. New York: Monthly Review Press.

Hartlyn, Jonathan (1998). "Political Continuities, Missed Opportunities, and Institutional Rigidities: Another Look at Democratic Transitions in Latin America." In *Politics, Society, and Democracy: Latin America*, ed. Scott Mainwaring and Arturo Valenzuela, 101–120. Boulder, CO: Westview Press.

Hellinger, Daniel C. (1991). *Venezuela: Tarnished Democracy*. Boulder, CO: Westview Press.

——— (2007). "When 'No' Means 'Yes to Revolution': Electoral Politics in

Bolivarian Venezuela." In *Venezuela: Hugo Chávez and the Decline of an "Exceptional" Democracy*, ed. Steve Ellner and Miguel Tinker Salas, 157–184. Lanham, MD: Rowman & Littlefield.

Hellman, Judith Adler (1992). "The Study of New Social Movements in Latin America and the Question of Autonomy." In *The Making of Social Movements in Latin America: Identity, Strategy, and Democracy*, ed. Arturo Escobar and Sonia E. Alvarez, 52–61. Boulder, CO: Westview Press.

Herman, Donald L. (1980). "The Christian Democratic Party." In *Venezuela at the Polls: The National Elections of 1978*, ed. Howard R. Penniman, 133–153. Washington, DC: American Enterprise Institute for Public Policy Research.

——— (1988). "Democratic and Authoritarian Traditions." In *Democracy in Latin America: Colombia and Venezuela*, ed. Donald L. Herman, 1–15. New York: Praeger.

Hernández, Carlos Raúl, and Luis Emilio Rondón (2005). *La democracia traicionada: grandeza y miseria del Pacto de Punto Fijo (Venezuela, 1958–2003)*. Caracas: Rayuela.

Herrera Campins, Luis (1979). "La sociedad comunitaria." In *Sociedad comunitaria y participación*, 61–67. Caracas: Editorial Ateneo de Caracas.

Herrera Salas, Jesús María (2005). *De cómo Europa se apropió de la leche de las madres africanas en el Caribe: un ensayo sobre "barbarie" y "civilización"*. Caracas: Editorial Tropykos.

——— (2007). "Ethnicity and Revolution: The Political Economy of Racism in Venezuela." In *Venezuela: Hugo Chávez and the Decline of an "Exceptional" Democracy*, ed. Steve Ellner and Miguel Tinker Salas, 99–118. Lanham, MD: Rowman & Littlefield.

Holloway, John (2005a). "A Debate Between John Holloway and Alex Callinicos: World Social Forum, 27 January 2005." *International Socialism* 108 (Spring): 112–128.

——— (2005b). *Change the World Without Taking Power*. London: Pluto Press.

Horowitz, Joel (1999). "Populism and Its Legacies in Argentina." In *Populism in Latin America*, ed. Michael L. Conniff, 22–42. Tuscaloosa: University of Alabama Press.

Howard, Harrison Sabin (1984). *Rómulo Gallegos y la revolución burguesa en Venezuela*. 2nd ed. Caracas: Monte Avila.

Huntington, Samuel P. (1991). *The Third Wave: Democratization in the Late Twentieth Century*. London: University of Oklahoma Press.

Inter-American Development Bank (1994). *Economic and Social Progress in Latin America: 1993 Report*.

Irwin, Domingo G. (2004). "Los militares y los civiles." In *La independencia de Venezuela: historia mínima*, 87–110. Caracas: Funtrapet.

Ishibashi, Jun (2001). "Hacia una apertura del debate sobre el racismo en Venezuela: exclusión e inclusión estereotipada de personas 'negras' en los medios de comunicación." In *Políticas de identidades y diferencias sociales en tiempos de globalización*, ed. Daniel Mato, 33–61. Caracas: Universidad Central de Venezuela.

Izarra, William E. (2001). *En busca de la revolución*. Caracas: Producciones Karol.

James, Daniel (2000). *Doña María's Story: Life History, Memory, and Political Identity*. Durham, NC: Duke University Press.

Jardim, Claudia (2005). "Prevention and Solidarity: Democratizing Health in Venezuela." *Monthly Review* 56, no. 8 (January): 35–39.

Jenkins, Keith (1997). *The Postmodern History Reader*. London: Routledge.

Karl, Terry Lynn (1987). "Petroleum and Political Pacts: The Transition to Democracy in Venezuela." *Latin American Research Review* 22, no. 1: 63–94.

——— (1997). *The Paradox of Plenty: Oil Booms and Petro-States*. Berkeley: University of California Press.

Kornblith, Miriam (2005). "Elections Versus Democracy." *Journal of Democracy* 16, no. 1 (January): 124–137.

Kozloff, Nikolas (2007). *Hugo Chávez: Oil, Politics, and the Challenge to the United States*. New York: Palgrave Macmillan.

Laclau, Ernesto (1977). *Politics and Ideology in Marxist Theory: Capitalism, Fascism, Populism*. London: New Left Books.

——— (2005). *On Populist Reason*. London: Verso.

Lander, Edgardo (2005). "Venezuelan Social Conflict in a Global Context." *Latin American Perspectives* 32, no. 2 (May): 20–38.

Lander, Luis (1981). Author interview with minister of public works during the *trienio*. October 20. Caracas, Venezuela.

Lanza, Eloy (1980). *El Sub-imperialismo venezolano*. Caracas: Editorial "Carlos Aponte."

Lara, William (2005). *MVR: De aparato electoral a partido político orgánico*. Caracas: n.p.

Lebowitz, Michael A. (2006). *Build It Now: Socialism in the Twenty-First Century*. New York: Monthly Review Press.

Leeuw, Hendrik de (1935). *Crossroads of the Caribbean Sea*. New York: Julian Messner.

Lepage, Freddy (2006). *En el nombre de la revolución*. Caracas: Debate.

Levine, Daniel (1973). *Conflict and Political Change in Venezuela*. Princeton: Princeton University Press.

——— (1978). "Venezuela Since 1958: The Consolidation of Democratic Politics." In *The Breakdown of Democratic Regimes: Latin America*, ed. Juan J. Linz and Alfred Stepan, 82–109. Baltimore: Johns Hopkins University Press.

——— (1995). "Legitimacy, Governability, and Reform in Venezuela." In *Lessons of the Venezuelan Experience*, ed. Louis W. Goodman et al., 223–251. Baltimore: Johns Hopkins University Press.

Lieuwen, Edwin (1965). *Venezuela*. 2nd ed. London: Oxford University Press.

Linz, Juan J., and Alfred Stepan, eds. (1978). *The Breakdown of Democratic Regimes: Latin America*. Baltimore: Johns Hopkins University Press.

Lombardi, John V. (1982). *Venezuela: The Search for Order; The Dream of Progress*. New York: Oxford University Press.

López Maya, Margarita (1994). "The Rise of Cause R: A Workers' Party Shakes Up the Old Politics." *NACLA Report on the Americas* 27, no. 5: 29–34.

——— (2003). "The Venezuelan Caracazo of 1989: Popular Protest and Institutional Weakness." *Journal of Latin American Studies* 35, no. 1 (February): 117–137.

——— (2004). *Del viernes negro al referendo revocatorio*. Caracas: Alfadil.

López Maya, Margarita, and Luis Lander (2005). "Popular Protest in Venezuela:

Novelties and Continuities." *Latin American Perspectives* 32, no. 2 (March): 92–108.

Lucena, Héctor (2007). "Sindicatos y Cooperativas: Encuentros y Desencuentros." In *Cooperativas, empresas, estado y sindicatos: Una vinculación necesaria*, ed. H. Lucena, 73–78. Barquisimeto, Venezuela: Universidad Centroccidental Lisandro Alvarado Fondo Editorial and Universidad de Carabobo.

Lynch, John (2006). *Simón Bolívar: A Life*. New Haven: Yale University Press.

Magdaleno, John (2003). "Plan en marcha para quebrar a los grandes." *VeneEconomia* [section "Gobierno y Política"] 20, no. 6 (March): 1–3.

Márquez, Patricia (1999). *The Street Is My Home: Youth and Violence in Caracas*. Stanford: Stanford University Press.

Martín, Américo (1975). *Los peces gordos*. Valencia, Venezuela: Vadell Hermanos.

Martz, John D. (1966). *Acción Democrática: Evolution of a Modern Political Party in Venezuela*. Princeton: Princeton University Press.

——— (1970). "Government, Democratic Opposition, and Extremists." In *Political Power in Latin America: Seven Confrontations*, eds. Richard R. Fagan and Wayne A. Cornelius, 53–59. Englewood Cliffs, NJ: Prentice Hall.

——— (1980). "The Evolution of Democratic Politics in Venezuela." In *Venezuela at the Polls: The National Elections of 1978*, ed. Howard R. Penniman, 1–29. Washington, DC: American Enterprise Institute for Public Policy Research.

——— (1995). "Political Parties and the Democratic Crisis." In *Lessons of the Venezuelan Experience*, ed. Louis W. Goodman et al., 31–53. Baltimore: Johns Hopkins University Press.

Martz, John D., and Enrique A. Baloyra (1976). *Electoral Mobilization and Public Opinion: The Venezuelan Campaign of 1973*. Chapel Hill: University of North Carolina Press.

Mayhall, Marguerite (2005). "Modernist but Not Exceptional: The Debate over Modern Art and National Identity in 1950s Venezuela." *Latin American Perspectives* 32, no. 2 (March): 124–146.

Maza Zavala, D. F. (1986). *Venezuela: historia de una frustración*. Interviewed by Agustín Blanco Muñoz. Caracas: UCV.

MBR-200 (1992). "Carta de los Oficiales del MBR 2000." In *Carta a los Militares de Nuestra Generación*, Enrique Ochoa Antich, 9–31. Caracas: Fuentes Editores.

McBeth, Brian S. (2001). *Gunboats, Corruption, and Claims: Foreign Intervention in Venezuela, 1899–1908*. Westport, CT: Greenwood.

McCaughan, Michael (2004). *The Battle of Venezuela*. London: Latin American Bureau.

McCoy, Jennifer L. (1989). "Labor and the State in a Party-Mediated Democracy: Institutional Change in Venezuela." *Latin American Research Review* 24, no. 2: 35–67.

——— (2004). "From Representative to Participatory Democracy? Regime Transformation in Venezuela." In *The Unraveling of Representative Democracy in Venezuela*, ed. J. McCoy and David J. Myers, 263–295. Baltimore: Johns Hopkins University Press.

——— (2005). "One Act in an Unfinished Drama." *Journal of Democracy* 16, no. 1 (January): 109–123.

Mijares, Augusto (1993). *The Liberator*. Caracas: North American Association of Venezuela.

Miquilena, Luis (2000). Interview with the author. March 29. Caracas, Venezuela.

Mohamedi, Fareed (2006). Author interview with consultant for PFC Energy. November 10. Washington, DC.

Moleiro, Moisés (1979). *El partido del pueblo: crónica de un fraude*. 2nd ed. Valencia, Venezuela: Vadell Hermanos Editores.

——— (1998). *El poder y el sueño*. Caracas: Planeta.

Molina, José E. (2004). "The Unraveling of Venezuela's Party System: From Party Rule to Personalistic Politics and Deinstitutionalization." In *The Unraveling of Representative Democracy in Venezuela*, ed. J. McCoy and David J. Myers, 152–178. Baltimore: Johns Hopkins University Press.

Moncada, Samuel (1985). *Los huevos de la serpiente: Fedecámaras por dentro*. Caracas: Alianza Gráfica.

Morales, Aurora (2004). Author interview with director of MVR Ideological Formation. March 30. Caracas, Venezuela.

Morón, Guillermo (1961). *Historia de Venezuela*. 3rd ed. Caracas.

——— (1971). *Historia de Venezuela: la nacionalidad*. Vol. 5. Caracas.

Müller Rojas, Alberto (2007). "La Fuerza Armada está politzada y partidizada." *Ultimas Noticias* (June 30): 22–23.

Muntaner, Carles (2005). "Is Chávez's Venezuela Populist or Socialist." *Counterpunch* (May 5).

Murillo, Maria Victoria (2001). *Labor Unions, Partisan Coalitions, and Market Reforms in Latin America*. Cambridge: Cambridge University Press.

Murmis, Miguel, and Juan Carlos Portantiero (1971). *Estudios sobre los orígenes del peronismo*. Buenos Aires: Siglo Veintiuno Argentina.

Myers, David J. (2004). "The Normalization of Punto Fijo Democracy." In *The Unraveling of Representative Democracy in Venezuela*, ed. J. McCoy and David Myers, 11–29. Baltimore: Johns Hopkins University Press.

Naím, Moisés (1993a). *Paper Tigers and Minotaurs: The Politics of Venezuela's Economic Reforms*. Washington, DC: Carnegie Endowment for International Peace.

——— (1993b). "The Launching of Radical Policy Changes, 1989–1991." In *Venezuela in the Wake of Radical Reform*, ed. Joseph S. Tulchin and Gary Bland, 39–94. Boulder: Lynne Rienner Publishers.

——— (2001). "The Real Story Behind Venezuela's Woes." *Journal of Democracy* 12, no. 2: 17–31.

Naím, Moisés, and Ramón Piñango (1984). "El caso Venezuela: una ilusión de armonía." In *El caso Venezuela: una ilusión de armonía*, ed. M. Naím and R. Piñango, 538–579. Caracas: Ediciones IESA.

Nash, June (1979). *We Eat the Mines and the Mines Eat Us: Dependency and Exploitation in Bolivian Tin Mines*. New York: Columbia University Press.

Nava, Julian (1965). "The Illustrious American: The Development of Nationalism in Venezuela Under Antonio Guzmán Blanco." *Hispanic American Historical Review* 45, no. 4 (November): 527–543.

Nixon, Richard (1990). *In the Arena: A Memoir of Victory, Defeat, and Renewal.* New York: Simon and Schuster.

Nuñez Tenorio, J. R. (1993). *La democracia venezolana: the big business.* Caracas: Editorial Tropykos.

——— (1998). *La lucha contra el Puntofijismo corrupto neoliberal.* Los Teques: Editorial A.L.E.M.

Ochoa Antich, Fernando (2000). "Política Exterior: Irresponsabilidad y Mesianismo." *El Universal*, August 22, 2000.

Oppenheimer, Andrés (2005). *Cuentos Chinos: El engaño de Washington, la mentira populista y la esperanza de América Latina.* Buenos Aires: Editorial Sudamericana.

——— (2006). "No alineados y petropopulismo." *Listindiario.com* [Dominican Republic], September 15.

Ortega Díaz, Pedro (1989). Interview with the author. April 22. Puerto La Cruz, Venezuela.

——— (2006). *El congreso de Panamá: la unidad latinoamericana.* Caracas: Ministerio de Comunicación e Información.

Ortiz, Nelson (2004). "Entrepreneurs: Profits Without Power?" In *The Unraveling of Representative Democracy in Venezuela*, ed. J. McCoy and David Myers, 71–92. Baltimore: Johns Hopkins University Press.

Parker, Dick (2007). "Chávez and the Search for an Alternative to Neoliberalism." In *Venezuela: Hugo Chávez and the Decline of an "Exceptional" Democracy*, ed. Steve Ellner and Miguel Tinker Salas, 66–74. Lanham, MD: Rowman & Littlefield.

Partido Comunista de Venezuela (1986). *Diputados comunistas rinden cuenta al pueblo: crisis y deuda externa 1976–1986.* Caracas: COTRAGRAF.

Peña, Alfredo (1979). *Conversaciones con Carlos Andrés Pérez.* Vol. 2. Caracas: Ateneo de Caracas.

Pensamiento político venezolano del siglo XX: Gobierno y época del Presidente Isaías Medina Angarita (1987). Vol. 33. Caracas: Congreso de la República.

Pérez, Carlos Andres (1982). Interview with the author. April 15. Caracas, Venezuela.

Pérez Martí, Felipe (2004). Author interview with former planning minister. April 29. Washington, DC.

Petkoff, Teodoro (1989). "La Venezuela acorralada explotó." *27 de febrero.* Congressional speech, March 6. Caracas: Ediciones Venezuela-MAS.

——— (2000). *La Venezuela de Chávez: una segunda opinión.* Caracas: Grijalbo.

——— (2005). *Dos Izquierdas.* Caracas: Alfadil Ediciones.

Picón Salas, Mariano (1949). *Comprensión de Venezuela: antologías y selecciones.* Caracas: Ministerio de Educación Nacional.

Pino Iturrieta, Elías (1991). "Rasgos y limites de la restauración liberal." In *Cipriano Castro y su época*, 9–25. Caracas: Monte Avila.

——— (2003a). "Idolos compartidos." *El Universal*, February 17.

——— (2003b). "San Cipriano y su pontífice." *El Universal*, February 2.

——— [interviewee] (2004). "Ausencia de liderazgo condena al Chavismo." *La Voz* [daily newspaper, Miranda State], October 24.

Pividal, Francisco (1979). *Bolívar: pensamiento precursor del imperialismo.* Caracas: Ateneo de Caracas.

Plaza, Helena (1978). *El 23 de enero de 1958.* Caracas: Garbizu and Todtmann.

Polanco Alcántara, Tomás (1990). *Juan Vicente Gómez: aproximación a una biografía.* Caracas: Italgráfica.

———(1991). "Esquema bibliográfica." In *Cipriano Castro y su época*, 27–56. Caracas: Monte Avila.

Powell, John Duncan (1971). *Political Mobilization of the Venezuelan Peasant.* Cambridge, MA: Harvard University Press.

Pressly, Thomas (1954). *Americans Interpret Their Civil War.* Princeton: Princeton University Press.

Proceso Político (1978). *CAP: 5 años, un juicio crítico.* Caracas: Editorial Ateneo de Caracas.

Punto Socialista (1984a). "Refinanciamiento sin sacrificio social." *Punto Socialista* 8 (January): 29–30.

———(1984b). "Hasta hoy había funcionado implícitamente el Pacto Social..." *Punto Socialista* 11 (April): 4–7.

Quintero, Inés (2004). "¿Fue la independencia una revolución social?" In *La independencia de Venezuela: historia mínima*, 147–166. Caracas: Funtrapet.

Quintero, Rodolfo (1970). *El petróleo y nuestra sociedad.* Caracas: UCV.

Rabe, Stephen G. (1982). *The Road to OPEC: United States Relations with Venezuela, 1919–1976.* Austin: University of Texas Press.

——— (1988). *Eisenhower and Latin America: The Foreign Policy of Anticommunism.* Chapel Hill: University of North Carolina Press.

Raby, D. L. (2006). *Democracy and Revolution: Latin America and Socialism Today.* London: Pluto Press.

Rakowski, Cathy (2003). "Women's Coalitions as a Strategy at the Intersection of Economic and Political Change in Venezuela." *International Journal of Politics, Culture, and Society* 16, no. 3 (March): 387–405.

Ramírez, Kléber (1991). *Venezuela: La IV República (o la total transformación del Estado).* Caracas: Venezuela por Cromotip.

Ramos Jiménez, Alfredo (2006). "Democracia y liderazgo político: una relación conflictiva en la experiencia venezolana." In *Debate sobre la democracia en América*, ed. José María Cadenas, 13–35. Caracas: UCV.

Rangel, Domingo Alberto (1988) [1966]. *La revolución de las fantasías.* Caracas: Grijalbo.

——— (1998). *Venezuela en tres siglos.* Caracas: Vadell Hermanos and El Centauro/Catalá.

——— (2001). *Gustavo Machado: un caudillo prestado al comunismo.* Caracas: El Centauro.

Rangel, José Vicente (1969). *Expediente negro: el caso Lovera.* Caracas: Ediciones Muralla.

Ranis, Peter (2005). "Argentina's Worker-Occupied Factories and Enterprises." *Socialism and Democracy* 19, no. 3: 93–115.

Ratliff, William (1999). "Development and Civil Society in Latin America and Asia." *Annals of the American Academy of Political and Social Science* 565 (September): 91–112.

Ray, Talton F. (1969). *The Politics of the Barrios of Venezuela.* Berkeley: University of California Press.

Rincón N., Fredy (1982). *El Nuevo Ideal Nacional y los planes económico-militares de Pérez Jiménez, 1952–1957.* Caracas: Centauro.

Rippy, J. Fred (1958). *Latin America: A Modern History.* Ann Arbor: University of Michigan Press.

Rivas Rivas, José (1987). *Las tres divisiones de AD: causas y consecuencias.* 2nd ed. N.p.: Eduxere.

Roberts, Edwin A. (2005). "From the History of Science to the Science of History: Scientists and Historians in the Shaping of British Marxist Theory." *Science & Society* 69, no. 4 (October): 529–558.

Robinson, William I. (2004). *A Theory of Global Capitalism: Production, Class, and State in a Transnational World.* Baltimore: Johns Hopkins University Press.

Rodríguez, Angel (2007). "Cooperativa de Mantenimiento y Servicio de Enelbar." In *Cooperativas, empresas, estado y sindicatos: Una vinculación necesaria,* ed. H. Lucena, 247–250. Barquisimeto, Venezuela: Universidad Centroccidental.

Rodríguez Araque, Alí (1997). *El proceso de privatización petrolera en Venezuela.* N.p.: Impregraf.

Rodríguez Campos, Manuel (1994). "Federacion, Economia y Centralismo." In *Antonio Guzmán Blanco y su época,* ed. I. Quintero, 81–102. Caracas: Monte Avila.

Romero, Carlos A. (2004). "The United States and Venezuela." In *The Unraveling of Representative Democracy in Venezuela,* ed. J. McCoy and David Myers, 130–151. Baltimore: Johns Hopkins University Press.

Ron, Lina (2003). *Lina Ron habla: su verdad histórica.* Caracas: Editorial Fuentes.

Rosas, Alexis (2005). *La masacre de Cantaura.* Caracas: Editorial Texto.

Ruptura [Comisión Ideológico] (1977). *El imperialismo petrolero y la revolución venezolana: las ganancias extraordinarias y la soberanía nacional.* Vol. 2. Caracas: Editorial Ruptura.

Salamanca, Luis (1998). *Obreros, movimiento social y democracia en Venezuela.* Caracas: UCV.

Salas, Yolanda [author and interviewer] (2004). *Manuel Piar: El héroe de múltiples rostros (una aproximación a la historia desde la perspectiva de la memoria colectiva).* Caracas: FUNDEF.

Salcedo-Bastardo, J. L. (1979). *Historia fundamental de Venezuela.* 8th ed. Caracas: UCV.

Salgado, René (1987). "Economic Pressure Groups and Policy-Making in Venezuela: The Case of FEDECAMARAS Reconsidered." *Latin American Research Review* 22, no. 3: 91–105.

Sanin [Alfredo Tarre Murzi] (1983). *Los Adecos en el poder.* Caracas: Publicaciones Seleven.

Sanoja, Mario, and Iraida Vargas Arenas (2002). *El Agua y El Poder, Caracas y la Formación del Estado Colonial Caraqueño: 1567–1700.* Caracas: Banco Central de Venezuela.

——— (2004). *Razones para una revolución.* Caracas: Monte Avila Editores.

Sartori, Giovanni (1976). *Parties and Party Systems: A Framework for Analysis.* Cambridge, UK: Cambridge University Press.

Schlesinger, Arthur M. (1965). *A Thousand Days: John F. Kennedy in the White House.* Boston: Houghton Mifflin.

Schönwälder, Gerd (2002). *Linking Civil Society and the State: Urban Popular*

Movements, the Left, and Local Government in Peru, 1980–1992. University Park, PA: Pennsylvania State University.

Serbín, Andrés (1995). "A New Approach to the World? The *Gran Viraje* and Venezuela's Foreign Policy." In *Lessons of the Venezuelan Experience*, ed. Louis W. Goodman et al., 365–386. Baltimore: Johns Hopkins University Press.

Silva Calderón, Alvaro (2006). "Trayectoria de la nacionalización petrolera." *Revista Venezolana de Economía y Ciencias Sociales* 12, no. 1 (January-April): 109–123.

Silvert, Kalman H. (1961). *The Conflict Society: Reaction and Revolution in Latin America.* New Orleans: Hauser Press.

Siso Martínez, José Manuel (1973). *105 años de vida repúblicana.* Caracas: Ministerio de Educación.

Sosa, Arturo A., and Eloi Lengrand (1981). *Del garibaldismo estudiantil a la izquierda criolla: los orígenes marxistas del proyecto de A.D. (1928–1935).* Caracas: Ediciones Centauro.

Soto, Hernando de (1989). *The Other Path: The Invisible Revolution in the Third World.* New York: Harper & Row.

Spenser, Daniela (2005). "Cuba: New Partners and Old Limits." *NACLA: Report on the Americas* 39, no. 2 (September-October): 25–28.

Stambouli, Andrés (2002). *La política extraviada: una historia de Medina a Chávez.* Caracas: Fundación para la Cultura Urbana.

Suárez Figueroa, Naudy (1982). "Los socialcristianos en el trienio: 1946–1948." In *Los copeyanos*, 75–113. Caracas: Centauro.

Tablante, Carlos (2003). *Venezuela herida: pacto por la democracia del futuro.* Caracas: Los Libros de "El Nacional."

Taylor, Philip Bates (1968). *The Venezuelan Golpe de Estado of 1958: The Fall of Marcos Pérez Jiménez.* Washington, DC: Institute for the Comparative Study of Political Systems.

Tinker Salas, Miguel (forthcoming). *The Enduring Legacy: Oil, Culture, and Society in Venezuela.* Durham, NC: Duke University Press.

Toro Jiménez, Fermín (2006a). *Formación, mediatización y degradación de la soberanía de Venezuela 1830–1998: reflexiones a propósito de la constituyente.* Ministerio de la Cultura: Caracas.

——— (2006b). *Los mitos políticos de la oligarquía venezolana.* Ministerio de la Cultura: Caracas.

——— (2006c). Interview with the author. March 10. New York.

Trejo, Hugo (1977). *La revolución no ha terminado . . . !* Valencia, Venezuela: Vadell Hermanos.

Trinkunas, Harold A. (2004). "The Military: From Marginalization to Center Stage." In *The Unraveling of Representative Democracy in Venezuela*, ed. J. McCoy and David Myers, 50–70. Baltimore: Johns Hopkins University Press.

——— (2005). *Crafting Civilian Control of the Military in Venezuela: A Comparative Perspective.* Chapel Hill: University of North Carolina Press.

Ugalde, Luis (2004). "La costosa emancipación nacional." In *La independencia de Venezuela: historia mínima*, 35–86. Caracas: Funtrapet.

Uslar Pietri, Arturo (1959). "El drama de la Federación." *El Nacional*, February 20, 1959.

Valecillos, Héctor (2005). *Ilusiones y mentiras del Chavismo: Crónicas de la degredación del país II*. Caracas: UCV.

Valencia Ramírez, Cristóbal (2007). "Venezuela's Bolivarian Revolution: Who Are the *Chavistas?*" In *Venezuela: Hugo Chávez and the Decline of an "Exceptional" Democracy*, ed. Steve Ellner and Miguel Tinker Salas, 121–139. Lanham, MD: Rowman & Littlefield.

Vallenilla Lanz, Laureano (1990). *Cesarismo democrático: estudios sobre las bases sociológicas de la constitución efectiva de Venezuela*. Caracas: Monte Avila.

Velasco, Alejandro (2002). "The Hidden Injuries of Race: Democracy, Color, and Political Consciousness in Contemporary Venezuela." M.A. thesis, Duke University.

Velásquez, Ramón J. (1979). *Venezuela moderna: medio siglo de historia, 1926–1976*. 2nd ed. Caracas: Editorial Ariel.

Weyland, Kurt (2001). "Will Chávez Lose His Luster?" *Foreign Affairs* 80, no. 6 (November-December): 73–87.

——— (2002). *The Politics of Market Reform in Fragile Democracies: Argentina, Brazil, Peru, and Venezuela*. Princeton: Princeton University Press.

Whitaker, Arthur P., and David C. Jordan (1966). *Nationalism in Contemporary Latin America*. New York: Free Press.

Wise, George S. (1951). *Caudillo: A Portrait of Antonio Guzmán Blanco*. New York: Columbia University.

Wright, Winthrop R. (1990). *Café con Leche: Race, Class, and National Image in Venezuela*. Austin: University of Texas Press.

Yarrington, Doug (2003). "Cattle, Corruption, and Venezuelan State Formation During the Regime of Juan Vicente Gómez, 1908–1935." *Latin American Research Review* 38, no. 2: 9–33.

Yépez Castillo, Aureo, and Emilia de Veracoechea (1997). *Historia de Venezuela*. Caracas: Editorial Larense.

Zago, Angela (1998). *La rebelión de los ángeles: los documentos del movimiento*. Caracas: Impresores Micabú.

Index

▼

About the Book

IN THIS fresh look at Venezuelan politics, Steve Ellner emphasizes the central significance of the country's economic and social cleavages.

Ellner's journey through modern Venezuelan history—observing popular masses and social actors as much as political elites and formal institutions—fundamentally informs his analysis of Hugo Chávez's presidency and the "Bolivarian Revolution" at its core. Perhaps equally important, as he explores the rise of *Chavismo*, opposition within the country and abroad, internal tensions in the *Chavista* movement, and the trajectory of the Chávez government domestically and on the international stage, he sheds new light not only on Venezuela but also on the recent political turmoil elsewhere in Latin America.

Steve Ellner is professor of history at the Universidad de Oriente in Venezuela. His recent publications include *Neoliberalismo y Anti-Neoliberalismo en América Latina* and *Venezuela: Hugo Chávez and the Decline of an "Exceptional Democracy"*(coedited with Miguel Tinker Salas).